P9-AFK-576

FITNESS
A Lifetime
Commitment

Third Edition

DAVID K. MILLER
T. EARL ALLEN

University of North Carolina at Wilmington

Macmillan Publishing Company
New York
Collier Macmillan Publishers
London

Copyright © 1986, by Macmillan Publishing Company,
a division of Macmillan, Inc.
Copyright © 1982, 1979 by Burgess Publishing.
Printed in the United States of America

Library of Congress Cataloging in Publication Data

Miller, David K. (David Keith)
   Fitness: a lifetime commitment.

   Bibliography: p.
   Includes index.
   1. Physical fitness. 2. Exercise. 3. Exercise—
Physiological aspects. I. Allen, T. Earl (Thomas Earl)
II. Title.
RA781 .M464   1986   613.7   85-25481
ISBN 0-02-381271-0

Macmillan Publishing Company
866 Third Avenue
New York, N.Y. 10022
Collier Macmillan Canada, Inc.

Printing 4 5 6 7 8 Year 7 8 9 0

ISBN 0-02-381271-0

To our wives,
Roselyn and Johanna

Contents

Foreword

In recent years, scientific research has markedly expanded the body of knowledge that links exercise to health promotion and disease prevention. As a result, health professionals and the lay public have come to accept regular participation in vigorous physical activity as an integral component of a healthy life-style. This pervasive recognition of the health benefits of exercise has had a profound impact on American society. Millions of adults have incorporated exercise into their daily regimen, exercise program providers have proliferated in both public and private sectors, and a massive industry has sprung up to provide exercisers with equipment, supplies, facilities, and information. America truly seems to have experienced a "fitness revolution."

Regrettably, however, the American fitness revolution has not been uniformly successful. Over half the adult population remain essentially sedentary. Many persons who initiate exercise programs fail to adhere to them. The fitness industry is populated by an alarming number of charlatans who promise vulnerable consumers unrealistic returns on what can be a substantial investment of money and time.

Many of the failings of the fitness movement can be explained by the public's lack of knowledge of the principles of exercise training. A knowledgeable exerciser is not likely to overtrain at the start of an activity program, does not pay for a health club membership he or she cannot use, and will not purchase a diet book that recommends a weight loss regimen that is biologically or behaviorally unsound.

Numerous techniques can be used to educate the public regarding proper exercise practices. One of the most promising is widespread exposure of high school and college students to organized courses of study on physical fitness. Such courses have the capacity to provide students with comprehensive, detailed, and practical learning experiences that promote permanent adoption of an active life-style. In such courses, students must be provided with support material that reinforces key concepts and that enables inquisitive students to saturate their need to know.

In the third edition of *Fitness: A Lifetime Commitment*, Professors Miller and Allen have produced a volume that is ideally suited to the college course on physical fitness. The book deals comprehensively with exercise by addressing the psychology as well as the physiology of exercise, by discussing both the health promotion and disease prevention benefits of exercise, and by describing the potential risks of physical activity. The authors understand well that they are addressing an intelligent, discerning audience and accordingly discuss the why as well as the how of exercise training. Importantly, the content of the book is up-to-date and well referenced. Just as importantly, the presentation style is attractive, readable, and pedagogically sound. The text is supported by clearly defined student objectives and by easily executed laboratory experiences.

The readers of *Fitness: A Lifetime Commitment* can be assured that the content of this book is current and accurate. In addition, they can be confident that the authors have included information that is important and relevant to their well-being. Finally, and perhaps most importantly, the readers can be certain that if they follow the recommendations of Professors Miller and Allen, their physical fitness, health, and quality of life will be enhanced.

Russell Pate, Ph.D., F.A.C.S.M.
University of South Carolina

Preface

The major objectives for the third edition of *Fitness: A Lifetime Commitment* remain the same as for the two previous editions: to provide the student information about the benefits of physical exercise, techniques for self-evaluation of physical fitness, and guidelines for preparation of a personalized exercise program that can be beneficial throughout life. Although this book is designed primarily for college men and women enrolled in courses in physical fitness, body conditioning, or foundations of physical activity, additions to the third edition increase its appropriateness for adult fitness groups.

Throughout this book, the terms *exercise* and *exercise program* are used. Unless otherwise stated, both are interpreted to mean an organized, regular program of physical activity designed to develop or maintain the components of physical fitness.

Some authors define physical fitness as the capacity for sustained physical activity without excessive fatigue or as the capacity to perform everyday activities with reserve energy for emergency situations. Many persons may incorrectly classify themselves as physically fit by these definitions, and accepting these definitions is especially incorrect when the relationships between inactivity and health are considered. For the purposes of this book, no definition of physical fitness is given. Rather, the concept is taken to include circulorespiratory endurance, muscular strength and endurance, flexibility, and weight management.

This edition does not represent a major change in the overall organization of the book; however, many additions and revisions have been made. New to this edition is a chapter on the advantages and disadvantages of various aerobic activities and a discussion of selection of exercise apparel. Although not a complete listing, representative changes include updated information about the total cholesterol/high-density lipoprotein (HDL) ratio as a predictor of coronary heart disease, alcohol and HDL, aging and physical activity, exercise during pregnancy, anabolic androgenic steroids and strength training, diet and weight management, and exercise and mood changes.

As in the previous editions, key terms, the pages on which they are found, and student objectives are listed at the beginning of each chapter. Fulfillment of the objectives will accomplish the purposes of the book. The key terms appear in boldface, and other words that we wish to emphasize are italicized.

Each chapter is designed to stand alone, and the sequence of chapters may be rearranged to meet the needs of a particular group of students. To develop a clear understanding of heart disease, exercise prescription, and training responses to exercise, the student should possess a basic knowledge of the anatomy and physiology of the circulatory, respiratory, and muscular systems. Chapters 9, 10, and 11 include this information for the student whose background is inadequate. In addition, important concepts other than those of basic anatomy and physiology are included in those chapters.

Included in the appendixes are the 12-minute walk/run and the 1.5-mile run tests for self-evaluation of circulorespiratory endurance with Cooper's tables for interpretation of results by age and sex. Also in the appendixes is a sample exercise prescription. A glossary is provided to clarify terms not fully defined in the text.

The 15 accompanying laboratory sessions provide another avenue for meeting the student objectives. These self-evaluation sessions also give the instructor and student an opportunity to assess the student's needs for an individualized physical fitness program. In addition, the inclusion of an exercise log enables the student to maintain a record of exercise participation throughout the course.

We wish to express our appreciation to the many students and colleagues who directly and indirectly contributed to the development of the three editions of this book and to the publishers who have graciously allowed the reproduction of tables. We especially wish to thank the reviewers of the final manuscript for this third edition: Henry DeLorme, Oakland University, Rochester, Mich.; Dale Mood, University of Colorado, Boulder; G. Dennis Wilson, Auburn University, Auburn, Ala.; Kenneth Ackerman, Southern Illinois University, Carbondale; and Patricia Schmitt, Del Mar College, Corpus Christi, Tex. Along with these five people, the following completed the initial survey questionnaire that gave direction to this revision: Leslie Self, Birmingham Southern College, Birmingham, Ala.; Elizabeth Stevenson, California State University, Sacramento; James McCormick, University of Topeka, Topeka, Kan.; Patty Long, Malone College, Canton, Ohio; John Sacchi, Middlesex County College, Edison, N.J.; and Jan Boyungs, Central Washington University, Ellensburg.

Most grateful acknowledgment is extended to Sharon Brewington and MaLou Stokes for their typing of the manuscript, to Talmsi Schultz and Jan Allen for the illustrations, and to Daniel Noel and Dillon Bryant for the photography. David Cameron, J. L. Doolittle, A. W. Faris, Ed Hooks, Marylou Morgan, and Doug Smith are thanked for their early reviews of the manuscript. A special debt is owed to Bob Clayton for his assistance and encouragement with the first edition.

Chapter One
INTRODUCTION

KEY TERMS

Body image (p. 3)   Self-concept (p. 3)
Hypokinetic disease (p. 4)   Self-esteem (p. 3)
Neuromuscular efficiency (p. 4)   Self-image (p. 3)

STUDENT OBJECTIVES

On completion of this chapter, the student should be able to:

1. Define the key terms listed above
2. Describe five major changes and problems that the human population has experienced in modern times
3. List and discuss at least six benefits to be gained from a regular exercise program

---

People are designed for physical activity. Primitive humans had to be able to run, climb, jump, and throw to provide for their needs and to escape constant threats to their lives. They *had* to be physically fit—only the fittest survived. This capacity for physical activity remains in modern people. Even the developing embryo moves within the uterus long before the mother becomes aware of it. After the infant is born, the parents can hardly wait for the child to crawl and walk, but encouragement to move is not really needed—the desire to walk, skip, run, and play is present from the start. Often during adolescence and adulthood, however, habits of inactivity are developed and permitted to become a part of daily living.

Development of these habits of inactivity is primarily due to the presence of labor-saving devices. One hundred years ago, only 6% of the energy used to produce goods was mechanical; the remaining 94% was generated by human or animal muscle power. Today, however, as much as 96% of all energy used is mechanical, and 70% of the working population performs nonphysical tasks. Power steering and power brakes, riding lawn mowers, remote-control television, and similar devices have made the American people weaker and lazier. Associated with this sedentary life-style are numerous health problems—degenerative and cardiovascular diseases, excessive weight gain, low back pain, and mental illness. Also, the **self-concept, self-image, body image,** and **self-esteem** of many individuals have suffered owing to lack of movement and physical deterioration.

In addition, people today have experienced more changes and crises than any other generation. The knowledge explosion and the use of computers, the continued growth in world population, the threat of nuclear war, economic instability, pollution, and the frenzied pace of living are but a few of the major changes and problems facing the world. Mental strain and stress have resulted from these changes and crises, creating a way of life that is biologically and psychologically unsuitable. To compensate for the daily pressures that they must face, people depend on coffee to awaken them in the morning, alcohol and tranquilizers to calm their disturbed nerves, and sleeping pills to help them rest at night. These drinks and pills have not succeeded in providing the desired results, however; mental illness is more prevalent now than ever before.

Even though these habits of inactivity have developed and our environment has changed, the important and basic human need for movement has remained. Movement is refreshing—the simple act of opening and closing the hand or tapping the foot can be a relief to someone who must sit or stand for a long period of time. The morning and afternoon breaks from one's work are often refreshing because of the moving or walking associated with them. Movement is necessary even during sleep to promote circulation.

Movement is also related to one's self-concept. Self-image, body image, and self-esteem constitute self-concept; an individual who ranks low on any one of them will probably have a poor self-concept. A successful exercise program can improve one's self-image and self-esteem. It can improve one's sense of well-being and help to develop a positive view of life. Also, movement and action are essential for the development of one's body image.

An individual who has a healthy body image, self-image, and self-esteem is more likely to attempt new physical activities, and participation in these activities can provide opportunities for social recognition and development of friendships. Various group activities can also develop one's ability to work harmoniously with others and to adjust to their wishes and feelings. Often a togetherness of the group emerges and carries over into situations other than those found in sports. Many persons fail to enjoy the social interaction that can be experienced in a program of physical activity owing to their unwarranted concern about physical appearance and performance and their low estimate of potential success. A specified level of physical fitness, which in turn may improve one's self-concept, should be developed prior to participation in leisure activities if maximum social benefits are to be gained from this participation.

Perhaps an even more important aspect of movement is the possible prevention of degenerative and cardiovascular diseases. The law of use and disuse dictates that one must use one's body if it is to be developed and maintained at a high level of efficiency, and that if one fails to do so, the body will deteriorate (**hypokinetic disease**). Increasing evidence supports the value of a regular exercise program to help keep the cardiovascular system as well as other systems of the body in good condition. Exercise develops the heart and lungs so that they are able to supply oxygen to the muscles without strain. Regular exercise has been reported to improve coronary circulation and to reduce the risk of obstructive arterial disease. An exercise program helps one to establish and maintain desirable weight and to prevent low back pain, loss of flexibility, and other degenerative diseases often associated with aging. Improved muscular strength and endurance, blood supply, innervation, and flexibility enhance **neuromuscular efficiency,** which increases the participant's chances for success in leisure activities.

In addition, emotional needs are related to the need for movement. The human body has an identical reaction to mental and physical stress. This means that a physically fit person is better prepared to adapt to and cope with mental stress. Physical activity provides an outlet that enables a person to let go, to release instinctive aggressive drives, and to relieve stifled anger and hostility. It also can be effective therapy for depression. Fulfilling the goals of an exercise program and experiencing the mental peace and physical relaxation that usually follow an exercise session enhance the participant's emotional health. Many Americans would be well advised to seek peace and relaxation this way rather than through alcohol or drugs.

From all the reasons given here, it should be apparent that a regular physical exercise program is not a luxury but a necessity. There are many types and variations of exercise programs, and each individual should select one according to personal interests and needs. Everyone should know the why as well as the how of physical exercise, however. More people would follow a regular exercise regimen if they truly understood its purpose.

Chapter Two
HEART DISEASE

KEY TERMS

Angina pectoris (p. 9)
Atherosclerosis (p. 9)
Coronary heart disease (CHD) (p. 7)
Fibrous plaque (p. 10)
High-density lipoprotein (HDL) (p. 13)
Hypercholesterolemia (p. 12)
Hyperlipidemia (p. 12)
Hypertension (p. 12)

Ischemia (p. 9)
Low-density lipoprotein (LDL) (p. 13)
Myocardial infarction (p. 9)
Retrograde murmur (p. 16)
Rheumatic heart disease (p. 17)
Serum cholesterol (p. 12)
Serum triglyceride (p. 12)
Stenosis (p. 16)

STUDENT OBJECTIVES

On completion of this chapter, the student should be able to:

1. Define the key terms listed above
2. Describe four steps in the progressive development of coronary heart disease
3. Identify three primary and eight secondary risk factors associated with the development of coronary heart disease according to the multiple risk factor theory

4. Identify safe ranges for blood pressure and desirable levels for serum cholesterol, serum triglyceride, and high-density lipoprotein-cholesterol
5. List six risk factors that are positively influenced by exercise
6. List three characteristics of a highly trainable postinfarction patient that are somewhat controllable

According to 1984 American Heart Association statistics, 42,750,000 Americans have one or more forms of heart or blood vessel disease. Of this number, about 37,330,000 have hypertension. Approximately 4,600,000 persons alive today have had a heart attack or are living with angina pectoris, 2,010,000 have rheumatic heart disease, and 1,870,000 are affected by the aftermath of nonfatal strokes.[1]

Cardiovascular diseases (CVD) are the major cause of death in the United States, representing just under 50% of all deaths in 1981.* Of this number, 56.5% resulted from heart attack and 16.6% from stroke. The remaining CVD deaths were attributable to such conditions as rheumatic heart disease, hypertensive disease, and congenital heart disease.[1] Such death is particularly tragic when it strikes persons in the prime of life. Statistics show that of all who die from CVD, more than 20% are less than 65 years old. Forty percent of the deaths in men ages 40 to 59 are due to a form of CVD called **coronary heart disease** (CHD).

As can be seen in Figure 2.1, the economic impact of these disorders is staggering. The total cost of CVD in 1984 was estimated to be $64.4 billion. This figure includes physician and nursing services, hospital and nursing home services, cost of medications, and lost work output due to disability. This represents an increase of $23.4 billion over

* Statistics presented in connection with CVD were taken from the latest material available (1981) from the National Center for Health Statistics U.S. Public Health Service, Department of Health and Human Services, and the American Heart Association (1984)

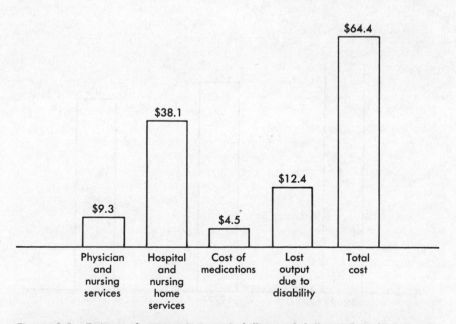

Figure 2.1. Estimated economic costs in billions of dollars of cardiovascular diseases by type of expenditure in the United States in 1984
(© Reproduced with permission. American Heart Association)

the $41 billion estimate of 1980. The real tragedy is that much of the expense and suffering might be avoidable.

Paradoxically, though the cost of CVD has continued to rise dramatically, the past decade has seen the death rate from CVD decline only slightly (Figure 2.2). Even so, health care professionals are reluctant to conclude that a reduced occurrence of CVD is responsible. They prefer to explain the decreasing mortality rates by citing improved medical diagnostic ability and disease management techniques as well as a general public that is more enlightened about CVD. We believe that basic knowledge of causes, preventive measures, and available modern treatments should enable one to respond intelligently to CVD danger signs that signal impending serious risk if unheeded. To that end, a few of the more common types of heart disorders are listed and discussed. Where appropriate, the role of exercise as a preventive or treatment tool is given. Forms of CVD described are:

1. CHD (resulting in angina pectoris or myocardial infarction)
2. Congenital defects
3. Valvular lesions
4. Rhythm disorders
5. Rheumatic heart disease

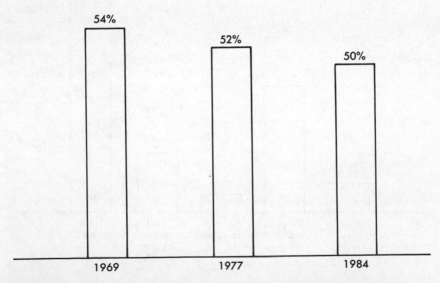

Figure 2.2. Percentage of deaths due to cardiovascular diseases in the United States 1969-1984 (Data adapted from the American Heart Association)

CORONARY HEART DISEASE

As can be seen from information previously presented, CHD is one of the most important and prevalent types of CVD. It is characterized by a reduction of the open area (lumen) in one or more of the coronary arteries. These important arteries encircle the heart muscle (myocardium) and supply it with oxygen and other nutrients. (See Figure 9.2.)

Atherosclerosis

Atherosclerosis is a major contributor to the development of CHD. This progressive pathologic condition does not suddenly appear one morning in middle age, but rather develops over a long period of time. The etiology of atherosclerosis is controversial. Whatever the cause, *lesions* develop in the walls of the coronary arteries. Over the years, this pathologic process continues until blood flow is seriously reduced (a condition known as **ischemia**) or even until the vessel becomes completely blocked. The slowly developing atherosclerotic process finally becomes dramatically manifested in the occurrence of angina pectoris or myocardial infarction.

Angina Pectoris

Angina pectoris means chest pain. This disorder is caused by the inability of the coronary arteries to supply the myocardium (heart muscle) with adequate oxygen. Pain is usually absent when at rest, is precipitated by physical exertion, and usually subsides with cessation of activity. It is described as excruciating, often radiating from the sternum to the shoulders, jaw, and arms. Depending on the severity of the condition, treatment includes diet and drug therapy, exercise, or surgical procedures.

Myocardial Infarction

A **myocardial infarction** is a heart attack. The term *infarct* refers to an area of dead tissue resulting from inadequate circulation in the myocardium. If a coronary artery becomes blocked by a clot (thrombus) or by some other material, the tissue beyond that point is deprived of blood. The tissue dies (necrosis), and the area is permanently damaged. If the damaged area is large enough, the victim dies. A mild infarction can be treated successfully, and many patients can be rehabilitated. As with angina pectoris, diet and drug therapy and exercise are important in the recovery of postinfarction patients.

DEVELOPMENT OF ATHEROSCLEROSIS

The Process

Autopsy examination of the coronary arteries of soldiers (whose average age was 22 years) killed in the Korean and Vietnamese conflicts showed evidence of significant atherosclerotic coronary artery disease (60 and 45%, respectively). In the Vietnam data, approximately 5% of those studied had at least one of the three major coronary arteries almost completely blocked or all three vessels involved to a significant degree. These data clearly demonstrate that atherosclerosis is not just a disease of the aged but also is manifested early in life.

One of the major efforts in the United States to trace the development of atherosclerosis was begun in 1947 under the direction of the International Atherosclerosis Project. Researchers in this project collected approximately 30,000 aortas and coronary arteries from around the world and made cross-sectional analyses of subjects from birth to age 70. From the data, the pathologic process of atherosclerosis was established as follows:[32]

1. Below age 10—Fatty streaks first appear in the aorta as the result of *lipid* deposition in the arterial intima (lining). This is considered benign, since it appears to occur in populations of children all around the world, regardless of diet, exercise level, or genetic background.
2. Age 10 to 20—Fatty deposits begin to appear with increasing frequency in the coronary arteries themselves. This occurs particularly in Western populations.
3. Age 20 to 40—The lipid materials continue to build up in the arterial wall until age 35 or 40, when they begin to change into **fibrous plaque** and become covered by fibrous scars. Most authorities believe that this development of fibrous plaque marks the point of no return—once plaque formation occurs, the process appears to be irreversible. The process can be somewhat arrested, but the scars will not disappear as do the fatty streaks.
4. Age 40 and beyond—Finally, the areas of fibrous plaque develop into more complicated lesions involving further lipid deposition, thrombus formation, and eventual death of the tissue beyond the clot.

During the last 30 years, both epidemiological and experimental findings have made it increasingly clear that any one of a number of factors, possibly acting alone or in combination with other factors, can initiate the atherosclerotic process. The pieces of the puzzle are finally coming together. For example, improved understanding of the underlying mechanisms of lesion formation now enables scientists to link together the *lipid infiltration hypothesis* and the *endothelial injury-platelet aggregation hypothesis.*[31] In the 1970s, development of the *monoclonal cell proliferation theory* further enhanced our understanding of the progressive pathologic process of atherosclerosis and added a new dimension for exploration.[3] (See glossary for explanation of these terms.)

MULTIPLE RISK FACTOR THEORY

The most widely accepted theory concerning development of atherosclerosis is the multiple risk factor theory. Epidemiologic research points toward a multifactorial cause involving identifiable factors or combinations of factors as being responsible for increasing one's risk of the disease developing.[30] Some of the factors are statistically more strongly associated with the premature development of atherosclerosis and are identified as *primary risk factors;* others, which are less strongly associated, are considered as *secondary risk factors.* The following are considered primary risk factors:

1. Hypertension (high blood pressure)
2. Hyperlipidemia (abnormally high levels of serum triglyceride or serum cholesterol or both in circulating blood)
3. Cigarette smoking (Figure 2.3)

Following closely behind and not necessarily listed in order of importance are these secondary risk factors:

4. Obesity
5. Sedentary living habits
6. Psychological or emotional stress
7. *Glucose* intolerance (diabetes mellitus)
8. Positive family history of heart disease
9. Sex (male)
10. Age (old)
11. Low HDL levels

Hypertension

Hypertension (high blood pressure), salt intake, and obesity are all interrelated.[8] Except in extreme cases, blood pressure can be reduced by the control of salt intake, diet, weight, and exercise. In extreme cases, drug therapy becomes necessary and is effective. Medical researchers are seeing alarmingly higher blood pressure in American children today than in the past. Although blood pressure tends to increase with age, there is no reason to accept values higher than those listed:

Less than 5 years	120/80 mm Hg
Five to 10 years	135/85 mm Hg
Adolescent	140/85 mm Hg
Adult	145/90 mm Hg

Hyperlipidemia

Hyperlipidemia (elevated **serum triglyceride** or **serum cholesterol** or both) has been implicated as an important risk factor in the development of CHD, although many researchers attach more importance to **hypercholesterolemia** (elevated serum cholesterol) alone.

Cholesterol is produced by almost all cells of the body (endogenous production), especially by those of the liver. Large amounts are also ingested in the typical American diet. Individual differences in ability to transport and metabolize it may lead to an abnormally high serum cholesterol level, which has been purported to result in lipid deposition in the arterial lining. Assuming that low levels are desirable, probably the best way to reduce serum cholesterol is dietary intervention. Although earlier research[10, 11, 15, 25, 27] reported regular vigorous exercise to be helpful in cholesterol reduction, more recent research,[18]

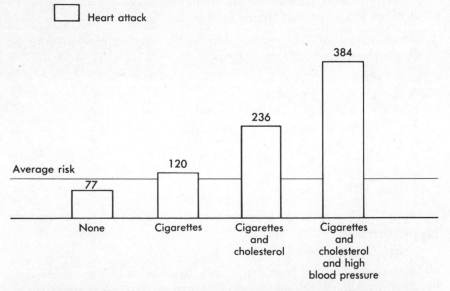

Figure 2.3. Danger of heart attack increases with number of risk factors present. For illustration purposes, chart uses abnormal systolic blood pressure of 180 mm Hg and cholesterol level of 310 mg/100 ml of blood in a 45-year-old man (© Reproduced with permission. American Heart Association)

using improved experimental design, suggests that exercise effectively reduces only the triglyceride component of blood lipids. Possibly a cholesterol-lowering effect is specific to some individuals only. Until research defines clearly the role of cholesterol in the development of CHD, it seems prudent to maintain cholesterol levels below 165 and 200 mg/100 ml of blood in children and adults, respectively. Cholesterol intake should not be restricted in children during their first year or so as it is important in the development of some of the components of the nervous system.

Cholesterol Subclasses

The manner in which cholesterol travels in the bloodstream now appears to be more important than the serum level. The major blood lipids, including cholesterol and triglyceride, are insoluble in plasma and must combine with plasma proteins to achieve solubility (hence the name *lipoproteins*). The four major lipoprotein classes are chylomicrons, very-low-density lipoproteins (VLDL), **low-density lipoproteins (LDL),** and **high-density lipoproteins (HDL).**

Chylomicrons are composed primarily of triglyceride. They originate in the intestine from dietary fat and are metabolized rapidly in the bloodstream. VLDL is the main carrier of triglyceride and is produced primarily in the liver and small intestine. It is degraded in the blood fairly rapidly and eventually becomes LDL. LDL consists of about 60 to 75% cholesterol, and is the major carrier of cholesterol to the cells.

Both the liver and the small intestine are thought to be involved in the production of HDL. When secreted directly from these organs, HDL is an immature sort of empty biconcave sac. During its maturation, HDL is thought to assist in cholesterol removal from the tissue with the help of an enzyme called LCAT.[14, 22]

Another theory considers the possibility that HDL might also inhibit the deposition of LDL in arterial cells by interfering with cholesterol binding sites. Further investigation will be necessary to define accurately the exact biochemical mechanism responsible for the apparent cholesterol scavenging activity of HDL. Although present evidence suggests the occurrence of a reverse cholesterol transport, and although epidemiologic studies suggest that high levels of HDL protect against CVD, the antiatherogenic effect of the HDL mechanism has not been clearly established.[20]

After the adolescent years, HDL levels in males decline from about 55 to about 45 mg/100 ml of blood and remain there until beyond age 50. Some researchers think that if only one risk factor is considered, a low HDL level is the best single predictor of future coronary artery disease. To determine the degree of risk posed by low HDL, divide the total cholesterol value by HDL cholesterol. A ratio of 5 for men or 4 for women suggests average risk. Lower ratios indicate reduced risk.[6]

Triglyceride may be ingested in the diet, or it may be synthesized within the body during carbohydrate or fat metabolism or both. Dietary prudence quite effectively keeps the triglyceride levels in most people below the maximum allowable 150 mg/100 ml of blood recommended by the National Institutes of Health. Equally effective in triglyceride control is vigorous aerobic physical activity.[18]

Cigarette Smoking

Most are aware of the association of chronic cigarette smoking and the risk of lung cancer. Few realize that the relationship between cigarette smoking and CHD is even stronger. Smoking only one pack per day is sufficient to increase the risk of myocardial infarction three times over that of a nonsmoker.

The potentially damaging acute effects are numerous. Heart rate and blood pressure are increased almost immediately. Nicotine is a coronary vasoconstrictor and myocardial irritant. These actions, coupled with increased levels of carbon monoxide in the blood, reduce myocardial oxygen supply and render the heart more susceptible to potentially dangerous dysrhythmias. Smoking has also been shown to decrease serum HDL levels.[7] The waste caused by so insignificant and useless an act as cigarette smoking is regrettable.

RISK FACTOR REDUCTION

Except for age, sex, and a positive family history for CHD, the remaining risk factors can be reduced, controlled, or eliminated completely. Exercise either directly or indirectly can play a significant role in improving a poor risk factor profile.

Relative to the three primary risk factors, exercise can directly exert positive influences on two. In many hypertensive individuals, regular endurance exercise tends to normalize blood pressure. Although the more well-designed cholesterol studies do not show that serum cholesterol decreases as a result of training, two important lipid alterations do occur. First, an almost immediate reduction in plasma triglyceride levels occurs and holds for approximately 24 to 36 hr. Secondly, after a period of several months, a change in the plasma HDL/LDL ratio occurs. HDL is increased with a concomitant decrease in LDL, although total cholesterol may remain unchanged.

Cigarette smoking might be influenced positively as many people who are serious enough to commit to a regular exercise program recognize the health hazards of smoking and voluntarily reduce the number of smokes per day or stop altogether.

With respect to the secondary risk factors, exercise can assist in weight reduction in the overly fat individual by increasing the number of Calories used in a given period. In addition, a beneficial increase in basal metabolic rate may occur as well as a change in the body's setpoint for fat storage. (See p. 139.)

The risk generated by sedentary living is eliminated by regularly engaging in a physically vigorous life-style. Research results have demonstrated conclusively that vigorous exercise is an excellent method for relieving emotional stress while improving CV fitness. Although the mechanisms are not clear, changes in brain chemistry may be involved. (See Chapter 8.)

Regular exercise enhances the transport of blood glucose into cells. This does not mean that exercising diabetics no longer need insulin. It does mean that the insulin requirement might be somewhat less for insulin-dependent diabetics who exercise regularly.

HDL cholesterol is increased after a few months of regular endurance exercise at an appropriate intensity.

OTHER HEART DISORDERS

Although the heart disorders described below are no less important than those previously mentioned, they occur less frequently and, with the exception of rheumatic heart disease, are not preventable.

Congenital Defects

Congenital defects are abnormalities that are present at birth as a result of some genetic disturbance or prenatal developmental accident. Examples are atrial and ventricular septal defects produced by the failure of the heart to make postnatal adaptive changes from fetal circulation to normal circulation, coarctation of the aorta (an obstructive abnormality), and circulatory shunt disorders relating to the failure of certain fetal vessels to close at birth. Although exercise per se cannot remove these defects, psychological outlook and physiologic condition can be improved in those for whom exercise is not contraindicated. Persons with these defects must be handled individually with regard to the level of exercise that can be tolerated.

Valvular Lesions

Abnormalities of the heart valves can occur congenitally, result from some infectious disease, or develop over the years as a result of wear and tear and mineral deposition in the valve leaflets. Some are functionally significant and others are not. The problems associated with these types of disorders are usually twofold. First, if a valve fails to close properly, there is a backward flow (**retrograde murmur**) of blood into the chamber from which it came. This produces a volume overload and means that the affected chamber has to compensate to keep up. The defective valve is said to be *incompetent*. Second, in obstructive valvular disease, the improper formation or operation of a valve often obstructs flow through the orifice—a problem known as **stenosis.** In this case, emptying pressures higher than normal must be generated within the chamber. The usual result is pathologic enlargement (disproportionate change in the length/width ratio of myocardial cells) of that chamber (hypertrophy). It is not uncommon for a valve to become both incompetent and stenotic.

Initially, these disorders are clinically detected as abnormal heart sounds *(murmurs)* when a physician listens to the heart (auscultation). Since the 1950s, the more serious valvular lesions have been investigated by invasive techniques such as cardiac catheterization. In this procedure, tiny tubes (catheters) are threaded through vessels in the arms or legs and inserted into the chambers of the heart. Pressures in the various heart chambers can then be measured during the different phases of the cardiac cycle, and the degree of valvular incompetence can be evaluated. Use of X-ray photography to trace blood flow patterns and echocardiography to observe valve action and wall motion enable physicians to assess the seriousness of a diseased valve. Fortunately, many of the more serious problems can be corrected surgically, with the patient returning to an almost normal life-style after a short convalescent period.

In the past, physicians tended to discourage physical activity for people with heart murmurs. Unfortunately, this advice produced an unnecessarily large number of cardiac cripples. Except in cases of relatively severe mitral or aortic stenosis in which the risk of sudden death during exercise is high, more enlightened physicians no longer restrict activity levels because of heart murmurs. Instead, they usually encourage each individual to engage in almost any activity and allow the condition to become self-limiting. In other words, when the circulatory demands of an activity become so severe that the heart cannot pump an adequate amount of blood, fatigue ensues and the individual voluntarily slows the pace or stops to rest.

No evidence shows that exercise can improve the functional ability of an incompetent or stenotic valve, but exercise-induced bradycardia (decreased heart rate), compensation of the myocardium, and peripheral muscular adaptation are known to reduce cardiac work for a given level of activity. Any adaptation that can decrease cardiac work must be viewed as a beneficial response.

Disorders of Rhythm

Rhythmic disturbances, many of which are relatively harmless, frequently occur in apparently healthy individuals. They are manifest in the form of an unexplained, excessively rapid heart rate (tachycardia), extra (ectopic) beats, or skipped beats. Clinical diagnosis can explain some of the abnormalities, but many are transient, occurring in the absence of any pathologic condition, and are therefore inexplicable. Excessive fatigue, chronic emotional stress, overuse of caffeine and nicotine, and too little exercise have been implicated.

Mild cases of rhythmic dysfunction can be controlled by drug therapy. More severe disorders may require surgical implantation of artificial pacemaker devices.

Rheumatic Heart Disease

The American Heart Association estimates that 100,000 children and 1,910,000 adults were living with **rheumatic heart disease** in 1981.[1] This disease is caused by rheumatic fever, which is usually thought of as a childhood disease because it most frequently strikes between the ages of 5 and 15. This disease is always preceded by a streptococcal infection—usually a sore throat. If allowed to go untreated, this disease can cause permanent damage to the heart valves.

Rheumatic heart disease not only can shorten life but also can seriously reduce the quality of life. Although mortality from this disease has declined sharply since 1940, incidence rates remain too high for a preventable disease. The first step toward prevention is identification of the streptococcal infection followed by effective treatment using penicillin or its substitutes in penicillin-sensitive persons.

PREVENTIVE MEASURES IN CHD

The medical community generally agrees that premature development of CHD can, to a large degree, be prevented in many people. Once it has progressed to the stage of fibrous plaque formation, prospects for reversal are gloomy. Not to destroy all hope, however, a few reports describe success in reversing the process using exercise, diet, and sometimes drug therapy.[19, 28, 29] If further research supports these claims, the current position on irreversibility of the process will have to be altered.

At the present time, prevention of premature CHD appears to rest with the early identification of the coronary-prone individual and subsequent control of the risk factors previously described in this chapter. While it has been shown that progress is being made in modifying risk factors,[30] conclusive evidence that risk factor modification actually reduces morbidity or mortality from CHD has not been presented. Recent studies have attempted to supply this evidence.

In the Multiple Risk Factor Intervention Trials Project (MRFIT)[26] sponsored by the National Heart, Lung, and Blood Institute, almost 13,000 high-risk, middle-aged men were randomly divided into two groups and studied for 6 years. One group received a special intervention program designed to help them stop smoking cigarettes and reduce elevated serum cholesterol and blood pressure levels. The other group received only their usual medical care. Both groups demonstrated considerable success in reducing the three risk factors studied. No difference was observed between the groups relative to the development of CHD or in the number of deaths from CHD. A slightly lower than predicted number of deaths and infarction was observed in both groups, however. Although the results suggest a benefit in risk factor reduction, the evidence was not considered conclusive.

The failure of this study to demonstrate clearly a positive relationship between risk factor reduction and risk allows for several conclusions. One is that only the three primary risk factors were considered, suggesting that their interaction with the so-called secondary risk factors may be more important than was thought. Another is that waiting until becoming high risk in middle age may be too late. Finally, the treatment that the usual care group received might have been as effective as the care that the special intervention group received.

Possibly the most acclaimed study reported in the 1980s was The Lipid Research Clinics Coronary Primary Prevention Trial Results.[23] This study showed that reducing one primary risk factor—elevated blood cholesterol—decreased the risk of death or nonfatal infarction from CHD.

In this study, 3806 asymptomatic middle-aged men (35 to 59 years) whose plasma cholesterol equaled or exceeded 265 mg/100 ml of blood were divided into a treatment group and a control group and observed for about 7 years. The treatment group received a cholesterol-lowering drug, cholestyramine, and the control group received a placebo. Neither group was aware of what they were taking. Results revealed that the cholestyramine group experienced 8 fewer fatal (30 to 38) and 28 fewer nonfatal (130 to 158) heart attacks. Lowering cholesterol 8% at the levels studied was conclusively shown to represent a 19% decline in risk. Those members who were able to lower total cholesterol as much as 25% developed only half the incidence of CHD as did those whose cholesterol remained unchanged.[23] Some have interpreted this to mean that a 1% reduction in cholesterol means a 2% reduction in risk.[24]

From the results of these two studies, which suggest benefits from risk factor reduction, as well as other studies not mentioned, continued efforts to maintain a low risk factor profile throughout life appear to be the prudent course of action.

The Role of Diet

Given that hyperlipidemia is a primary risk factor and that decreasing one's risk factor profile might reduce the occurrence of premature CHD, knowledge of dietary methods for normalizing blood lipids becomes important.

Some individuals have such sensitive feedback mechanisms for internal cholesterol control that blood levels remain within acceptable ranges regardless of diet. Most, however, are not so fortunate and need to restrict the daily cholesterol intake to less than 300 mg. Because saturated fat is thought to elevate blood cholesterol by stimulating endogenous cholesterol production in the liver, intake restriction of this dietary fat is equally important. Careful monitoring of these two dietary lipids can decrease serum cholesterol by 15 to 20% in hyperlipidemic individuals.

Like cholesterol, HDL levels may also be influenced by dietary components. Calories, alcohol, carbohydrates, and dietary fats have all been implicated.[2] For example, some studies have shown that when a high percentage of the diet is supplied by carbohydrates, a modest decrease in HDL results. In such cases, a small decrease in serum cholesterol is also observed so that the serum cholesterol/HDL ratio is not disturbed. The effects of dietary fat on HDL are less consistent.

In studies of dietary influence on HDL, the strongest and most consistent association has been between alcohol intake and HDL. These studies have repeatedly demonstrated that moderate use of alcohol increases HDL levels.[9] Most of these studies, however, measured only total HDL concentration. Because of improved techniques, HDL can now be subfractionated into HDL_2 and HDL_3. *Only the HDL_2 fraction is considered to be antiatherogenic.* HDL_2 is known to be higher in women, long-distance runners, and children than in the average sedentary adult. HDL_3 is not elevated in these people and is presently considered to be unrelated to CHD. Recent studies have shown that when alcohol is ingested, the resulting increase in total HDL is due to an increase in HDL_3 and therefore should not be interpreted as an antiatherogenic benefit.[13, 21]

In view of this evidence, it would be unconscionable to recommend that nondrinkers begin using alcohol to raise HDL levels as a means of preventing CHD. To continue the use of alcohol as a means of preventing CHD as was suggested in earlier studies has no support from current research. On the other hand, those who use alcohol in moderation probably should not be advised to discontinue, at least not for medical reasons. These people should be made aware, however, that heavy usage unquestionably enhances the development of several severe CV and other health problems.[16, 17] Furthermore, the potential for socioeconomic trauma that is associated with alcohol abuse cannot be ignored.

At the present time, eating a normal balanced diet in the proportions recommended by the Senate Select Committee on Nutrition and Human Needs appears to be sound dietary advice for the prevention of premature CHD. (See Chapter 7.)

The Role of Exercise

For years, many have claimed that vigorous exercise throughout life is a major deterrent to the development of CHD. A former president of the American Medical Joggers Association even went so far as to claim that people who train for and complete marathons do not develop CHD. He was challenged by colleagues from around the world, and evidence from autopsy findings was presented that dispelled the myth that marathon running provides immunity to CHD. Although the incidence is lower in people who adopt the life-style of the marathon runner, whether it is accurate to infer that running (exercise) is responsible for this phenomenon or whether these individuals select this most strenuous type of exercise because of some genetic predisposition remains highly controversial.

It has already been pointed out that moderate exercise does appear to exert a positive influence on several risk factors. Evidence is now convincing that exercise increases the level of HDL cholesterol, which is interpreted as a protective mechanism against lipid deposition in blood vessel walls.[12, 34, 35] Regular exercise is also one of the best methods for decreasing blood pressure in some individuals, and its value in weight management is well documented. Furthermore, regular exercise is effective in reducing emotional stress and the amount of insulin required by diabetics. Undoubtedly exercise is valuable therapy for reducing risk factors.

The question of how much one should exercise to reduce the risk of CHD is as yet unanswered. Present opinions range from as little as 15 min triweekly to as much as 6 mi or 1 hr of daily continuous running at a good pace if significant protection against CHD is to occur. Until well-controlled scientific research provides an answer, it should be assumed that, to a point, the benefit derived is generally proportional to the exercise input. This concept is discussed more fully in Chapters 3 and 4.

CARDIAC REHABILITATION

If preventive measures have been begun too late and a cardiac incident occurs, modern medical technology can, in many cases, enable a patient to be rehabilitated. Coronary bypass surgery for bypassing arterial occlusions, valve replacement by open-heart surgery, and pacemaker implants are important achievements that have become fairly common. More recently, transluminal coronary angioplasty has allowed surgeons to reopen some obstructed arteries without opening the chest as is required in the coronary bypass operation. In this procedure, a tiny balloon-tipped catheter is threaded to the obstruction site in the partially occluded vessel. Inflation of the balloon compresses the lipid material against the vessel wall. This technique has only been successful, however, when used before the lesion has developed into fibrous plaque.

The medical literature is saturated with reports of the therapeutic value of exercise as one mode of rehabilitating patients predisposed to CHD. With few exceptions, cardiac patients respond to physical training in much the same manner as do healthy individuals. In addition to reconditioning the heart, exercise reconditions the skeletal muscles, which is considered to be of equal benefit. Since posttraining heart rate and blood pressure are both lower at comparable work levels, cardiac work is reduced and functional cardiac reserve power is thereby increased.[4, 33]

Although many heart attack patients have made remarkable recoveries through rehabilitative efforts involving changes in life-style, not all individuals respond well to physical training. Dr. John Cantwell, co-director of cardiac rehabilitation at Georgia Baptist Hospital, has outlined characteristics of a highly trainable postinfarction patient as follows:[5]

1. Less than 55 years old
2. Uncomplicated inferior myocardial infarction
3. Able to achieve greater than 85% of age-predicted maximum heart rate during an exercise test
4. Less than 20% body fat
5. Nonsmoker or ex-smoker
6. Former athlete (physically well-trained individual)

Note that items 4, 5, and 6 are somewhat controllable, and that 6 suggests the value of a physically active adolescence and young adulthood.

REFERENCES

1. American Heart Association. 1984. *Heart facts 1984.* Dallas: American Heart Association.

2. American Society for Clinical Nutrition. 1979. Symposium: Report on the task force on the evidence relating six dietary factors to the nation's health. *American Journal of Clinical Nutrition* 32(12):2621–2748 (suppl.).

3. Benditt, E. 1977. The origin of atherosclerosis. *Scientific American* 236(2):74–85.

4. Bruce, R. A. 1973. Principles of exercise testing. In *Exercise testing and exercise training in coronary heart disease,* edited by J. P. Naughton and H. K. Hellerstein. New York: Academic Press.

5. Cantwell, J. D. Presentation, Quinton Exercise Stress Testing Seminar, Atlanta, January 1978.

6. Cooper, K. H. 1982. *The aerobics program for total well being.* New York: Bantam Books.

7. Criqui, M. H. et al. 1980. Cigarette smoking and plasma high density lipoprotein cholesterol. *Circulation* 62 (suppl. 4):70–76.

8. Dustan, H. P. 1979. Research contributions toward prevention of cardiovascular disease: Research related to the underlying mechanisms in hypertension. *Circulation* 60(7):1566–1568.

9. Ernst, N. et al. 1980. The association of plasma high density lipoprotein cholesterol with dietary intake and alcohol consumption. *Circulation* 62 (suppl. 4):41–52.

10. Fox, S. M., and Haskell, W. L. 1968. Physical activity and the prevention of heart disease. *Bulletin of the New York Academy of Medicine,* 2d series, 44:950, August.

11. Gustafson, A. 1971. Effect of training on blood lipids. In *Coronary heart disease and physical fitness,* edited by O. A. Larsen and R. O. Malmborg. Baltimore: University Park Press.

12. Hartung, G. H. et al. 1980. Relation of diet to high-density-lipoprotein cholesterol in middle-age marathon runners, joggers, and inactive men. *New England Journal of Medicine* 302(7):357–361.

13. Haskell, W. L. et al. 1984. The effect of cessation and resumption of moderate alcohol intake on serum high-density-lipoprotein subfractions. *New England Journal of Medicine* 310(13):805–810.

14. Havel, R. J. 1979. High-density lipoproteins, cholesterol transport, and coronary heart disease. *Circulation* 60(1):1–3.

15. Joseph, J. J., and Bena, L. L. 1977. Cholesterol reduction—a long term intense exercise program. *Journal of Sports Medicine and Physical Fitness* 17(2):163–168.

16. Klatsky, A. L. 1979a. Alcohol and cardiovascular disorders. *Primary Cardiology* 5(9):86–95.

17. ———. 1979b. Alcohol and cardiovascular disorders. *Primary Cardiology* 5(10):76–83.

18. Lampman, R. M. et al. 1978. Effectiveness of unsupervised and supervised high intensity physical training in normalizing serum lipids in men with type IV hyperlipoproteinemia. *Circulation* 57(1):172–180.

19. Leonard, J. N., Hofer, J. L., and Pritikin, N. 1974. *Live longer now*. New York: Grosset and Dunlap.

20. Levy, R. I., and Rifkind, B. M. 1980. The structure, function and metabolism of high-density lipoproteins: A status report. *Circulation* 62 (suppl. 4):4–8.

21. Lieber, C. S. 1984. To drink (moderately) or not to drink? *New England Journal of Medicine.* 310(13):846–848.

22. Lindgren, F. T., ed. 1979. Symposium: High density lipoproteins (HDL). Champaign, Ill: American Oil Chemists' Society.

23. Lipid Research Clinics Program. 1984a. The lipid research clinics coronary primary prevention trial results. I. Reduction in incidence of coronary heart disease. *Journal of the American Medical Association* 251(3):351–364.

24. ———. 1984b. The lipid research clinics coronary primary prevention trial results. II. The relationship of reduction in incidence of coronary heart disease to cholesterol lowering. *Journal of the American Medical Association* 251(3):365–374.

25. Milesis, C. A. 1974. Effects of metered physical training on serum lipids of adult men. *Journal of Sports Medicine and Physical Fitness* 14:8–13.

26. Multiple Risk Factor Intervention Trial Research Group. 1982. Multiple risk factor intervention trial. Risk factor changes and mortality results. *Journal of the American Medical Association* 248(12):1465–1477.

27. Pollack, M. J. et al. 1969. Effects of frequency of training on serum lipids, cardiovascular function and body composition. In *Exercise and fitness,* edited by D. B. Frunks. Chicago: Athletic Institute.

28. Pritikin, N., and McGrady, P. M., Jr. 1980. *The Pritikin program for diet and exercise*. New York: Bantam Books.

29. Schettler, G. et al., eds. 1977. *Atherosclerosis IV*. New York: Springer-Verlag.

30. Stamler, J. 1979. Research related to risk factors. *Circulation* 60(7):1575–1587.

31. Steinberg, D. 1979. Research related to underlying mechanisms in atherosclerosis. *Circulation* 60(7):1559–1565.

32. Strong, W. B. 1975. The natural history and pathogenesis of

atherosclerosis: Pediatric aspects. Presented at the Southeast Regional Meeting of the American College of Sports Medicine, Columbia, S.C., November.

33. Wenger, N. K. 1979. Research related to rehabilitation. *Circulation* 60(7):1636–1639.

34. Wood, P. D., and Haskell, W. L. 1979. The effect of exercise on plasma high density lipoproteins. *Lipids* 14(4):417–427.

35. Wood, P. D. et al. 1977. Plasma lipoprotein distribution in male and female runners. *Annals of the New York Academy of Sciences* 301:748–763.

Chapter Three
THE EXERCISE PRESCRIPTION

Although strenuous physical activity is not a panacea for all the ills of humankind, it is widely accepted that a regular program of vigorous, rhythmic exercise enhances the quality of life by increasing the physical capability for work and play.[3] On the basis of current evidence, it is unjustifiable to conclude that exercise alone is the key to the prevention of heart disease.[1] Each year, however, the data become increasingly favorable in support of continued vigorous physical activity throughout life as a valuable adjunct to the elimination of certain risk factors such as cigarette smoking, high blood pressure, and high blood lipids in reducing the probability that coronary heart disease (CHD) may develop.

While exercise has been established to be valuable in the rehabilitation of individuals who have certain types of cardiovascular disease

(CVD),[6] and even though the literature supports exercise as a strong contributor to the prevention of atherosclerotic coronary artery disease, some should be cautious about engaging in an unsupervised vigorous program of physical training. Does this mean that exercise is dangerous? Not necessarily. For persons under age 35 who have none of the primary risk factors, the chance of bodily damage from sensible physical exercise is so remote that it can be disregarded. Some individuals, however, could benefit greatly from certain types of exercise regimens at specified tolerance levels, but engagement in more strenuous activity might be extremely hazardous or even fatal. For a few, almost any level of exercise is so dangerous that the risks of mortality far outweigh any small benefits to be gained; these people should not exercise.

The problem then is to determine for each individual the amount of risk involved, the kind of program that is in order, and the level of exercise that can be safely tolerated. The solution to the problem lies in the analysis of data collected during a procedure designed to evaluate the functional capacity of an individual. This procedure, commonly called a **stress test** or a *graded exercise test,* should be performed prior to participation in any strenuous exercise program.

THE STRESS TEST

A stress test usually consists either of riding a stationary bicycle (bicycle ergometer) or walking or running or both during a multistage treadmill test (Figure 3.1) while one's blood pressure, electrocardiogram (ECG), and general response to exercise are monitored by a physician. In either case, the work load is gradually increased in a stepwise fashion until a predetermined target heart rate is attained, the person can no longer continue, or symptoms of CVD are observed, which dictate that the test should be terminated. The primary purpose of the test, when directed by a physician, is to identify the presence of silent ischemic heart disease by means of the ECG in the absence of clinical symptoms. Although testing of persons under age 35 without significant risk factors is not likely to identify more than one case in a hundred, ischemic responses can be expected with greater frequency as age increases. In addition to revealing the presence of latent ischemic heart disease, the test is often useful for other reasons[3]—to evaluate cardiovascular function capacity, to evaluate response to conditioning, and to increase individual motivation.

Who Should Have a Stress Test?

Ideally, all who plan to engage in strenuous exercise would be well advised to take a physician-administered stress test first. Even in apparently healthy, **asymptomatic** young adults, the test can be

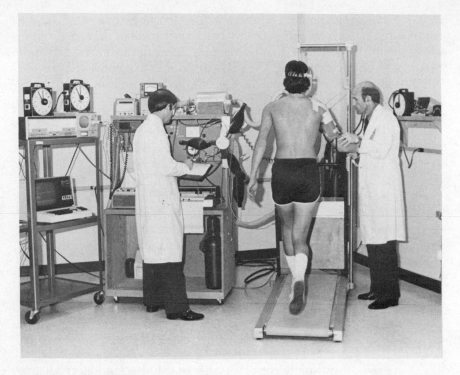

Figure 3.1. Treadmill stress test

valuable to establish an ECG baseline, which can be compared with the results of some future test if the question of abnormality should arise. Realistically, however, graded exercise tests are quite expensive, and testing sites are often not conveniently located for those who might desire to be tested. Fortunately, people who are able to exercise safely can usually be identified with proper screening during a routine medical examination, including a review of family history of heart disease and a routine ECG. On the basis of the findings of such examinations, the American College of Sports Medicine Committee on Exercise and Stress Testing has recommended that candidates for exercise be classified and advised as follows:[1]

1. For asymptomatic individuals under age 35 with no previous history of CVD and without any of the CHD primary risk factors, the risk involved in the increase of habitual physical activity is low enough that special medical clearance is not required. If questionable symptoms develop or if this individual has not had a medical examination during the previous two years, consultation with a physician would be wise before proceeding with an exercise program.

2. For those 35 years of age or younger who have had or who show evidence of CVD or who have significant combinations of positive family history of CVD, elevated blood pressure (hypertension), hyperlipidemia, diabetes mellitus, cigarette smoking, or obesity, medical clearance is highly recommended prior to any significant increase in physical activity level.
3. Regardless of health status, all persons above age 35 are advised to receive medical clearance before they increase activity levels. Furthermore, all persons over age 35 and all those under age 35 who are either high risk or **symptomatic** are advised to take an ECG-monitored graded exercise test conducted under the supervision of a qualified physician prior to any major increases in exercise.

GUIDELINES FOR THE EXERCISE PRESCRIPTION

Best results from any training program are assured when the exercise regimen is prepared on scientifically sound principles and is based on the results of a preliminary evaluation of the subject's circulorespiratory (CR) function, health, interests, motor proficiency, and available facilities.[2] Eight steps are easily identifiable in the development of an individualized exercise prescription. They are (1) medical clearance, (2) identification of a personal fitness goal, (3) some form of CR fitness evaluation (e.g., Cooper's 12-Minute Run, Harvard Step Test), (4) selection of a training style or styles, (5) establishment of exercise frequency, (6) establishment of exercise intensity, (7) determination of the duration of each exercise session, and (8) periodic reevaluation of CR fitness and program adjustment if necessary. The steps described above are applicable for use by any age group. Remember, however, that as age increases, medical clearance becomes more important and that a longer period is required to experience improvement.

Step One: Medical Clearance

If CHD risk factors, overt symptoms of cardiac impairment, or age (see p. 12) suggests that exercise might not be well tolerated, medical clearance should be sought before an individual engages in any significant increase in physical activity. If, however, there are no contraindications to physical activity, it is not hazardous for most people to develop and engage in individualized exercise programs.

Step Two: Goal Identification

Because exercise benefits are closely related to the type of training one employs, it is imperative that the desired level of fitness be identified. Equally important is the definition of the desired type of fitness (e.g., strength, CR endurance, speed). Those who want to run marathons require different styles and levels of training from those who prefer to participate in recreational activities that use different muscle groups and demand lower levels of CR endurance.

Step Three: Circulorespiratory Fitness Evaluation

Unless one falls into a category that requires a physician-administered stress test, less sophisticated, self-administered tests are helpful in estimating CR fitness levels. Examples of such tests are the 12-min run, the 1.5-mi run, or the Harvard Step Test. These tests are described in Appendixes A and B and Laboratory Exercises 5 and 6. Additional tests are available for walking, cycling, and swimming.[4] None of these tests should be used until moderate aerobic exercises have been employed for a few weeks. Younger individuals generally require a shorter period of preparation than older ones.

Step Four: Selection of a Training Style and Exercise Type

Selection of the type of exercise and the training style is critical to the success of an exercise program for at least two reasons. First, the appropriateness of these two choices determines whether the training results will be consistent with the goals that have been identified. Second, the style must provide a pleasant training experience or the long-term commitment to exercise is not likely to persist. Varying both training style and surroundings relieves the boredom that so often sets in when the same routine is followed over an extended period.

The most basic principle behind any type of training is that it should overload the body beyond normal daily demands. Second, training has a specificity effect: only the body part that is overloaded improves, and the improvement is specific to the type of exercise used. Because of this, several types of exercise are available. (See Chapter 5 for explanation of various appropriate activities.) The training effect expected from each type is important to know. To become physically fit, one needs to devise a program that stresses work in CR endurance, muscular endurance, strength, and flexibility. Chapter 4 provides more detailed information about training styles and their effects.

Circulorespiratory Endurance

If a training regimen were to contain only one type of exercise, then one that develops CR endurance would be preferable. Running, swimming, and cycling are three commonly chosen activities used to develop *aerobic power*. When properly engaged in, these types of movements overload the oxygen-transport system and result in an increase in CR endurance. Any activity that involves the large-muscle groups of the body in continuous, rhythmic, *dynamic contraction* at the appropriate intensity is satisfactory.

Muscular Strength and Endurance

Methods of developing strength and methods of developing endurance lie at opposite ends of a continuum. Strength is best developed by high-resistance, low-repetition exercises, which are dynamic. On the other hand, to improve either CR or muscular endurance, one must alter the traditional strength-training procedure by increasing repetitions.

If one wants to develop both strength and muscular endurance, strength is usually the initial concern until the desired level is achieved. Then the regimen is altered to provide increased endurance. (See Chapter 4.)

Isometric exercise has been proved effective in increasing strength; however, we have two serious reservations about recommending it. First, research indicates that *isometric contraction* appears to enhance strength most at the angle at which contraction occurs. Second, static straining is potentially dangerous to poorly conditioned individuals and persons with compromised CV function. At any rate, neither isometric nor dynamic resistive exercise is effective in the improvement of CR endurance to any appreciable degree.

Flexibility and Relaxation Activities

As a result of inactivity or aging, the range of motion in joints progressively decreases. Maintaining flexibility is highly desirable and can be achieved by slow stretching movements. A posture at the limit of one's range of motion should be held momentarily, then followed by a further effort to stretch the joint and the corresponding muscle groups. Rapid, forced, ballistic bouncing is not recommended because tissue damage might occur. It has been suggested that this type of bouncing might even be detrimental to flexibility, owing to muscular response to the *stretch reflex*. Additional information on flexibility can be found in Chapter 6.

In recent years, more emphasis has been placed on relaxation activities. (See Chapter 8.) The key lies in identifying the source of muscular tension. Relaxation is then achieved by vigorous contraction of that particular muscle group while breathing freely, after which a conscious attempt at complete muscular relaxation is made. These exercises are most effectively used during the warm-up and cool-down periods of an exercise session.[1]

Steps Five, Six, and Seven: Selecting Training Frequency, Intensity, and Duration

Training frequency, intensity, and duration are interrelated in the exercise prescription. Even if one variable is altered, a concomitant adjustment in one or both of the remaining variables can be made to produce the same result. Thus, these variables can be manipulated to prevent injury in the initial stage of a regimen and to ward off boredom or to increase the training stimulus during some later stage.

When planning an exercise program, one does well to remember that the initial improvement in sedentary individuals generally occurs in proportion to the amount of work accomplished. Later, as the physical condition improves, further increases in the work load elicit diminished gains in relation to work input. This necessitates periodic revisions of the exercise prescription if continued improvement is desired. At some point, however, when improvement is no longer the goal, the program changes to one of maintenance. Thus, when one is faced with decisions about how often (frequency), how long (duration), and how hard (intensity) the exercise program should be, two major criteria should be kept in mind: first, the entry level of the participant, and second, the goals and how soon they must be achieved.

Except for very deconditioned people, fewer than three workouts per week appears to be insufficient to produce measurable training benefits. Three workouts per week have been demonstrated to be beneficial for most sedentary persons. After a moderate level of training has been attained, however, the frequency usually must be increased if continued improvement is to be observed. Therefore, after the initial triweekly period, and except in the case of those who are preparing for competition, training frequency should be increased to four or five weekly sessions interspersed with occasional rest days. The rest days allow the body to rebuild tissues that inevitably become worn and injured, and they offer psychological relief to those who become bored with the regularity of the regimen.

The question often arises as to how the work sessions should be spaced when there are fewer than five per week. Participants have traditionally been advised to space training sessions symmetrically on alternate days throughout the week, although conclusive scientific data are not currently available. In one study involving the arrangement of triweekly training sessions, the improvement made by a group that worked for three consecutive days and rested for four was not different from the improvement made by a group that symmetrically spaced training and rest days.[5] Despite the evidence of improved aerobic power with nonsymmetrical spacing of training sessions, the effectiveness of exercise in the reduction of serum triglyceride levels for 24 to 36 hr after a vigorous workout appears to make symmetrical spacing more advisable.

Intensity and duration are inversely related. For the development of CR endurance, it seems more desirable to increase the duration (within reasonable limits) at the expense of intensity rather than vice versa, particularly in symptomatic individuals over 35 years old. An exercise session should include an initial 5- to 10-min warm-up period (longer for the older and the less well conditioned) and should end with approximately 10 min of cool-down and relaxation activities. A minimum of 20 min of aerobic exercise, exclusive of warm-up and cool-down, is recommended.

Determining the intensity of exercise is probably the most important part of an exercise prescription. Always remember that training effects ensue only if the amount of the overload (training stimulus) is greater than some minimal amount of work necessary to maintain normal physiologic function and that the level of this stimulus varies among individuals.

Researchers have fairly well defined the threshold necessary to produce measurable gains in aerobic capacity as roughly 60% of one's **maximum heart rate range** (maximum heart rate minus resting heart rate). Just as one can train at an intensity too low to be of any benefit (i.e., below 60%), training can also be more rigorous than necessary to accomplish the desired goals. Except in the case of athletes preparing for world class competition, training at intensities greater than 85 to 90% of one's aerobic capacity is unnecessary. Furthermore, too high a training level might even be hazardous to those with exercise limitations.

One of the most frequent mistakes made by those who are beginning exercise regimens is to work too hard too soon. The resultant general malaise and localized muscular soreness experienced by formerly sedentary people are often a turning off rather than a turning on to exercise. In addition, failure to allow adequate time for the musculoskeletal system to adapt to this new form of stress too often results in painful overuse injuries that could be avoided by slowly, progressively increasing the amount of exercise as tolerance improves. There is no hurry, no deadline to meet, because we are talking about a lifetime commitment—not a crash program to develop fitness.

The training effect appears to be dependent, at least in part, on the total amount of work accomplished. The initial workouts should be low intensity with musculoskeletal adaptations as the primary goal.

After this initial phase, the intensity can be safely increased to 60 to 75% of the maximum heart rate range. Work at this level should produce recognizable improvement in 6 to 8 weeks, and substantial improvement within 6 to 8 months. Thereafter, the rate of improvement will likely decline. Until one becomes well conditioned, work above the 60 to 75% level is not well tolerated and therefore is not recommended. In practical terms, one should feel fully recovered within approximately 1 hr after exercise. Otherwise, the program is too severe.[1]

Quantifying Intensity

Several indices are available to quantify the intensity of a training program. The wise participant learns the technique of self-monitoring responses to the training stimulus, both during the workout and over the long term. Because heart rate, work load, and oxygen uptake are linearly related in the normal workout ranges, any of these is suitable for monitoring training intensity. Heart rate is the easiest to monitor and is probably used most frequently. To determine resting heart rate, the first and second fingers are placed lightly on the carotid artery, which is located in the neck (Figure 3.2). The pulsations are counted for 30 sec and multiplied by 2 to find the number of beats per minute. Only one carotid should be selected for *palpation,* and the pressure should be very light to prevent stimulation of the *barorecep-tors,* which reflexly reduce heart rate. In addition, if an estimate of exercise heart rate is desired, measurement must be made during the *10 sec immediately* following the cessation of exercise. Other sites may be used to monitor heart rate, including the wrist or by placing the open hand over the left breast area during or immediately following exercise.

The heart rate at which one should work can be calculated easily (Table 3.1), as is demonstrated in the following problem. Assume that an exercise prescription calls for work at 60% of the maximum heart rate range. Assume a maximum heart rate of 200 beats per minute (bpm) (this is the predicted value for a normal 20-year-old) and a resting heart rate of 70 bpm. The effective or maximum heart rate range is calculated by subtracting the resting heart rate from the maximum heart rate, which gives a potential increase of 130 bpm. This figure is then multiplied by 0.6 (for a 60% increase), which gives 78 bpm and is added to the resting rate. The target heart rate for satisfying the prescribed intensity level is therefore 78 + 70 = 148 bpm. The resting and maximum heart rate values may change from person to person, along with the intensity percentage to be calculated; however, the procedure for calculation does not change (Figure 3.3). If maximum heart rate is not known, a generally acceptable estimate can be made by subtracting one's age in years from 220.

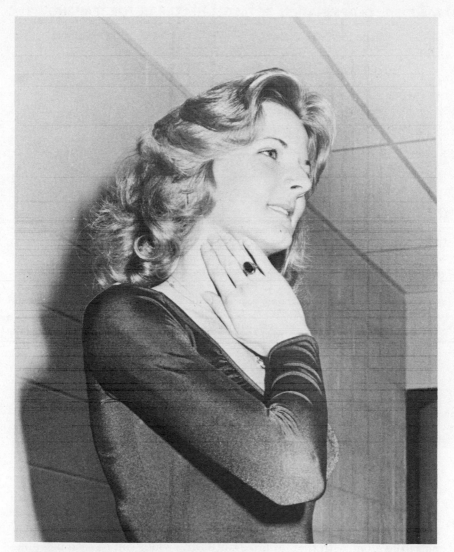

Figure 3.2. Palpation of carotid pulse

An alternative method to the use of the heart rate as an index of circulatory stress is gaining wider acceptance among exercise physiologists and medical personnel. This method employs multiples of the resting metabolic rate (**MET**), which represent the amount of oxygen used in the performance of various activities (expressed as milliliters of oxygen consumed per kilogram of body weight per minute). One MET is approximately 3.5 ml/kg/min. Two METs represent work requiring 7.0 ml/kg/min, 3 METs represent 10.5 ml/kg/min, and so on.

TABLE 3.1. DETERMINATION OF TARGET HEART RATE FOR TRAINING

Steps for Calculation		Sample	
1. Predicted maximum heart rate[a] (use actual rate if known)	= _____	(200)	200
2. Resting heart rate (end of week 1)	= _____		−70
3. Maximum heart rate range	= _____		130
4. Percentage desired for training (use 60%, 70%, 80%)	= × _____		×0.60
5. Multiply step 3 by step 4	= _____		78
6. Resting heart rate	= + _____		+70
7. Target heart rate for training (end of week 1)	= _____		148

NOTE: Periodic revision of target heart rate will become necessary as resting heart rate changes.

[a]If maximum heart rate is not known, a generally acceptable estimate can be made by subtracting one's age from 220. See M. Karvonen, K. Kentala, and O. Muslala, The effects of training heart rate: A longitudinal study. *Annales Medicinae Experimentalis et Biologiae Fenniae* 35:307–315, 1957.

The maximum functional capacity of most sedentary individuals is about 8 to 10 METs, and in highly trained athletes, about 16 to 20 METs. Accordingly, a work intensity of 4 METs represents 50% of the functional capacity of an individual whose maximum capacity is 8 METs, whereas this same load represents only 25% of the capacity of an athlete whose maximum is 16 METs. Consequently, the intensity represented by an MET is absolute in terms of the amount of oxygen consumed but relative with respect to the functional capacity of an individual. That is to say, 8 METs might be all that one individual can tolerate, but it might tax another individual at only 50%. Some common activities along with their approximate MET value can be seen in Table 7.12.

A third method of quantifying the level of the training stimulus makes use of the number of Calories required for a particular workout. Although appropriate for any exerciser, it is particularly attractive to those who plan to use exercise to assist in weight reduction. To use the method, one needs only to consult Table 7.12 or one similar.

Assume that the exercise prescription for a 150-lb person calls for a 200 Cal/day workout to assist in weight reduction and that the participant's exercise choice is jogging. Table 7.12 shows that jogging at 5 mph requires an energy expenditure of 0.0667 Cal/lb/min. Multiplied

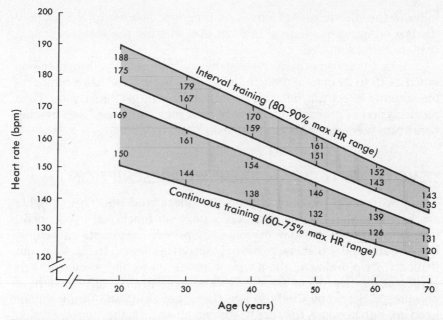

Figure 3.3. Training heart rate (HR) zones for increasing aerobic capacity. (Rates were calculated using the Karvonen formula and assuming a resting HR of 75 bpm and a maximum HR of 220 − age.)

by this person's body weight (150 lb), the energy cost becomes about 10 Cal/min (0.0667 Cal/lb/min × 150 lb). Expending 200 Cal by jogging at the rate of 5 mph would require approximately 20 min (200 Cal ÷ 10 Cal/min).

Regardless of the method used to quantify the intensity of work during an exercise session, it is wise to "listen" to your body. What is an acceptable work intensity on a given day may be entirely too difficult on another day when ensuing illness, injury, adverse environmental conditions, fatigue, or a combination of these calls for a reduction in work intensity. Any good training program employs a varied style to prevent boredom, allows for easy days following hard training days, and provides for occasional days without training at all to allow the body to rest. Our body has a way of telling us these things if we are only sensible enough to learn the language and listen.

Step Eight: Periodic Reevaluation

Most people make measurable improvement during the first 6 to 8 weeks of regular training, providing the exercise prescription is appropriate. Therefore, periodic evaluation of progress is an important index to the effectiveness of a training program. The results tell not only if one is adapting at a normal rate but also whether the goals set in step two are being achieved.

As fitness improves, resting heart rate usually decreases—as much as 15 to 20 bpm in some individuals. This means that a comparable training effect can be achieved at a lower target heart rate. Thus recalculation of a new training heart rate zone using the lower resting heart rate becomes necessary (Tables 3.1 and 3.2).

DEVELOPMENT OF AN EXERCISE PRESCRIPTION

Scott and Cindy are 19-year-old college students. Their weights are only slightly above normal. They have no functional impairment, and they are not regular exercisers. Sporadic attempts at tennis, basketball, and other recreational activities leave them sore and demonstrate a decline in the physical fitness they enjoyed during their earlier years. Several of their friends are physically active and have encouraged Scott and Cindy to join them, but Scott and Cindy cannot keep up. Furthermore, they are unsure about their ability to recondition themselves properly. Using the steps outlined in this chapter, they could proceed as follows.

Looking at the guidelines for the exercise prescription, they find themselves in a category that does not demand special medical clearance. Even so, they should use good common sense as they train and listen to their body for signals that might warrant medical advice.

Next, they set their training goals. They have heard and read about the many benefits of regular exercise, and they admire the self-confidence and apparent physical fitness displayed by their friends who

TABLE 3.2. RECORD OF RESTING HEART RATE

	Resting Heart Rate	Target Heart Rate
End of week 1		
End of week 2		
End of week 3		
End of week 4		
End of week 8		
End of last week		

are runners. Although not now possible, they eventually would like to join the friends in their daily 2 to 3 mi runs, which are usually covered at a pace of about 8.5 min/mi.

Having chosen this goal, they need to evaluate their present level of CR fitness so as to initiate an appropriate training stimulus. To accomplish this, Scott and Cindy self-administer the 12-min run (see Laboratory Exercise 5) and find that they can complete only 1.3 and 1.2 mi, respectively, in the allotted time. These results indicate that their CR fitness is only fair. (See Appendix A.)

The training style most likely to help Scott and Cindy initially will be an interval approach involving brief periods of work interspersed with rest periods of equal length. As their exercise tolerance improves, they should work toward a continuous effort by gradually increasing the length of the work periods while decreasing the time spent resting.

Adhering to the general principle that those in average or poorer fitness categories need to train three times per week, they select Monday, Wednesday, and Friday as their training days. (Scott and Cindy might like to train 5 days/week for faster progress, but they are aware that overuse at any point in training, and particularly during the early weeks, increases the possibility for musculoskeletal injury.) After 3 or 4 weeks they might try increasing the frequency of the workouts to 4 or 5 days/week so long as their backs, legs, ankles, and feet do not indicate ill effects.

Scott and Cindy are concerned about how intense their workout should be. Looking through an old college text, they find that they are not likely to experience any significant improvement unless they work in excess of 60% of their maximum heart rate range. Using the procedure described in Table 3.1, Scott calculates his target heart rate to be 149 bpm. He should not exceed 75% of his maximum heart rate range (168 bpm), so that the work does not become uncomfortably difficult during the relatively long periods of continuous work. Having determined this range, he should try to reach the minimum stimulus (heart rate = 149) after about 3 min of work. By approximately halfway through the workout, he should be at 65 or 70% of his maximum heart rate range (heart rate = 155 to 162). He should approach the upper limit to the training range (heart rate = 168) by the end of the workout.

Because Cindy's resting heart rate (80 bpm) is higher than Scott's (70 bpm), her minimum target heart rate (153) will be somewhat higher, as will her training range (153 to 171). In spite of these small differences, she must follow the same principles of training relative to target heart rate and training range that have been prescribed for Scott. This will probably mean that if Cindy and Scott wish to train together, she will have to work at a greater relative work load owing to her smaller and less efficient CR system. That is to say, at a given running pace, a greater demand is usually placed on the female's CR system than on that of her male partner.

The last critical decision Scott and Cindy have to make concerns the length of each workout. Ultimately, the greater the quantity of work (to a point), the greater the benefit. A realistic approach, however, must take into account their personal fitness goals as well as the time they are willing to devote to training. They must also remember that intensity, duration, and frequency are interrelated and can be manipulated in various combinations to produce the desired result. Two general principles will be helpful here: the principle of working within a training heart rate range, and the principle that about 300 Cal should be expended at the appropriate heart rate for CR benefits to accrue.[2]

In the early stages (first 3 to 5 weeks) of their training regimen, they should settle for 15 to 20 min of triweekly walking or jogging, at least until their musculoskeletal system can endure greater stress. After they have gradually worked up to about 2 continuous mi (within the prescribed heart rate range), their speed over this distance should be increased to provide the necessary overload for continuing improvement. Periodic reevaluation (every 4 to 6 months) of CR fitness is advisable to determine if the training regimen remains adequate.

Aging and Physical Activity

The aging process has predictable effects on one's body that result in a gradual decline in functional capacity. This decline is characterized by the following physiological changes:

1. Increased body fat
2. Increased blood pressure
3. Decreased flexibility
4. Decreased muscular strength and endurance
5. Decreased CR endurance
6. Decreased skeletal strength

That some of these changes are seen in inactive individuals of any age strongly suggests that the decline does not have to be accepted as a natural consequence of aging and is therefore inevitable. Research supports that much of the decline in functional capacity is more the result of hypokinetic disease than the aging process. In fact, evidence substantiates that every one of the changes listed, except some cases of blood pressure, can be reversed, or at least have the rate of progression slowed by proper physical activity.

Although hypokinesis results in declining functional capacity at any age, the rate of decline is accelerated in the over-25 age group. It is critical, therefore, that the aging individual understands the urgency of becoming or remaining active or both. It must also be emphasized that age is no barrier to exercise and that the aging body will respond to physical training in the same manner as the young body. The only real difference is that the time (weeks or months) required for the response will be longer, and the ultimate level that can be achieved will likely be lower as age increases.

The guidelines used to prescribe exercise for young and older populations are generally not different. The oldster is well advised to be more cautious relative to some aspects, however. The advice on medical clearance (p. 29) and the general precautions provided at the end of this chapter are particularly important to the older exerciser. Just remember that to train (exercise) at one's own pace while listening for body signals of overexertion can be enjoyable and fulfilling at any age.

Precautions

In general, apparently healthy, asymptomatic persons whose functional capacities are at least 8 METs can participate safely in an unsupervised conditioning program. For symptomatic persons, regardless of their functional capacities, or for asymptomatic persons whose functional capacities are less than 8 METs, supervised exercise programs are advised, at least until it is deemed safe for them to exercise on their own.[1] Additional precautions seem warranted as follows:[3]

1. Exercise should be avoided when it can aggravate a minor illness, injury, or infection or retard recovery from illness. Even when one simply does not feel well, exercise might be postponed, because illness might be incipient.
2. Strenuous exercise is hazardous in unusual environmental conditions (heat and humidity), during times of emotional stress, or immediately after ingestion of a heavy meal. In these cases, the intensity must be decreased or the exercise even postponed.
3. Cool-down periods should occur in the same environment as the exercise. In no case should one move from a cooler to a warmer environment during a cool-down period after strenuous exercise. (See next item.)
4. Hot showers, sauna baths, and steam rooms should be avoided during the immediate postexercise period, particularly by the over-35 age group. The increased metabolic activity that occurs during exercise liberates a tremendous amount of heat energy that must be dissipated. Conditions that inhibit heat removal (e.g., warmer environments, hot showers) increase the work of the circulatory system. For some, this added circulatory stress may precipitate a heart attack.

Summary

In summary, the following considerations appear to be reasonable when one makes a commitment to exercise throughout life:

1. Preliminary determination of individual functional capacity in relation to the degree of risk involved in exercise, with subsequent medical clearance or restriction.
2. Development of an appropriate exercise prescription, scientifically based on individual objectives, needs, functional capacity, and interests.
3. Regular, prudent participation in the prescribed regimen, with attention to safety precautions and contraindications to exercise.
4. Periodic reassessment of functional capacity in terms of adaptation to training, with subsequent adjustment of the prescription if indicated.

REFERENCES

1. American College of Sports Medicine. 1975. *Guidelines for graded-exercise testing and exercise prescription*. Philadelphia: Lea and Febiger.
2. ———. 1980. *Guidelines for graded-exercise testing and exercise prescription*. 2d ed. Philadelphia: Lea and Febiger.
3. American Heart Association. 1972. *Exercise testing and training of apparently healthy individuals: A handbook for physicians*. New York: American Heart Association.
4. Cooper, K. H. 1982. *The aerobics program for total well-being*. New York: Bantam Books.
5. Moffatt, R. J., Stamford, B. A., and Neill, R. D. 1977. Placement of triweekly training sessions: Importance regarding enhancement of aerobic capacity. *Research Quarterly* 48(3):583–591.
6. Naughton, J. P., and Hellerstein, H. K., eds. 1973. *Exercise testing and exercise training in coronary heart disease*. New York: Academic Press.

Chapter Four
TRAINING PROGRAMS AND THEIR EFFECTS

STUDENT OBJECTIVES

On completion of this chapter, the student should be able to:

1. Define the key terms listed above
2. Differentiate between types of training programs with regard to expected benefits
3. Develop an individualized training program for improving circulorespiratory endurance
4. Develop an individualized training program for improving strength
5. Describe the procedure used in circuit training
6. List the physiologic adaptations to endurance training
7. List the physiologic adaptations to strength training
8. List six functional abnormalities that may occur when anabolic androgenic steroids are used by males and by females
9. List six exercise-induced injuries
10. List six problems that might result from inappropriate exercise during pregnancy

PRINCIPLES OF TRAINING

Van Huss et al.[65] list several goals that supposedly motivate people to train. Some of the more common ones are:

1. Development of physique
2. Improvement of general physical condition
3. Increase in proficiency in sport skills

4. Weight control
5. Rehabilitation from injury or disease
6. Protection from injury

The training procedures used to accomplish these ends take various forms. As was indicated in Chapter 3, one must decide the benefits desired before formulating a training program. Only after personal objectives are clearly identified can decisions regarding exercise type, frequency, and intensity be made. It is essential that individuals desiring to train understand the principal concepts basic to the development and maintenance of any training program.

First, the **specificity effect** of training mentioned in Chapter 3 should be emphasized. This means that one benefits only in specific ways from particular kinds of training. For example, if one engages in activities that primarily involve the legs, then the arms do not benefit. Training is even more specific to limbs or muscle groups. Roberts and Alspaugh[52] clearly demonstrated this in a cycling and running experiment. Thirty-six subjects were initially tested on a bicycle ergometer and a motor-driven treadmill, after which they were randomly assigned to two different training groups. One group trained by pedaling a stationary bicycle and the other group by running on the treadmill. At the end of 6 weeks, each group was retested on both the bicycle and the treadmill. Interestingly, even though both training procedures involved leg work, the bicycle group improved only when tested on the bicycle ergometer, but the treadmill group improved on both the bicycle and the treadmill. From these data, cycling appears to be a more specific exercise, while running appears to be a more general conditioner. Other experiments comparing arm work and leg work have produced similar results—improvement seems to be restricted to the location of the working muscles.[20] Obviously, however, local muscle groups do not improve appreciably without some adaptation of the central circulation to training. Consequently, when constructing training programs, one must be careful to select stimuli that elicit central circulatory adaptation as well as peripheral adaptation in those muscles doing the work.

Second, the principle of overload (see Chapter 3) must be reemphasized. Without a *stressor* (exercise) greater than that which is habitually encountered, no improvement will occur. The greater the overload, within certain limits, the greater the stimulus imposed.

Third, training must occur regularly at an intensity greater than a minimum threshold, or adaptation will not occur. The amount of the benefit, to a point, is roughly proportional to the amount of work accomplished.

Fourth, once the desired state of fitness is achieved, continued maintenance is necessary, or the training effect will be lost. The rate of decline varies among individuals, but appears to be influenced by a number of factors, including heredity; level, length, and type of prior training; and posttraining life-style. In general, physical fitness is lost more rapidly than it is achieved. A reasonable level of fitness can be maintained through biweekly or triweekly maintenance workouts depending on the level to be maintained.

TRAINING FOR CIRCULORESPIRATORY ENDURANCE

Circulorespiratory (CR) endurance (also called *aerobic power*) indicates a high state of efficiency of the circulatory and respiratory systems in supplying oxygen to the working tissue. Of all the benefits one might receive from physical training, increased CR endurance is perhaps the most important. A multitude of training styles can be used for CR improvement. Two of the most popular are described here.

Continuous Exercise

Running or jogging long, slow distances (LSD) is an excellent method of improving CR endurance. (**Jogging** is defined as a slow running pace of about 8 to 12 min/mi.) Depending on the individual's training objective, appropriate distances range from 2 to 6 mi at an intensity of between 6 and 15 min/mi. Whatever the distance, the pace must be severe enough to elicit a heart rate of at least 60% of the maximum heart rate range, as was described in Chapter 3. Generally, this works out to be about 150 beats per minute (bpm) for most people 18 to 25 years old.

The importance of the distance-intensity relationship can be seen clearly in the results of a study we conducted using 20 college-age women enrolled in a foundations class.[4] They ran 1.3 mi/day in symmetrically spaced triweekly sessions for 10 weeks. Although the women were aware of the intensity levels necessary to elicit a training response, they were not forced to work at any particular intensity; only the distance was required. A comparison of their treadmill performances before and after the training period revealed no changes in maximum oxygen uptake, heart rate response to a given submaximum work load, or maximum heart rate. We concluded that distance alone in the absence of some minimum level of intensity does not guarantee improvement in CR endurance.

Interval Training

Interval training has been well received as an outstanding method of developing aerobic power. In contrast to the LSD regimen, interval training is discontinuous. A typical interval workout consists of several (three to seven) work periods that are relatively short (usually 3 to 5 min each) and very strenuous (approximately 80 to 90% of maximum capacity). These are interspersed with rest periods during which the subject walks or jogs while partially recovering for the next work period. The length of the recovery period may be based on a previously set **work/relief** ratio of 1:1 or 1:2, or it may be judged sufficient when the heart rate has returned to 120 bpm.[41]

Interval-style training appears to have several advantages over continuous work.

1. The intensity of the work can be greater because the work periods are relatively short.
2. The total amount of work accomplished within a given time can be greater.
3. More work can be accomplished with less discomfort.
4. The flexibility of the program helps reduce the boredom of prolonged continuous exercise.
5. The methods available for increasing the work load are more flexible.

Important considerations in the construction of an interval program are:

1. The length of the work period. At least 3 to 5 min are required if aerobic power is the objective.
2. The length of the rest period. Acceptable ratios of work to relief are 1:1 to 1:2.
3. The intensity of the work. In most cases, 80 to 90% of maximum capacity is recommended.
4. The number of work periods.

As the individual adapts physiologically to the training stimulus, the work load can be increased by:

1. An increase in the length of the work period
2. A decrease in the length of the rest period
3. An increase in the intensity of the work period
4. An increase in the number of work periods
5. Any combination of the above

Apparently not all types of exercise are equally effective in improving aerobic power. For example, Fox et al.[29] reported posttraining increases in maximum oxygen uptake when several short sprints served as the training stimulus. The sprinting periods (15 to 30 sec each) were interspersed with rest periods in a work/relief ratio of 1:3. Using 10 subjects in a similar program, we were unable to replicate these results.[5] In another study, Allen, Byrd, and Smith[3] used triweekly sessions of circuit weight training to condition 33 college freshmen. During each 27-min workout, 30-sec work bouts were alternated with 60-sec rest periods (work/relief ratio of 1:2). Even though heart rates during the entire 27-min workout far exceeded the generally accepted threshold for the production of cardiovascular adaptation, no *hemodynamic* improvement was found. From these results, the conclusion is that high heart rates alone do not stimulate training benefits but that the type of exercise is important.

The appropriateness of using very short work intervals for development of aerobic power remains questionable. Reports of increasing aerobic power by means of work periods of less than 2 min should be accepted with reservations until more data supporting these claims can be assembled.

Suitable Activities

Several popular activities can improve CR fitness. To qualify, three criteria must be met. First, the activity must be primarily aerobic. This means that the CR system is capable of supplying most of the oxygen required by the working muscles during the activity. Second, the level of the work (training stimulus) must be great enough to tax the oxygen transport system. Third, the time spent in the activity must be long enough to engage the aerobic metabolism as the primary pathway for energy production. Activities that are suitable for improving CR endurance are described in Chapter 5. In general, however, activities that are rhythmic and that employ large muscles are most effective.

HEMODYNAMIC RESPONSES TO ENDURANCE TRAINING

The training programs previously described in this chapter elicit responses that are specific to the frequency, intensity, duration, and type of exercise employed. Furthermore, the changes of adaptation might differ with respect to the physiologic states—rest, submaximum work, and maximum work. The consensus of recent research appears to support the posttraining changes presented in Tables 4.1 and 4.2 and Figure 4.1.

TRAINING FOR STRENGTH

For many years, the main physiologic benefit ascribed to weight training has been the development of muscular strength. DeLorme[23] wrote that weight-training methods can be clearly divided into two

TABLE 4.1. HEMODYNAMIC CHANGES AT REST AND DURING SUBMAXIMUM AND MAXIMUM WORK AFTER SEVERAL WEEKS OF CIRCULORESPIRATORY ENDURANCE TRAINING

Parameter	At Rest	During Submaximum Work	During Maximum Work
Heart rate	Decrease	Decrease	No change; slight decrease
Stroke volume	Increase	Increase	Increase
Cardiac output	No change; decrease	No change; decrease[a]	Increase
Peripheral blood flow	Decrease	Decrease	Increase
Systolic blood pressure	Decrease; no change	Decrease; no change	Decrease; no change
Diastolic blood pressure	Decrease; no change	Decrease; no change	Decrease; no change
Oxygen extraction (ml O_2/100 ml blood)	No change; increase	No change; increase	Increase
Oxygen uptake (liters/min)	No change	No change decrease[a]	Increase

[a] Slight decrease is due to increased mechanical efficiency.

TABLE 4.2. PHYSIOLOGIC ADAPTATION OF VARIOUS PARAMETERS TO SEVERAL WEEKS OF CIRCULORESPIRATORY ENDURANCE TRAINING

Parameter	Adaptation
Fibrinolysis	Increase; no change
Hemoglobin (total)	Increase
Metabolic enzymes (aerobic)	Increase
Muscle capillarization	Increase; no change
Myocardial weight (animal studies)	Increase
Percentage of body fat	Decrease
Red blood cells per mm³	No change; decrease[a]
Serum cholesterol	No change
HDL-cholesterol	Increase
LDL-cholesterol	Decrease
Serum triglycerides	Decrease
Total blood volume	Increase

[a] Marathon training

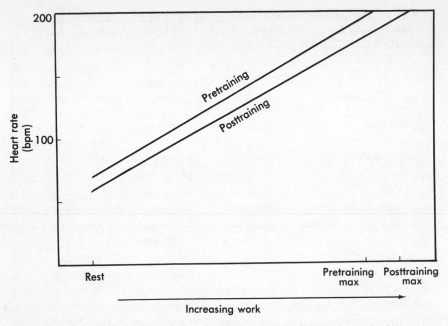

Figure 4.1. Heart rate response to given work loads before and after several weeks of endurance training

types: a high-resistance, low-repetition program for strength development and a low-resistance, high-repetition program for improvement of muscular endurance. He further suggested that either type is incapable of producing the results obtained by the other.

DeLorme's technique of *progressive resistance exercise,* generally accepted as the standard of weight training during the late 1940s, called for 7 to 10 bouts (**sets**) of repetitive exercise, each set consisting of 10 to 12 repetitions. His patients tried to increase the number of repetitions (**repetition max,** or **RM**) they could execute daily. At the end of each week, a new maximum resistance that could be handled through 10 repetitions (10 RM) was determined. The result was constant overload during the work period.

DeLorme and Watkins[24] later modified DeLorme's original statement on the necessary intensity and duration of the work bout; they recommended that workouts begin with only 50% of maximum contraction, to be increased to 100% at least once during the workout, and that the seven to ten sets be reduced to two or three. This procedure was questioned by Zinovieff[67], who advocated reversing the order in which resistance is applied, so that the heaviest loads would be encountered first and reduced systemically thereafter to keep pace with fatigue.

Since the time of these early conceptions of technique, weight training has been studied extensively by several investigators. Differences of opinion based on practical experience as well as on the results of experimental research abound. Berger[12,13,14,15] experimented with different combinations of repetitions and sets, attempting to identify the best method for developing strength. His findings supported the concept of high-resistance, low-repetition exercise recommended earlier by DeLorme. Furthermore, he concluded that a three-set, 6-RM regimen provided the best results. Workouts using heavier loads for fewer than 2 RM or lighter loads for more than 10 RM were unsatisfactory alternatives to the three-set, 6-RM combination.

More recently, however, Stone, O'Bryant, and Garhammer[60] reported a method for developing strength that integrates the traditional approach with periodization techniques employed by the successful Eastern European strength coaches as well as by many bodybuilders.

Hypertrophied muscle is generally accepted to have a higher potential for strength gain than nonhypertrophied muscle. According to Stone, O'Bryant, and Garhammer,[60] hypertrophy is best achieved using three to five sets of relatively high-volume, low-resistance exercise (8 to 20 RM). Once hypertrophy is achieved, three to five sets of 2 to 6 RM should be employed to produce the desired strength. In a study comparing this method with the traditional three-set, 6-RM method, these researchers reported the newer model to be superior to the more classical method for developing strength. Furthermore, the time required for a given amount of improvement was reduced with the newer model.[60]

Isotonic Contraction

The strength programs mentioned above all make use of isotonic, also called dynamic or moving, contraction. An isotonic contraction occurs when a muscle changes length and allows a joint to move through its complete range of motion. This occurs in natural movements such as walking and running, as well as in strength training when conventional weights, or weight-training machines such as Universal and Nautilus, are employed.

Isometric Contraction

A second type of contraction used to overload muscles is isometric. During isometric contraction, no shortening takes place—only straining against an immovable object. Since the work of Hettinger and Muller[36] was first reported, isometric exercise has been investigated extensively. Although not without opposition, some research supports isometrics as a useful method for developing muscular strength.[12,15,32,43,45]

Originally Hettinger and Muller reported that a single daily *static contraction* exceeding one third of the maximum strength of a muscle and held for a short period was able to produce the maximum rate of strength increase, whereas weekly contractions reduced the rate of gain by one third.[46] The reported rapid increases in strength, with a minimum amount of time involved and with no equipment necessary, have made isometrics attractive. Of several attempts[18,34] to reproduce Hettinger and Muller's original findings, however, only one[51] was successful. Because strength appears to increase significantly only at the angle of the contraction, we do not consider isometric exercise programs to be effective in the development of strength for activities requiring dynamic contractions. In addition, reports of hypertensive blood-pressure response during heavy isometric work[26] and increased resting diastolic blood pressure after an isometric training regimen appear to contraindicate extensive use of isometrics, especially by those with a compromised heart or impaired arterial walls.

Perhaps the most valuable use of isometric contraction is by people who have sendentary jobs. Daily isometric exercise can be performed whether seated or standing and without attracting attention. Moderate intensity contractions will serve to maintain muscle tone.

Isokinetic Contraction

Yet another type of strength training is isokinetic exercise. *Isokinetic contraction,* unlike isotonic and isometric contraction, provides maximum resistance to movement and a constant rate of movement, regardless of the changes in force that take place as leverage and mechanical advantage change. This is not true with conventional weights because after the initial force is applied, the ballistic effect reduces the muscle force necessary to complete the movement. In addition, at the end of most conventional lifts, *eccentric contraction* must be used to brake the inertia and return the weight to the prelift position.

Many advocate the eccentric portion as a valuable part of strength development. Isokinetic exercise, with the help of specially designed devices, eliminates the eccentric portion of the movement and provides for a constant resistance, regardless of changes in the force generated by the contracting muscle. This means that the muscle encounters maximum resistance throughout its range of motion. Although several studies support isokinetics as more effective than isotonics or isometrics in strength improvement,[37,44,53,64] it could be argued that elimination of eccentric contraction by isokinetics encourages an imbalance in opposing muscle groups and reduced coordination.

Steps in Developing a Strength Training Regimen

Traditional Approach

The following program is a cookbook approach to the formulation of one's own high-resistance, low-repetition program for strength development.

1. Identify the muscle groups in which an increase in strength is desired.
2. Select appropriate lifts to stimulate those muscles.
3. Arrange the order of lifts in such a manner that the same muscle groups are not used consecutively.
4. For each lift, determine the maximum amount of weight that can be moved for a set of five repetitions. This amount becomes the 5 RM.
5. The training regimen consists of three sets for each lift. Beginning with the 5 RM, try to work up to a maximum of eight repetitions for each lift during each of the first two sets.
6. When eight repetitions can be accomplished in each of the first two sets and exceeded in the third set, increase the resistance (at the beginning of the next training session) for that particular exercise until a new 5 RM (step 3) is established.
7. Lift triweekly on nonconsecutive days.

In our laboratory, 33 students using this program had an average gain in strength of 39% over a 12-week training period. The least improvement of the six muscle groups employed was 26%. The greatest amount of improvement, in the leg press, was 71%.[3]

Alternate Approach

The following program is a straightforward approach for increasing strength at an optimum rate. It was constructed from a model developed by Dr. Michael Stone at the National Strength Research Center of Auburn University and employs the periodization concept. Initially, a high-volume, low-intensity regimen is followed to produce muscular hypertrophy. Finally, a low-volume, high-intensity program is used to increase strength in the hypertrophied muscle. Strength gains in a group using this model are reported to be significantly higher than in a group using the three-set, 6-RM program after 6 weeks of training.[60] The following eight steps should be helpful in personalizing this model:

1. Identify muscle groups to be strengthened.
2. Determine the kinds of lifts to be used.
3. Determine the 10 RM.

4. For 3 weeks employ three to five sets at 10 RM, 3 or 4 days/week.
5. For 4 weeks employ three sets at 5 RM, 3 or 4 days/week.
6. For 4 weeks employ three sets at 2 to 3 RM, 3 or 4 days/week.
7. Convert to a maintenance regimen or a program of active rest (training at a recreational level using low volume and low intensity).
8. Repeat the cycle.

RESPONSES TO STRENGTH TRAINING

The hemodynamic improvements that occur after several weeks of endurance training are not observed after strength training of equal duration. Certain *histological* and biochemical changes are observed in the trained muscles, however.

1. Muscle fibers increase in size. An increase in the number of muscle fibers has been reported, but the evidence is not convincing. At any rate, this is secondary in importance to individual fiber hypertrophy.
2. Contractile force (strength) increases.
3. Hypertrophy of connecting tendons, ligaments, and supporting bony structures takes place.
4. Articular cartilages become thicker and more compressible.
5. Oxidative enzyme concentration decreases.
6. Mitochondrial volume density decreases.[42]

ANABOLIC ANDROGENIC STEROIDS

Some strength training enthusiasts and bodybuilders have attempted to maximize muscle response to the training stimulus by taking anabolic androgenic steroids (AAS) orally or by injection. In general, these drugs produce a masculinizing effect in both sexes and enhance protein synthesis. Their use during training can produce considerable hypertrophy and significant increases in strength in some people. Of the many issues involved in the use of these drugs, perhaps the most important is how AAS affect the health of those who use them. Serious and sometimes irreversible physiological changes as well as psychological abnormalities accompany AAS usage[8,40,62,63] and should not be ignored by a potential user. Although a detailed discussion of the topic is beyond the scope of this book, a partial listing of reported adverse responses to AAS is given in Table 4.3. Use of these potentially dangerous drugs is highly discouraged except where therapeutic prescription is necessary.

TABLE 4.3. SELECTED ADVERSE EFFECTS OF ANABOLIC ANDROGENIC STEROIDS ON MALES AND/OR FEMALES

Liver disease, including cancer
Accelerated cardiovascular disease
Decreased HDL-cholesterol
Increased serum cholesterol
Elevated blood pressure
Hyperinsulinism
Altered glucose tolerance
Decreased testicular size
Reduced sperm count
Increased virilization
Irreversible hirsutism
Irreversible clitoral enlargement
Menstrual abnormalities
Male pattern baldness
Aggressive behavior
Psychological disorders
Premature epiphyseal closure (youths)

CIRCUIT TRAINING

Circuit training was introduced by Adamson[2] in the late 1950s. This method can be used to improve general body condition or can be combined with resistive exercises in a program of circuit weight training for the development of strength or muscular endurance.

The classic circuit program consists of 9 to 12 exercise stations arranged in a circuit. After choosing the amount of work to be performed at each station, the person is timed during three laps around the circuit (with no rest between exercises or laps). The time recorded is reduced by one third; the resulting figure is the target time. When the person successfully completes the three laps within the target time, the amount of work at each station is increased, a new target time is established, and the training resumes. (See Laboratory Exercise 9.)

MUSCLE SORENESS

Some people experience muscle pain during the later stages of high-intensity exercise but almost everyone is familiar with the stiffness, soreness, and tenderness that occur a day or so following unaccustomed muscular exertion. This is normal and is observed after both strength and endurance work.

The pain that accompanies heavy exercise most likely results from the accumulation of metabolic products such as *lactic acid.* This pain is transitory and usually subsides shortly after the intensity of the exercise is reduced. Recovery appears to be enhanced by continued, very mild movement. This encourages removal of lactic acid from the affected muscles because circulation is allowed to continue at a relatively higher level than if the exercise were stopped abruptly.

The delayed-onset muscular soreness that follows unaccustomed muscular activity usually peaks 24 to 72 hr postexercise and then gradually subsides until it is unnoticed by the fifth to the seventh day.[9] At least three theories have been advanced to explain this soreness. Hough[38] hypothesized that the pain results from structural damage. DeVries[25] proposed that the soreness results from spasms of localized motor units in the affected muscles. Asmussen[10] and Komi and Buskirk[39] suggested that overstretching the muscle's elastic components during the eccentric phase of contraction produces the delayed pain.

In a study by Abraham,[1] the validity of each theory was tested experimentally. He reported that the evidence did not appear to support either the spasm or the muscle-damage theory, and that the delayed-onset soreness can most likely be attributed to alterations in the muscle connective tissue (elastic components). However, the soreness was found in muscles that performed concentric contractions as well as in those that performed eccentric ones.

Armstrong,[9] however, cites several studies that report the use of eccentric contraction as the most predictable way of producing delayed-onset muscular soreness.

Recovery from this type of soreness can be enhanced by warm compresses or warm baths, accompanied by light exercise to help prevent adhesions during the healing process.

EXERCISE INJURY

All who exercise should be aware that the benefits to be gained are not without concomitant risk of injury. In healthy individuals, exercise can induce injuries that range from minor aggravations to those so painful as to require complete immobilization during recovery. For others, such as postcoronary patients, persons in the coronary heart disease (CHD) high-risk category, and those with certain congenital abnormalities, some forms and levels of exercise can be hazardous—even life threatening. These people should exercise only under close medical supervision.

Each recreational activity has its own category of injuries that are peculiar to its demands. Although complete categorization and coverage are beyond the scope of this book, a few of the injuries most common to runners and bicyclists are described because these activities are probably the most popular forms of exercise that tend to generate injuries.

Running-Related Injury

In general, many of the overuse injuries incurred by runners could be prevented by adequate attention to strengthening anterior surface muscles and stretching posterior surface muscles. The low back problems frequently experienced result from muscle strength imbalances in the abdomen and lower spine area. A regular flexibility regimen coupled with bent-knee situps to strengthen abdominal muscles while at the same time increasing lower back flexibility has proved helpful.

Runner's Knee (Chondromalacia Patella)

Runner's knee is characterized by pain in the area of the knee. It has been described as the most frequent overuse injury in sports. According to Dr. George Sheehan,[57] four factors can act singly or in combination to produce an erosion of the cartilage covering the underside of the kneecap. These factors are structural instability of the foot, postural instability, leg-length discrepancy, and environmental stresses such as improper shoes or running on slanting surfaces. A weak quadriceps muscle (anterior thigh) has also been implicated.

To alleviate the condition, usually the foot must be treated rather than the knee. Foot supports called orthotics are placed in the shoes to assure balanced bone structure in the foot and ankle. Flexibility exercises are prescribed to stretch the shortened hamstring muscles. Lifts are used to equalize leg length. Properly constructed training shoes with adequate foot cushion are recommended.

Achilles Tendinitis

Achilles tendinitis is an inflammation of the heel cord (Achilles tendon) common in those who participate in running sports. Often the result of shortened calf muscles or of an abnormally formed foot that puts stress on the cord, it can be prevented by using stretching exercises to lengthen the calf and by inserting a wedge to elevate the heel adequately.

Use of ice on the area, heel lift orthotics, flexibility exercises, and avoidance of hill and speed running are recommended during the treatment and recovery period.[57,59]

Shinsplints

Shinsplints is a general term for pain over the anterior lower leg. It could result from a stress fracture of the lower leg bone (tibia), ischemia of the posterior leg compartment, or even soft-tissue injury and inflammation.[11] Overuse of the anterior compartment muscles, strength and flexibility imbalance of the lower leg muscles, a weak and excessively pronated foot, and improper shoes are factors often cited as contributing to the development of this disorder.

Treatment employs ice on the painful area, elevation, and rest, plus correcting the factors creating the problem.

Stress Fractures

Stress fractures are overuse injuries resulting from a series of submaximum stresses, any one of which is unlikely to cause a fracture. They are commonly seen in the long bones of the feet (metatarsals) and the bones of the lower leg (tibia and fibula) of middle- and long-distance runners.[55]

The chief symptom is diffuse pain that later localizes. This disorder is difficult to diagnose because these fractures may not be visible in an X-ray for several days.[50]

Colored Urine (Pigmenturia)

In some long-distance runners, the release of hemoglobin due to red blood cell destruction (hemoglobinuria) or of myoglobin during muscle damage (myoglobinuria) can result in pigmented urine during the first few hours after completing a run.[22] This type of pigmenturia is not dangerous nor is it an indication of a pathological condition. With adequate fluid replacement, the disorder usually corrects itself in a few hours.

Another form of pigmenturia results from red blood cells in the urine (hematuria) owing to bladder or urethra damage from repeated pounding of the bladder walls during long-distance running (usually 10,000 m or longer). This form usually corrects itself within 24 to 48 hr. In any of these pigmenturias, dark urine beyond 48 hr warrants prompt medical evaluation.

Of concern should be the underlying cause. Some doctors feel that the degree of exertion by the average jogger is not likely to produce hematuria from bladder trauma, and that all such first events should be clinically evaluated in light of the possibility of kidney or bladder tumors, cysts, stones, or other urinary disorders.[17,19] Others contend that first episodes that correct themselves are not usually dangerous and do not warrant the cost and inconvenience of complete urinary tract evaluation.[58]

Blacklock[16] suggested that hematuria from bladder trauma might be prevented if a critical volume of urine remains in the bladder to cushion the shock during exercise. To accomplish this, the runner refrains from complete bladder evacuation prior to running. Another technique involves full hydration prior to and during exercise.

Blisters and Stone Bruises

A blister is an escape of tissue fluid beneath the skin's surface caused by friction. Although debilitating to a runner, blisters usually heal relatively quickly compared with other exercise-induced injuries. Recovery time is prolonged, however, if improper care allows them to become infected.

Selection of properly fitting footwear, lubricating the areas of friction, and sensible care of the feet can prevent most blisters. When they do occur, the affected area should be cleansed with an antiseptic. The blister should then be lanced with a sterile needle at several points along its circumference and forcibly drained. The dead skin layer should be allowed to remain in place for protection. Surrounding the affected area with a thin felt or sponge doughnut helps to relieve pressure and eliminate friction until the area ceases to be tender.

Stone bruises of the heel surface or the ball of the foot are most often caused by running with inadequate foot cushion on rocky surfaces. Use of a sponge doughnut is about the only treatment unless one chooses to stay off the injured foot until it has healed.

Bicycling Injury

Poor riding position while bicycling encourages problems with the back, neck, and hands. The common cause is a combination of maladjustments that place the trunk too far forward. To see ahead, the neck must be hyperextended. Over a long ride, the required activity of the neck muscles may lead to severe localized neck pain or headache.

To support the trunk against gravity, either the muscles of the lower back must work continuously or the hands and arms must support the weight of the trunk. Continuous sharing of the load by the back muscles often leads to low back pain. Too much weight on the hands for extended periods can lead to serious neurological damage to the hand.

During the exaggerated trunk-forward position, typical hand placement on the handlebar subjects the ulnar nerve to severe punishment. In the hand, this nerve runs along the palmar surface on the side of the ring finger. Nerve fiber compression resulting from prolonged support of the trunk weight coupled with the periodic shocks transmitted from the riding surface through the frame results in a loss of the nerve's ability to transmit impulses. Symptoms of this injury are loss of sensation or tingling in the ring and little fingers on either or both hands and weakness in one or both hands; both symptoms may occur simultaneously. Compression neuropathy can result in irreversible damage to the ulnar nerve and permanent paralysis to the hand.

This disorder can be prevented by improved riding position, frequent change in hand position on the handlebar, and padding the handlebar or wearing padded gloves.[27]

Dehydration and Heat Illness

All exercisers should appreciate the necessity of water and electrolyte replacement when working in the heat. Weighing in before and after working out can serve as a guide to the amount of water that needs to be replaced. If a preworkout weight is 2% or more under that of the previous day, fluid replacement has probably been inadequate, and exercise should not be undertaken until rehydration has occurred. Generally, for each pound of water lost because of sweating, 1 pt of supplemental water is required.[30]

Replenishment of body fluid during or after exercise is limited by the rate at which the stomach empties. Gastric emptying is controlled by many factors including the volume of fluid ingested, its temperature, and its composition.

The optimal emptying rate occurs when the volume imbibed is kept between 400 and 600 ml (13.5 and 20 oz), the fluid temperature is about 5°C (41°F), and the sugar concentration remains below 2.5 gm/100 ml (0.9 oz/liter) of fluid.[21]

Although less critical than fluid replacement, electrolyte replacement is important for health maintenance. After acclimatization to exercising in the heat has occurred, dietary intake of sodium and potassium is usually sufficient to maintain safe levels except in those who sweat profusely. Even in these cases, supplemental salt is not required until more than 6 lb have been lost during one workout. The resulting deficit is then best handled by slightly increasing the amount of salt used at the table. Salt tablets are not recommended, because of the digestive disturbances so often related to their ingestion. *Caution:* If salt tablets are used, copious amounts of water are required (at least 1 pt per 7-grain tablet) or severe medical consequences might result.[30]

Inadequate water and electrolyte replacement and disregard of safe practices when working in the heat can lead to heat cramps, heat fatigue, and heatstroke. Symptoms of heat cramps and heat fatigue are usually transitory and disappear after a few hours of rest in a cooler environment and ingestion of fluids. Heatstroke, on the other hand, is life threatening, and most persons do not recover without prompt medical attention. Even then, permanent damage to the thermal regulatory mechanism usually results.

The best way to prevent heatstroke and other forms of heat illness is through adequate water and electrolyte replacement and the use of good judgment when working in the heat. The American College of Sports Medicine's position statement on such matters as fluid replacement while exercising is a helpful guide to follow.[7]

WOMEN AND TRAINING

In recent years women have become increasingly involved in physical activity and athletic competition. In most cases, the female response to physical training is identical to the male response. A few unique problems commonly occur in women, however.

Iron Depletion

After the onset of the menstrual cycle, some women become more susceptible to iron-related blood disorders because they lose iron during menstruation. Some studies have reported that prolonged, regular exercise (training) tends to aggravate this problem by reducing the body's store of iron. Although the literature is not in complete agreement,[49,66] sufficient evidence exists to suggest that women engaged in prolonged heavy training should have their serum iron levels monitored to determine whether they need supplemental iron.[31,47,48]

Menstrual Cycle and Exercise

The regularity of the menstrual period varies widely among healthy women, as does the degree of associated discomfort. The best advice regarding exercise during menstruation appears to be to listen to your body. If it says no, then exercise should be postponed, or at least curtailed, until normal vigor returns. Although exercising during menses is not harmful, heavy work may not be well tolerated. In our laboratory, some women experienced extreme discomfort during maximum treadmill testing while menstruating.

A growing amount of evidence suggests that severe, prolonged training, such as long-distance running, is associated with the cessation of menstrual periods (amenorrhea) and the absence of ovulation.[6,28,61] Whether this departure from normal reproductive function results directly from exercise or indirectly from the dramatic reduction of body fat typical of long-distance runners is not clear. Severe reduction of body fat in females inhibits the production of hormones that regulate the menstrual cycle. This appears to be transitory, however, and menstrual function returns to normal when training ceases or becomes less intense. Although heavy exercise is not recommended as a safe method of birth control, women trying to become pregnant should be aware that hard training may reduce fertility.

Breast Soreness

Breast soreness is a frequent complaint of many women who exercise regularly. Haycock and Gillette[35] reported that 72% of the female athletes they questioned experienced sore or tender breasts after exercise, most commonly after running. Although the reason for this soreness is not known, most theories attribute it to the stress produced on the underlying muscle and connective tissue by the horizontal and vertical motion of the breast during vigorous body movement. Furthermore, improperly supported breasts of some exercising women may result in damage to underlying muscle and connective tissue.

Apparently, other factors as well as breast size (mass) contribute to the discomfort. In a study designed to investigate breast soreness, Gehlsen and Albohm[33] studied 20 female athletes, 10 of whom had felt breast discomfort and 10 of whom had never felt breast discomfort. The bra cup sizes of the women in the discomfort group were 50% B, 20% C, and 30% D. The cup sizes of those who felt no discomfort were 90% B and 10% D. Biomechanical analysis of breast motion during running showed that two groups differed significantly only in the product of breast mass and velocity of movement. It was concluded that the breast mass, acting in conjunction with the velocity of breast movement, may be related to discomfort while jogging.

Studies of sport bra effectiveness have shown that breast motion can be controlled by a properly constructed bra.[33,54] The desirable qualities of such a bra as suggested by finalists in a women's marathon are firm lateral support; sufficient total support; no lace, padding, or underwires; an all-elastic back; and a wide variety of sizes. To prevent breast soreness and reduce the risk of premature breast sag, women who wear a B or larger cup size should consider wearing a sport bra when exercising.

Pregnancy and Exercise

Most professionals responsible for prenatal care agree that a healthy and physically fit woman fares better during pregnancy and delivery than one who is unfit. Even though existing studies on human pregnancy generally have not shown exercise to be harmful, evidence from animal studies, plus what is known about human response to exercise and training, raises serious questions about exercising during pregnancy that remain unanswered.

Dr. Mona Shangold, assistant professor of obstetrics and gynecology at Georgetown University School of Medicine and an enthusiastic runner, has listed the following concerns about exercising during pregnancy.[56]

1. Fetal oxygen deprivation (hypoxia)
2. Excessive temperature (hyperthermia)
3. Inadequate nutrition
4. Alterations in metabolism
5. Alterations in hormone production
6. Possible alterations in hormone response

During vigorous exercise, blood is diverted from some abdominal organs (e.g., kidney, intestines) to favor delivery to active skeletal muscles and the skin for energy production and cooling. If uterine blood flow is also reduced, oxygen deprivation could injure the developing fetus. The exercise intensity at which this might occur is not presently known. Dr. Shangold has suggested that exercise heart rates in the 140 to 160 bpm range may represent a safe intensity level.

Excessive temperature in early pregnancy produces birth defects, and in later pregnancy can induce premature labor. Although perhaps inconvenient, exercising pregnant women should monitor their body temperature at the conclusion of a session. If postexercise temperature (underarm or rectal) exceeds 101°F, efforts to hasten cooling should be undertaken.

Adequate birthweight is an important determinant of early survivability. Women who exercise heavily might not be able to consume enough calories and nutrients to provide energy for their exercise and at the same time allow for the 20- to 30-lb weight gain needed to ensure a healthy child at birth.

Vigorous exercise has also been shown to produce alterations in metabolism and hormone production. The effects of these changes on the developing child are not known at this time. Additionally, the possibility that responses to certain hormones may be altered should not be disregarded.

As might be expected, these concerns make advice about exercising during pregnancy somewhat controversial. There is no reason to tell healthy pregnant women not to exercise. In fact, they should be encouraged to do so within limits. The following plan represents a prudent approach that can help maintain a reasonable fitness level while protecting both the mother and the developing child.

1. Women who have been previously sedentary are not advised to start a *strenuous* exercise program after becoming pregnant. They are better advised to initiate a conservative program such as daily walking.
2. Women who are already training strenuously and become pregnant are best advised to gradually reduce the intensity during the course of pregnancy.
3. In either case, women should avoid training that
   a. Requires heart rates in excess of 160 bpm
   b. Extends over long periods (e.g., distance running)
   c. Is likely to produce dehydration or hyperthermia or both
   d. Is likely to increase the risk of abdominal trauma

Informed caution should be the guide during this time.

REFERENCES

1. Abraham, W. M. 1977. Factors in delayed muscle soreness. *Medicine and Science in Sports* 9(1):11–20.
2. Adamson, G. T. 1959. Circuit training. *Ergonomics* 2:183–186.
3. Allen, T. E., Byrd, R. J., and Smith, D. P. 1976. Hemodynamic consequences of circuit weight training. *Research Quarterly* 47:299–305.
4. Allen, T. E., and Miller, D. K. 1978. The effects of 10 weeks of running at volitional intensity on the cardiovascular systems of college women. *Journal of Physical Education and Recreation* 49(6):75–76.
5. ———. Sprint training for aerobic power. Unpublished report. Wilmington: University of North Carolina.
6. American College of Sports Medicine. 1979. Opinion Statement: Participation of the female athlete in long distance running. *Medicine and Science in Sports* 11(4):9.
7. ———. 1984a. Position statement: The prevention of heat injuries during distance running. *Medicine and Science in Sports and Exercise* 16(5):9–14.
8. ———. 1984b. Position statement: The use of anabolic-androgenic steroids in sports. *Sports Medicine Bulletin* 19(3):13–18.
9. Armstrong, R. B. 1984. Mechanisms of exercise-induced delayed onset muscular soreness: A brief review. *Medicine and Science in Sports and Exercise* 16(6):529–538.
10. Asmussen, E. 1956. Observations on experimental muscle soreness. *Acta Rheumatologica Scandinavica* 1:109–116.
11. Benas, D., and Jokl, P. 1978. Shin splints. *American Corrective Therapy Journal* 32(2):53–57.

12. Berger, R. A. 1962a. Comparison of static and dynamic strength increases. *Research Quarterly* 33:329–333.
13. ———. 1962b. Effect of varied weight training programs on strength. *Research Quarterly* 33:168–181.
14. ———. 1962c. Optimum repetitions for the development of strength. *Research Quarterly* 33:334–338.
15. ———. 1963. Comparison between static training and various dynamic training programs. *Research Quarterly* 34:131–135.
16. Blacklock, N. J. 1979. Bladder trauma in the long-distance runner. *American Journal of Sports Medicine* 7(4):239–241.
17. ———. 1980. Bladder trauma from jogging. *American Heart Journal* 99(6):813–814.
18. Bonde-Petersen, F. 1960. Muscle training by static, concentric, and eccentric contractions. *Acta Physiologica Scandinavica* 48:406–416.
19. *British Medical Journal.* 1979. The haematuria of the long-distance runner. 6183(2):159.
20. Clausen, J. P., Trap-Jensen, J., and Lassen, N. A. 1970. The effects of training on the heart rate during arm and leg exercise. *Scandinavian Journal of Clinical and Laboratory Investigation* 26:295–301.
21. Costill, D. L., and Saltin, B. 1974. Factors limiting gastric emptying during rest and exercise. *Journal of Applied Physiology* 37(5):679–683.
22. Daniels, J., Fitts R., and Sheehan, G. 1978. *Conditioning for distance running.* New York: John Wiley and Sons.
23. DeLorme, T. L. 1945. Restoration of muscle power by heavy resistance exercise. *Archives of Physical Medicine* 27:645–667.
24. DeLorme, T. L., and Watkins, A. L. 1948. Techniques of progressive resistance exercise. *Archives of Physical Medicine* 29:263–273.
25. deVries, H. A. 1966. Quantitative electromyographic investigation of the spasm theory of muscle pain. *American Journal of Physical Medicine* 45:119–134.
26. Donald, K. W. et al. 1967. Cardiovascular responses to sustained (static) contractions. *Physiology of Muscular Exercise.* American Heart Association Monograph no. 15, 15–30.
27. Faria, I. E., and Cavanagh, P. R. 1978. *The physiology and biomechanics of cycling.* New York: John Wiley and Sons.
28. Feicht, C. B. et al. 1978. Secondary amenorrhea in athletes, letter to the editor. *Lancet* 2(8100):1145–1146.
29. Fox, E. L. et al. 1973. Intensity and distance of interval training programs and changes in aerobic power. *Medicine and Science in Sports* 5:18–22.

30. Fox, E. L., and Mathews, D. K. 1981. *The physiological basis of physical education and athletics*. 3rd ed. Philadelphia: W. B. Saunders Company.

31. Frederickson, L. A., Puhl, J. L., and Runyan, W. S. 1983. Effects of training on indices of iron status of young female cross-country runners. *Medicine and Science in Sports and Exercise* 15(4):271–276.

32. Gardner, G. W. 1963. Specificity of strength changes of the exercised and nonexercised limb following isometric training. *Research Quarterly* 34:529–537.

33. Gehlsen, G., and Albohm, M. 1980. Evaluation of sports bras. *The Physician and Sportsmedicine* 8(10):89–97.

34. Hansen, J. W. 1961. The training effect of repeated isometric muscle contractions. *Internationale Zeitschrift fur Angewandte Physiologie* 18:474–477.

35. Haycock, C. E., and Gillette, J. 1976. Susceptibility of women athletes to injury. *Journal of the American Medical Association* 236:163–164.

36. Hettinger, T., and Muller, E. A. 1953. Muskelleistung und muskeltraining. *Arbeitsphysiologie* 15:111–126.

37. Hislop, H. J., and Perrine, J. J. 1967. The isokinetic concept of exercise. *Physical Therapy* 47(2):114–117.

38. Hough, T. 1902. Ergographic studies in muscular soreness. *American Journal of Physiology* 7:76–92.

39. Komi, P. V., and Buskirk, E. R. 1972. The effect of eccentric and concentric muscle activity on tension and electrical activity of human muscles. *Ergonomics* 15:417–434.

40. MacDougall, D. 1983. Anabolic steroids. *The Physician and Sportsmedicine* 11(9):95–99.

41. MacDougall, D., and Sale, D. 1981. Continuous vs. interval training: A review for the athlete and the coach. *Canadian Journal of Applied Sport Sciences* 6(2):93–97.

42. MacDougall, J. D. et al. 1979. Mitochondrial volume density in human skeletal muscle following heavy resistance training. *Medicine and Science in Sports* 11(2):164–166.

43. Mathews, D. K., and Kruse, R. 1957. Effects of isometric and isotonic exercises on elbow flexor muscle groups. *Research Quarterly* 29:26–37.

44. Moffroid, M. et al. 1965. A study of isokinetic exercise. *Physical Therapy* 49(7):735–747.

45. Morehouse, C. A. 1967. Development and maintenance of isometric strength of subjects with diverse initial strength. *Research Quarterly* 38:449–456.

46. Muller, E. A. 1958. Training muscle strength. *Ergonomics* 2:216–222.
47. Nickerson, H. J., and Tripp, A. D. 1983. Iron deficiency in adolescent cross-country runners. *The Physician and Sportsmedicine* 11(6):60–66.
48. Pate, R. R. 1983. Sports anemia: A review of the current research literature. *The Physician and Sportsmedicine* 11(2):115–131.
49. Puhl, J. L., and Runyan, W. S. 1980. Hematological variations during aerobic training of college women. *Research Quarterly* 51(3):533–541.
50. Quigley, T. B., ed. 1979. *1979 Yearbook of sports medicine.* Chicago: Year Book Medical Publishers.
51. Rarick, G. L., and Larsen, G. L. 1958. Observations on frequency and intensity of isometric muscular effort in developing static muscular strength in postpubescent males. *Research Quarterly* 29:333–341.
52. Roberts, J. A., and Alspaugh, J. W. 1972. Specificity of training effects resulting from treadmill running and bicycle ergometer riding. *Medicine and Science in Sports* 4:6–10.
53. Rosentswieg, J., and Hinson, M. M. 1972. Comparison of isometric, isotonic and isokinetic exercises by electromyography. *Archives of Physical Medicine and Rehabilitation* 53(6):249–252.
54. Schuster, K. 1979. Equipment update; Jogging bras hit the streets. *The Physician and Sportsmedicine* 7(4):125–128.
55. Scriber, K., and Burke, E. J., eds. 1978. *Relevant topics in athletic training.* Ithaca, N.Y.: Movement Publications.
56. Shangold, M. M. 1983. Reproductive function of the female athlete. Symposium of American College of Sports Medicine Annual Meeting, Montreal.
57. Sheehan, G. 1978. *Medical advice for runners.* Mountain View, Calif.: World Publications.
58. Siegel, A. J. 1979. Exercise related hematuria: Findings in a group of marathon runners. *Journal of the American Medical Association* 241(4):391–392.
59. Smart, G. W., Tauton, J. E., and Clement, D. B. 1980. Achilles tendon disorders in runners—a review. *Medicine and Science in Sports and Exercise* 12(4):231–243.
60. Stone, M. H., O'Bryant, H., and Garhammer, J. 1981. A hypothetical model for strength training. *Journal of Sports Medicine and Physical Fitness* 21:342–351.
61. Strauss, R. H., ed. 1979. *Sports medicine and physiology.* Philadelphia: W. B. Saunders Company.

62. Strauss, R. H. et al. 1983. Side effects of anabolic steroids in weight-trained men. *The Physician and Sportsmedicine* 11(12):87–98.
63. Taylor, W. N. 1982. *Anabolic steroids and the athlete.* Jefferson, N.C.: McFarland.
64. Thistle, H. G. et al. 1967. Isokinetic contraction: New concept of resistive exercise. *Archives of Physical Medicine and Rehabilitation* 48(6):279–282.
65. Van Huss, W. D. et al. 1969. *Physical activity in modern living.* 2d ed. Englewood Cliffs, N.J.: Prentice-Hall.
66. Wirth, J. C. et al. 1978. The effect of physical training on the serum iron levels of college-age women. *Medicine and Science in Sports* 10(3):223–226.
67. Zinovieff, A. N. 1951. Heavy resistance exercises. *British Journal of Physical Medicine* 14:129–132.

Chapter Five
AEROBIC ACTIVITIES

KEY TERMS

Aerobic dance (p. 71)   Rope skipping (p. 72)
Bicycling (p. 71)   Swimming (p. 73)
Jogging and Running (p. 72)   Walking (p. 73)

STUDENT OBJECTIVES

On completion of this chapter, the student should be able to:

1. Contrast the aerobic activities listed above
2. Describe the properties of a good aerobic dance and running shoe
3. Describe the appropriate exercise attire for hot and cold environments

---

Many activities are suitable for improving circulorespiratory (CR) fitness. In addition to fulfilling the criteria described in Chapter 4 (i.e., aerobic in nature, adequate intensity and duration), the activity should be enjoyed by the participant. Most people will not make a lifetime commitment to participate in a physical activity that they do not enjoy.

Six popular aerobic activities that meet these requirements are **aerobic dance, bicycling, jogging** or **running, rope skipping, swimming,** and **walking.** Other excellent activities, such as cross-country skiing, hiking, and rowing, will not be discussed here. Regardless of the type of aerobic program selected, the individual should incorporate these general principles into any exercise prescription:

1. Plan for adequate warm-up, cool-down, and stretching. Flexibility exercises should be performed before and after some activities (e.g., running).
2. Use slow progression when increasing duration and intensity of the exercise. Too much too soon causes overuse injury.
3. Reduce the intensity or duration or both of the program on hot, humid days.

4. Remain aware of your body, that is, only attempt what the body says to attempt. Be alert to fatigue and early signs of injury.
5. Allow a minimum of 6 to 8 weeks to observe any physical benefits of the program.

AEROBIC DANCE

Aerobic dance is rhythmic movement—walking, jogging, running, hopping, skipping, calisthenics—performed to music. The usual routine consists of warm-up calisthenics, 30 to 35 min of vigorous aerobic movement, and 5 min of cool-down activities. Heart rate is monitored during the session to determine the intensity of the exercise.

Moderate-intensity aerobic dance sessions are comparable to ice skating at 9 mph, walking at 3.5 mph, or bicycling at 10 mph; high-intensity sessions are equivalent to 0.5 hr of vigorous basketball, cycling at 13 mph, or swimming at 55 yd/min.[4] In caloric terms, the average size female uses 3.96 Cal/min in the low-intensity routine, 6.28 Cal/min in the medium-intensity routine, and 7.75 Cal/min in the high-intensity routine. The average size man uses 4.17 Cal/min in the low-intensity routine, 6.86 Cal/min in the medium-intensity routine, and 9.44 Cal/min at the high-intensity level.[4]

Many different aerobic dance routines are available on records and tapes, enabling the individual to exercise in the home. The routines should be performed on wood or carpeted surfaces, and aerobic dance shoes should be worn. Unconditioned individuals should be cautious when first participating in aerobic dance classes. If exercising with conditioned individuals, they may attempt to perform at too high a level, resulting in extreme fatigue or injury.

BICYCLING

Even though an excellent activity for all ages, bicycling is especially good for the overweight and unfit who might have leg and foot problems with weight-bearing activities. Most people enjoy bicycling and do not consider it as work.

Perhaps such an attitude is the biggest disadvantage of a bicycling program. Because individuals do not consider it as work, they often do not perform at an intensity to promote CR benefits. It is necessary to pedal uphill or faster to elevate the heart rate. A nice easy pace, however, may provide mental benefits.

There are a few minor problems with this activity. In addition to being limited by the weather, finding an appropriate place to cycle may be difficult. Use of a stationary bicycle eliminates these problems and can provide the same CR benefits.

JOGGING AND RUNNING

For both jogging and running, the heart rate should be monitored to determine the intensity of the exercise. These are excellent aerobic activities that can be regulated easily, and can be done by any healthy person who does not have foot or joint problems.

To aid in preventing injury, maintain correct form.[1]

1. Keep the head up to avoid the tendency to watch the feet.
2. Keep the back straight but naturally comfortable. Do not throw back the shoulders and stick out the chest.
3. Tuck in the buttocks. In this position, a hypothetical line drawn through the shoulders and hips should be vertical or nearly so.
4. Bend the elbows, hold slightly away from the body, and carry slightly above hip or belt level. Do not hold out like wings or press to the chest.
5. Keep the body straight as the legs move freely from the hips. Lift the legs from the knees while relaxing the ankles. Do not overstride; each foot should fall just under the knee. The foot-strike should not produce a slapping action. The jarring that this causes in the leg must be absorbed by the muscles to prevent injury, wasting energy that could be used running. Of the following three methods for footstrike, use the most comfortable.
   a. With the heel-to-toe method, one should land on the heel, then rock forward to take off from the ball of the foot. This method is least wearing because the heel cushions the landing and the forward rocking distributes the pressure.
   b. With the flat-foot method, the foot falls under the knee in a quick, light action and the entire foot lands on the ground at the same time. This type of landing provides a wide surface area to cushion the footstrike. The foot should not be driven down but should be allowed to pass beneath the body.
   c. In the ball-heel-ball method, the runner first lands on the ball of the foot, settles to the heel, and takes off from the ball of the foot. This method is more efficient when attempting to run faster.

ROPE SKIPPING

Rope skipping can increase the heart rate substantially and be quite strenuous. In fact, it may be too severe for the average, untrained adult beginning a fitness program. A person should be able to walk briskly for 2 or 3 mi before beginning a rope skipping program. The initial program should consist of alternate bouts of skipping for 20 to 30 sec and equal or longer times for rest.[2] The total jumping time should be limited to 4 to 5 min/day until the individual is ready to progress.

When energy expenditure (Calories burned per minute) comparisons are made at the same heart rate, jogging appears to be better for the development of CR endurance because it involves more muscle mass than skipping in place.[2] To provide the equivalent physiological benefits, the intensity and duration of rope skipping should be at least as great as for jogging. Do not be misled by claims that jumping rope for 10 min is equivalent to 30 min of jogging. Furthermore, rope skipping, like running in place, is performed on the balls of the feet. Since over long periods of time this can cause injury and pain to the feet, wearing shoes with a good cushion is especially important for this activity.

SWIMMING

Swimming is an excellent aerobic exercise. Because it is a non-weightbearing activity and involves the major muscles of the body, swimmers are able to swim several miles or for long periods of time without the risk of joint or muscle injury. However, a few disadvantages in selecting swimming are: the individual must be a fairly competent swimmer, an aquatic facility must be available, and participants in water activities sometimes encounter ear or eye infections or sinus problems.

WALKING

Performed at progressively increased rates and distances, walking can provide sufficient stimulus to bring about CR benefits, especially for poorly conditioned or older individuals. In a walking program, joint irritation and muscle soreness are less likely with consequent low risk to the heart and blood vessels. Most walking participants remain within the recommended exercise guidelines; however, to produce CR endurance, the minimum threshold intensity level must be reached.

Any type shoe that is comfortable, provides support, and has a good cushion may be worn when walking for an extended time. Many individuals prefer running shoes during their walking exercise.

EXERCISE ATTIRE

With so many different styles of exercise clothing and shoes on the market, the consumer sometimes faces a difficult decision in the selection. The following guidelines should be followed when purchasing exercise attire, especially shoes and clothing for aerobic dance and running.

Aerobic Dance Shoes

Aerobic dance should be performed in shoes designed to take the stress of repeated shock to the feet, ankles, lower legs, and knees.[3] Running shoes are not appropriate because they break down with the sliding and twisting motions, and the elevated heel could cause ankle injury.

The sole of the aerobic dance shoe should be thick and have zigzag lines that go from side to side. The rubber heel should be directly beneath the heel of the shoe (i.e., no flair) to provide ease in executing sideward movements.

The shoe should have a lot of cushioning in the arch and heel and be very flexible. Little foot flexibility can occur when dancing if the shoe does not bend well.

The lacing style should provide five or six eyelets closely spaced on top of the instep. Wide lacing from the base of the toes across the entire instep provides less support for lateral movement. In addition, this type of shoe (low-tops) may tend to make the foot roll outward, causing ankle injury.

Shoe tops made of nylon are cooler than leather tops. Leather or suede along the toe area protects the nylon and provides a longer shoe life.

Aerobic Dancing Clothing

Comfort and ease of movement are the primary considerations in selection of aerobic dance clothing.[3] Under warm conditions, wear as little as is decently possible. Cotton shorts and a cotton tee shirt, leotards, cotton exercise body suits, or swimsuits are appropriate.

When dancing in a cool environment, dress in layers. Warm-up sweatsuits or jogging suits may be worn, and tights are especially appropriate. As the body temperature increases, some clothing may be removed. Proper-fitting socks will help to prevent blisters and keep the feet dry.

Running Shoes

When running on anything other than sand, the impact of footstrike goes into the sole of the foot and proceeds to jolt the foot, ankle joint, knee, hip, and back. For this reason, a good running shoe is especially important.[5] Cheaply made running shoes greatly increase the risk of injury.

To select a good running shoe, check the sole, heel, arch, material, and fit. The sole should be hard; it can have a flat surface or a rigid rubber design called waffles. Select the design that feels best. Between the sole and the foot are two cushions. The top cushion should be three times the thickness of the bottom cushion. These cushions help to alleviate the impact of the footstrike. The heel should be snug, and the arch should be strong and supportive.

The top of the shoes are made of canvas, nylon, or leather. Canvas is not very supportive and usually stretches. Leather is most supportive but permits the least amount of breathing. Nylon is supportive and permits breathing. The best combination is leather for support and nylon for air.

The shoe should have forefoot flex and should fit with about a thumbnail's space between the big toe and the toe of the shoe. Both the right and left shoes should feel comfortable on the feet.

Running shoes are made for forward rocking motion and should not be worn for participation in basketball, racquet sports, or aerobic dance. They can cause ankle injuries in sports that require side-to-side movements or pivots. In addition, the runner should be aware of the difference between training shoes and racing shoes. Training shoes are heavier and have higher heels and thicker soles. Training shoes should be used for routine running. A knowledgeable salesperson can be helpful to a beginning runner who is buying running shoes.

Running Clothing

Running clothing should be light, permit freedom of movement, and be appropriate for weather conditions.[5] The following items typically are worn by runners:

Tank top	Made of cotton and a light color
Shorts	Made of nylon or cotton—nylon usually preferred since cotton can cause chafing on some individuals
Socks	Regular cotton socks in cold weather and low-cut in hot weather
Warm-up suit	Only necessary in very cold weather; lightweight nylon suit with layers of clothing underneath preferred by many runners

Without being indecent, the runner should wear as little clothing as possible during hot, humid weather. During cold weather, layers of lightweight clothing are preferable to thick, bulky clothing. In addition, if mittens and a stocking cap are worn, the runner can better tolerate a cold environment.

REFERENCES

1. Bowerman, W. J., and Harris, W. D. 1967. *Jogging*. New York: Grosset and Dunlap.
2. Getchell, B., and Clearly, P. 1980. The caloric costs of rope skipping and running. *The Physician and Sportsmedicine* 8(2):56–60.
3. Mazzeo, K., and Kisselle, J. 1984. *Aerobic dance: A way to fitness*. Englewood, Colo.: Morton Publishing.
4. Schuster, K. 1979. Aerobic dance: A step to fitness. *The Physician and Sportsmedicine* 7(8):98–103.
5. Squire, B., and Krise, R. 1982. *Improve your running*. Brattleboro, Vt: Stephen Greene Press.

Chapter Six
FLEXIBILITY

Flexibility is the ability of an individual to move the body joints through a maximum range of motion without undue strain. It is not a general factor but is specific to given joints and to particular sports or physical activities. It is more dependent on the soft tissues (ligaments, tendons, and muscles) of a joint than on the bony structure of the joint itself.[2] The bony structures of certain joints, however, do place limitations on flexibility as illustrated by the extension of the elbow or knee. Similarly, *hyperextension* of the spinal column is limited by the position and shape of the spinous processes, as bending or abduction is limited by the position and shape of the transverse processes.

Flexibility is also related to body size, sex, age, and activity. Any increase in body fat usually decreases flexibility. Females are generally more flexible than males of the same age. From birth to old age, a gradual decrease in flexibility occurs as the soft tissues lose their extensibility.[4] This decrease is usually caused by failure to maintain an active program of movement through a complete range of motion.

Active individuals tend to be more flexible than inactive individuals, because flexibility is predominantly a function of habits of movement. The soft tissues or joints tend to shrink and thus lose extensibility when the muscles are maintained in a shortened position, as happens in sedentary individuals. Habitual postures and chronic heavy work through restricted ranges of motion also can lead to adaptive shortening of muscles. Physical activity with wide ranges of movement helps prevent this loss of extensibility. In summary, flexibility is related to habitual movement patterns for each individual and for each joint, and age and sex differences are secondary rather than innate.[4]

EFFECTS OF INFLEXIBILITY

Flexibility is an important aspect of physical fitness, and its lack can create disorders or functional problems for many individuals. Anyone with a stiff spinal column is at a disadvantage in many physical activities and also fails to get full value from the shock-absorbing arrangement of the spine when walking, running, or jumping. Lack of flexibility in the back can also be responsible for bad posture, compression of peripheral nerves, painful menstruation, and other ailments.[4] Short muscles limit work efficiency. They become sore when they perform physical exertion, and, without a good range of movement, the individual is more likely to incur torn ligaments and muscles during activities. In summary, individuals with good flexibility have greater ease of movement, less stiffness of muscles, enhancement of skill, and less chance of injury during movement.

DEVELOPMENT OF FLEXIBILITY

It is impossible to state how much flexibility is desirable, but everyone should strive to prevent loss of flexibility during the aging process. Of the soft tissues, the muscles are most affected by stretching exercises, and both the **static stretch** (a holding position) and the **ballistic stretch** (a bouncing motion) are effective in the development of flexible joints. However, the use of a fast, forceful, bobbing type of stretching induces the **stretch reflex,** which could result in injury to muscle tissue. The amount and rate of the stretch reflex contraction vary directly in proportion to the amount and rate of the movement that causes the stretch. The faster and more forceful the stretch, the faster and more forceful the reflex contraction of the stretched muscle. Static stretching is recommended because it will not induce the stretch reflex. In addition, it poses less danger of exceeding the extensibility limits of the tissues involved, requires less expenditure of energy, and provides greater relief from muscle soreness.[1]

Stretching should never proceed to the point of actual pain and subsequent soreness. Some discomfort can be expected, but any after-effects should be noted and given time to repair.

Little is known about the minimum requirement for producing gains in flexibility, but experience has shown that improvement is most likely to result from *distributed practice* rather than from *massed practice*.[2] Sets of stretches for each specific flexibility are better done throughout the day than all at once. Daily exercise, or at least 5 days/week, is also recommended. Once the desired flexibility has been attained, 3 days of exercise per week are probably adequate to maintain flexibility.[2]

The most important specific flexibilities are probably neck and shoulder flexion, back extension, hip flexion, and posterior lower-leg extension (ankle flexion). Hip flexion is performed with the knees straight to stretch the hamstrings (posterior upper-leg muscles). Tight hamstrings cause an improper pelvic tilt, which is a potential contributor to low back pain or problems.[2]

GUIDELINES FOR DEVELOPMENT OF FLEXIBILITY

The following guidelines are recommended for flexibility programs.[2]

1. Practice regularly. Flexibility exercises should be performed several times per day and at least 5 days/week.
2. Flexibility is highly specific to each joint and activity; therefore, flexibility exercises are highly specific.
3. Stretch gently and gradually to prevent soreness and damage to tissues. Hold the stretch position for 20 sec.
4. The extent of stretching should be gradually and progressively enlarged with full extension, flexion, or both being placed on the joint.
5. Flexibility can accompany strength development if exercises are performed through the full range of joint movement.

MEASUREMENT OF FLEXIBILITY

Flexibility is not a general factor but is specific to each joint. No single test, therefore, can measure the flexibility of all the major joints of the body. In addition, there are two types of flexibility tests:

1. Relative flexibility tests are designed to be relative to the length or width of a specific body part. In these tests, the movement and the length or width of an influencing body part are measured.

TABLE 6.1. FLEXIBILITY CLASSIFICATIONS

	Shoulder Lift (in.)	Trunk Extension (in.)	Sit and Reach (in.)
Men			
Excellent	26 or more	23 or more	7 or more
Good	23–25	20–22	4–6
Average	20–22	18–19	1–3
Below average	19 or less	17 or less	0
Women			
Excellent	25 or more	20 or more	8 or more
Good	21–24	17–19	5–7
Average	18–20	15–16	2–4
Below average	17 or less	14 or less	0–1

Sources: C. B. Corbin et al., *Concepts in physical education,* 2d ed., Dubuque, Iowa: William C. Brown, 1974; and R. V. Hockey, *Physical fitness—the pathway to healthful living,* 3rd ed., St. Louis: C. V. Mosby, 1977.

2. Absolute flexibility tests are designed to measure only the movement in relation to an absolute performance goal.

The following absolute flexibility tests provide an indication of flexibility in various parts of the body. (See Table 6.1 for desirable scores for these tests.)

The shoulder lift test (Figure 6.1) measures flexibility of the shoulders and the shoulder girdle.

1. Lie prone on the floor. Touch the chin to the floor and extend the arms forward directly in front of the shoulders.
2. Hold a stick or ruler horizontally with both hands. Keep the elbows and wrists straight.
3. Raise the arms upward as far as possible with the chin still touching the floor. Measure the distance in inches from the bottom of the stick or ruler to the floor.

Figure 6.1. Shoulder lift test

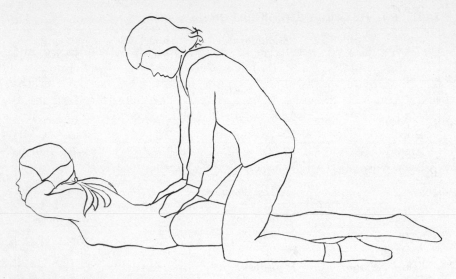

Figure 6.2. Trunk extension test

The trunk extension test (Figure 6.2) measures flexibility of the trunk.

1. Lie prone on the floor with a partner holding the buttocks and legs down.
2. With fingers interlocked behind the neck, raise the chest and head off the floor as far as possible. Measure the distance in inches from the floor to the chin.

The sit and reach test (Figure 6.3) measures flexibility of the trunk and hips.

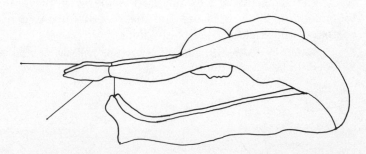

Figure 6.3. Sit and reach test

1. Sit on the floor with legs fully extended and feet flat against a bench turned on its side.
2. While a partner holds the knees straight, bend forward and extend the arms and hands as far as possible.
3. Measure the distance from the fingertips to the edge of the bench. If the fingers do not reach the edge, the distance is expressed as a negative score; if they reach beyond the edge, it is expressed as a positive score.

The procedures shown in Figures 6.4 through 6.7 can also be performed to measure flexibility.[3]

Figure 6.4. Normal flexibility of neck allows chin to move close to upper chest

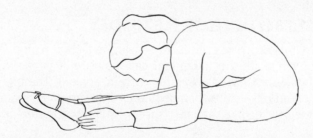

Figure 6.5. Normal flexibility of hips and lower back allows flexion to about 135 degrees in a young adult

Figure 6.6. Normal flexibility of hamstring muscle allows straight-leg lifting to 90 degrees from supine position

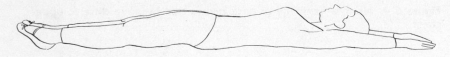

Figure 6.7. Normal flexibility of chest muscles allows arms to be flexed to 180 degrees at shoulders

EXERCISES TO DEVELOP FLEXIBILITY

The following exercises are designed to develop flexibility throughout the body. An individual can choose not to perform all the exercises but only to select ones for certain areas of the body. All the exercises should have a duration of 20 sec; they should be repeated three times and performed on at least three different occasions during the day.

Figure 6.8. Shoulder and pectoral stretch

1. Stand in a doorway and grasp the doorjamb above the head.
2. Lean forward through the doorway until stretch is felt.
3. Stretch a little farther each time.

Figure 6.9. Shoulder and pectoral stretch

1. Stand and hold a towel behind the hips, with the elbows straight and the palms toward the rear.
2. Lift the hands backward as high as possible.
3. Stretch a little farther each time. Do not bend forward.

Figure 6.10. Shoulder and pectoral stretch

1. Stand and hold a towel in front of the body, with the elbows straight and palms down, about 18 in. apart.
2. Slowly lift the towel forward and overhead.

Figure 6.11. Shoulder stretch

1. Bring the right hand over the right shoulder to the upper back.
2. Bring the left hand under the left shoulder to the upper back.
3. Hook the fingers of the two hands together and pull.

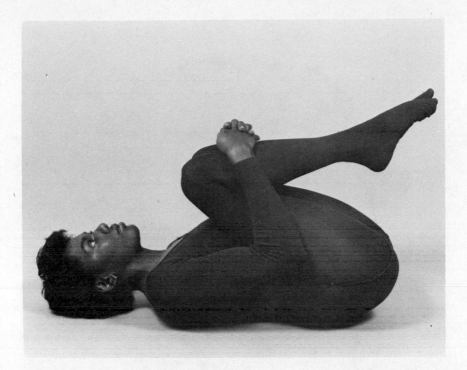

Figure 6.12. Back extensors stretch

1. Lie supine with the knees flexed and the feet flat on the floor.
2. Pull in the stomach and bring both knees toward the center.
3. Grasp the knees and pull them toward the chest.

Figure 6.13. Back extensors stretch

1. Sit with the legs crossed and the arms folded across the chest.
2. Tuck the chin and curl forward. Try to touch the forehead to the knees.

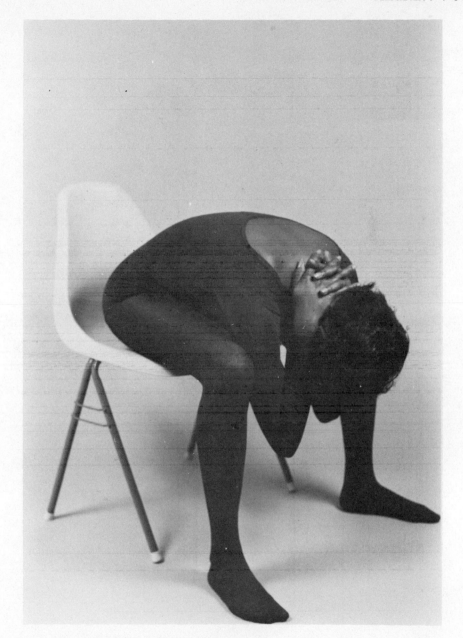

Figure 6.14. Back extensors stretch

1. Sit in a chair with the feet about 24 in. apart.
2. Bend forward, with the arms and shoulders between the knees.
3. Attempt to touch the elbows to the floor.
4. Stretch until stretch discomfort is felt in the lower back.

Figure 6.15. Upper trunk stretch

1. Lie prone with the hands in the push-up position.
2. Extend the arms fully to raise the shoulders and upper back. Keep the pelvis and legs on the floor.

Figure 6.16. Lower trunk stretch

1. Lie prone, bend the lower legs, and reach back and grasp the ankles.
2. Pull slowly and hold the head up.

Figure 6.17. Lateral abdominal stretch

1. Stand and hold a towel overhead with the hands about 12 in. apart, the elbows straight, and the feet 18 to 24 in. apart.
2. Bend to one side as far as possible. Keep the elbows straight.
3. Bend to the other side.

Figure 6.18. Lateral abdominal stretch

1. Stand with the feet together and the right side toward the wall, about 18 in. from the wall.
2. Place the right hand and forearm against the wall at shoulder level. Place the heel of the left hand on the left hip.
3. Contract the abdominal and gluteal muscles and push with the hand on the hip to move the hips toward the wall. Keep the body straight and facing forward.

Figure 6.19. Trunk twister

1. Sit on the floor with the legs crossed.
2. Twist the body to the right and reach to touch the floor behind the back with both hands.
3. Repeat for the left side.

Figure 6.20. Lower back and hamstring stretch

1. Sit on the floor with the legs straight and the feet together.
2. Bend forward and grasp the outer sides of the legs as far down as possible. Pull the head downward. Attempt to grasp the outer borders of the feet.

Figure 6.21. Hamstring stretch

1. Stand with one leg crossed in front of the other and with the feet close together. The front leg holds the rear leg back and straight.
2. Slowly bend over and attempt to place the hands on the floor.
3. Repeat with each leg.

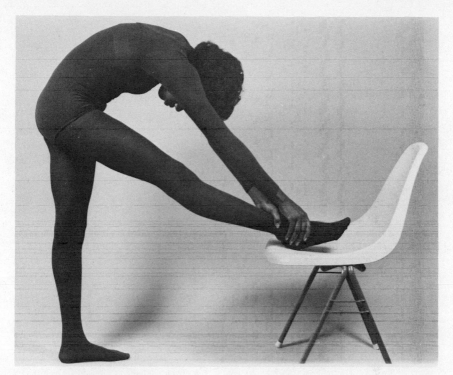

Figure 6.22. Hamstring stretch

1. Straighten one leg, lock the knee, and place the leg on a footstool.
2. Keep the other leg straight and bring the head to the knee of the extended leg, or toward the knee until stretch discomfort is felt.
3. Repeat with each leg.
4. Progress to the use of a chair and finally a table as improvement takes place.

Figure 6.23. Heel cord, gastrocnemius, and soleus stretch (lower leg)

1. Stand with the face to the wall and place the palms against the wall at arm's length and at shoulder height. Keep the feet flat and the body in a straight line.
2. Lean forward and let the elbows bend until stretch discomfort is felt. Do not allow the heels to rise off the floor.

Figure 6.24. Lower leg stretch

1. Step forward with either leg.
2. Keep the back leg straight with the foot straight ahead and the heel on the floor.
3. Bend the front leg to stretch the back leg until stretch discomfort is felt.
4. Step farther ahead with the front leg to gradually increase the distance between the feet.

Figure 6.25. Foot and ankle stretch

1. Sit on the feet with the toes and ankles stretched backward.
2. Balance with both hands on the floor just behind the hips.
3. Raise the knees slightly from the floor.

REFERENCES

1. deVries, H. A. 1974. *Physiology of exercise for physical education and athletics,* 2d ed. Dubuque, Iowa: William C. Brown.
2. Johnson, P. B. et al. 1975. *Sport, exercise and you.* New York: Holt, Rinehart and Winston.
3. Neilson, N. P., and Jensen, C. R. 1972. *Measurement and statistics in physical education.* Belmont, Calif.: Wadsworth Publishing.
4. Rasch, P. J., and Burke, R. K. 1974. *Kinesiology and applied anatomy.* 5th ed. Philadelphia: Lea and Febiger.

Chapter Seven
NUTRITION AND WEIGHT MANAGEMENT

KEY TERMS

Adequate diet (p. 107)
Adipose tissue (p. 106)
Basal metabolic rate (BMR) (p. 134)
Caloric balance (p. 105)
Calorie (p. 134)
Hyperlipidemia (p. 114)
Metabolism (p. 134)

Negative caloric balance (p. 146)
Obese (p. 105)
Overweight (p. 105)
Positive caloric balance (p. 105)
Setpoint theory (p. 139)

STUDENT OBJECTIVES

On completion of this chapter, the student should be able to:

1. Define the key terms listed above
2. List the four major reasons why individuals are overweight or obese
3. List the four functions of adipose tissue
4. Describe five effects of being overweight or obese
5. Define *saturated* and *unsaturated fat, carbohydrate, protein, mineral, vitamin,* and *water* and list the functions of each of these substances
6. State adequate percentages of carbohydrate, protein, and fat in the diet
7. Define *cholesterol* and *triglyceride* and list the functions of these substances; state their relations to cardiovascular disease
8. Define *fiber* and list the reasons for its inclusion in the diet
9. Describe the problems associated with the excessive consumption of salt, sugar, and fast foods
10. Describe ectomorph, mesomorph, and endomorph body types
11. Describe the problems associated with weight reduction through diet modification only
12. Describe the advantages of a weight-reduction

program that combines
exercise with a small
decrease in caloric intake

13. Design a weight-reduction
program that combines
exercise with a small
decrease in caloric intake

The way to a man's heart is through his stomach. How often have we all heard this statement? The prevalence of flabby waists indicates that many persons believe it. Even though Americans enjoy the most diverse food supply in the world, a tragic fact is that a large percentage of them are overweight or obese. From 1970 to 1979, the weight of Americans increased an estimated 5 to 7%.[6] Today more than 80 million Americans are **overweight** in that their percentage of body fat exceeds a desirable level, and 40 million are **obese,** which means that their body fat content exceeds 25% (men) or 30% (women) of the total body weight.[5,18] This excess weight is not limited to the older population, as 20 to 30% of teenagers are overweight.[4] Indeed, overfatness is a national problem.

Various causes have been suggested to explain overweight and obesity, the major reasons being inactivity, overeating, emotional problems, and physiological disturbances. The last two involve only a small percentage of overweight people, and it is these individuals who need medical help. Inactivity and overeating are without a doubt the major causes of excess weight in this nation's population. These two factors are related because weight gain occurs if caloric intake exceeds energy expenditure. Inactivity takes on greater significance in combination with modern dietary habits. A physically active person today eats as much as a moderately active person did a century ago but is less active than a sedentary person was then.[36] Indeed, the single factor most frequently held responsible for excess weight and obesity is lack of exercise.[23]

If caloric intake and energy expenditure are equal, **caloric balance** results, and no weight gain occurs. Parents often overfeed young children or allow between-meal snacks and sweets but fail to encourage habits of activity. Later, during the sedentary years of adulthood, creeping obesity occurs because caloric intake exceeds metabolic use or needs, which produces a **positive caloric balance.**

Because so many Americans are overweight, an array of ideas, devices, and diets has guaranteed easy methods of weight control or weight reduction, and people have spent billions of dollars annually hoping that such methods will work. Also, much publicity has promoted the value of special diets and supplements to be used with exercise programs. Unfortunately, most of these methods are not based on scientific evidence, and their promoters are more interested in money than in the health of the public.

EFFECTS OF EXCESS WEIGHT

Adipose tissue, a type of connective tissue in which many of the cells are filled with fat, is located throughout the body and serves several functions. Found underneath the skin, it helps reduce the loss of body heat. It also serves as a reserve fuel supply, which, if needed, can be returned to the cells by the blood and oxidized to produce energy. Adipose tissue is also present as support and protection around certain internal organs and delicate structures such as blood vessels and nerves, around joints as padding, and in the marrow of the long bones.[22] The body needs adipose tissue and should never lack it, but serious problems can develop if excess fat accumulates. Many persons only become concerned about their weight because of their physical appearance, but the direct relationship between fat beneath the skin and internal fat around the body organs creates other reasons for concern.

Life insurance companies have stated that overweight individuals are poor risks compared with persons of normal weight, because life expectancy is shorter if the percentage of body fat is excessive. The death rate is increased 30% for persons who are 15 to 24% overweight and as much as 80% for those who are 35% or more overweight.[29]

Diseases of the heart and circulatory system are often associated with obesity. High blood pressure is twice as frequent and arteriosclerosis (hardening of the arteries) is three times more frequent in obese individuals.[23] For every 5 lb of excess fatty tissue, 4 to 5 additional mi of blood vessels and capillaries must be formed to supply the tissue with needed blood. This places an increased burden on the heart and can contribute to the development of cardiovascular disease and diminish the chances of recovery from a heart attack.

In addition, overweight and obese individuals have more problems with their muscles and joints, more low back problems, and a higher incidence of ruptured intervertebral disks. Excess weight creates respiratory difficulties and increases the probability that varicose veins will develop. Diabetes and problems during pregnancy occur more often, and accidental deaths are more frequent among obese individuals. Being overweight or obese is a threat to the quality and length of one's life.

FUNCTIONS OF FOOD

The term *balanced diet* designates relationships among various nutrients in an individual's diet. When fewer varieties of foods were available in the early days of nutritional science, much emphasis was placed on balancing the carbohydrate, fat, and protein in the diet. Research has since shown that the functions of all nutrients—vitamins, minerals, proteins, fats, carbohydrates, and water—are closely related in cellular metabolism. Hence the term **adequate diet,** rather than *balanced diet,* should probably be used to refer to all these relationships.

The best-known and most widely recognized adequate diet consists of groups of foods that provide significant amounts or recommended daily allowances of important nutrients. Foods are grouped into the Basic Four: (1) milk and milk products, (2) meat, fish, and poultry, with nuts and legumes as alternates, (3) fruits and vegetables, and (4) breads and cereals.

When examining their diet, too many individuals consider only the number of Calories consumed. The requirement for vitamins, minerals, and other nutrients as well as Calories should be considered.[37]

Fats

Fats, or lipids, composed of carbon and hydrogen and containing little oxygen, have the highest energy content of any food (Table 7.1). They yield more than twice the number of Calories per gram than do carbohydrates and proteins.

Dietary fat serves to (1) promote satiety or staying power during the slow process of digestion, (2) enhance flavor and palatability, and (3) help provide and transport the fat-soluble vitamins A, D, E, and K. Body fat serves to (1) store energy, (2) support and protect vital organs, (3) insulate the body against the environment, and (4) store fat-soluble vitamins.[9]

Classification of fats is based on the number of hydrogen atoms combined with carbon atoms. *Saturated fats* are those in which the maximum number of hydrogen atoms are attached to the carbon atoms. They harden at room temperature. Saturated animal fats are found in

TABLE 7.1. ENERGY SUPPLIED BY THE THREE BASIC TYPES OF FOOD

Type of Food	Energy (Cal/gm)
Carbohydrates	4.1
Fats	9.3
Proteins	4.1

beef, lamb, pork, ham, butter, cream, whole milk, and cheeses made from cream and whole milk. Saturated vegetable fats are found in many solid and hydrogenated shortenings, coconut oil, cocoa butter, and palm oil (used in commercial cookies, pie fillings, and nondairy milk and cream substitutes).

Unsaturated and *polyunsaturated* fats have fewer hydrogen atoms per carbon atom than saturated fats. They are usually liquid at room temperature. They are found mostly in vegetable foods and in vegetable oils such as those derived from corn, cottonseed, safflower, sesame seed, soybean, and sunflower seed.[2]

It is important to know the difference in these fats because they produce different physical effects in the body. Many nutritionists and cardiologists believe that consumption of saturated fats increases blood cholesterol levels.[11] Studies comparing the diets and blood lipid levels of various societies support this belief. In one such study, three groups of healthy young urban Ethiopian men differing in dietary pattern were observed.[30] The results showed striking increases in blood lipids when the diet assumed more Western characteristics. Some nutritionists also believe that consumption of polyunsaturated fats tends to reduce blood cholesterol levels in many individuals.[15] How this reduction takes place is unknown. If cholesterol is taken from the blood and deposited in tissues of the body, this particular decrease in plasma cholesterol may not be beneficial. Until the mechanism for the decrease is identified, the percentages of fats recommended by the Senate Select Committee on Nutrition and Human Needs should probably not be exceeded. (See page 123.)

In addition, a diet high in saturated fats may be directly or indirectly related to the development of cancer of the colon, stomach, esophagus, breast, liver, uterus, and prostate gland. Again, studies of diets in various nations support this belief.[14] For example, the United States has a high fat intake and a high incidence of breast cancer; Japan has a low intake and a low incidence of breast cancer. Possibly a high intake of fats enhances the activity of cancer-producing agents, or the fats act as carriers of these agents to their site of action.

At the turn of the century, the American diet consisted of about 33% fat, but today the proportion has increased to 40 to 45%. Most nutritional experts agree that this percentage should be no more than 25 to 30% and that at least one half to two thirds of this total should be unsaturated and polyunsaturated fats.

Carbohydrates

Carbohydrates, which make up 45 to 50% of the American diet, are organic compounds that commonly include starches and sugars and are found in various fruits, vegetables, grains, and sweets. These compounds are broken down into glucose, a simple sugar that the body uses as its primary source of energy. The majority of the carbohydrate intake should be in the form of starches. In the United States, however, sugar provides more than 50% of the carbohydrate intake and between 20 and 25% of the total caloric intake.[24]

Proteins

Proteins are organic compounds that are needed to build and repair body tissues. They make up approximately 10 to 15% of the American diet. Red meats are excellent sources of protein, as are fish, poultry, milk, grains, nuts, and legumes. The body cells do not ordinarily use protein for energy; they do so only if carbohydrate and fat supplies have been depleted. Protein is required especially during pregnancy. Even though caloric intake should decrease with age, the need for protein does not.

Minerals

The body needs *minerals* in various amounts as building materials for certain tissues and as body regulators. The more common ones are listed in Table 7.2; others include chlorine, cobalt, copper, fluorine, manganese, molybdenum, selenium, sulfur, and zinc. Minerals such as sodium and potassium can be lost though exercise, but an adequate diet will replace them without the addition of supplements.

Vitamins

Vitamins function in the utilization and absorption of other nutrients and serve as components of various enzyme systems. They do not supply energy to the cells. They differ greatly in chemical composition and are found in various quantities in different foods. They must be obtained through the diet.

Vitamins are divided into two groups on the basis of their solubility. The fat-soluble vitamins, A, D, E, and K, are found in foods associated with lipids. They are normally not excreted in the urine but tend to remain stored in the body in moderate quantities (Table 7.3). Owing to such reserves, the body is not absolutely dependent on a day-to-day supply. The water-soluble vitamins, B-complex and C, are excreted in excess through the urine and are not stored in the body in appreciable quantities[11] (Table 7.4).

Because many people believe that high doses of vitamin supplements promote good health, they annually spend millions of dollars on

TABLE 7.2. MINERAL SOURCES, FUNCTIONS, ADULT REQUIREMENTS, AND DEFICIENCY DISORDERS

Mineral	Sources	Functions	Adult Requirement	Deficiency Disorders
Calcium	Milk, most dairy products, shellfish, egg yolk, green vegetables	Major component of skeleton & teeth; essential for clotting of blood, normal functioning of nerve tissue	800 mg	Rickets (principal cause is deficiency of vitamin D), demineralization of bone
Iodine	Seafoods, vegetables grown on iodine-rich soils, iodized salt	Formation of thyroid hormone	0.15–0.30 mg	Goiter
Iron	Liver, lean meats, shellfish, egg yolk, dried fruits, nuts, green leafy vegetables	Oxygen transport & cellular respiration	10–15 mg	Anemia
Magnesium	Almonds, lima beans, peanuts, peas, pecans, brown rice, whole wheat, walnuts	Activation of many of body's enzymes; cardiac & skeletal muscles & nervous tissue depend on proper balance between calcium & magnesium	300 mg	True dietary deficiency has not been reported; can result from severe renal disease, hepatic cirrhosis, sustained losses of gastrointestinal secretions

TABLE 7.2./ continued

Phosphorus	Milk, fish, poultry, eggs	Important role in muscle energy metabolism; carbohydrate, protein, & fat metabolism; nervous-tissue metabolism; normal blood chemistry; skeletal growth; tooth development; transport of fatty acids	800 mg	Deficiency rarely found; abnormal ratio of calcium & phosphorus interferes with absorption of both elements
Potassium	Bananas, beets, molasses, sweet potatoes, green vegetables	Influence on contractility of smooth, skeletal, & cardiac muscle; affects excitability of nerve tissue	. . . .	Deficiency rarely found, but can cause muscular weakness & nervous irritability
Sodium	Celery, beet greens, kale, sodium chloride (salt)	Important in acid-base balance & osmotic pressure of extracellular fluids	2.5 gm	Muscular cramps, weakness, headache, interference with heat-regulating power of body

TABLE 7.3. FAT-SOLUBLE VITAMIN SOURCES, FUNCTIONS, ADULT REQUIREMENTS, AND DEFICIENCY DISORDERS

Vitamin	Sources	Functions	Adult Requirement	Deficiency Disorders
A	Liver, eggs, fish-liver oils; as carotene (converted to vitamin A) in dark green & deep yellow vegetables & yellow fruits	Normal growth of epithelial tissues, normal vision, growth of bones & teeth	5000 IU	Night blindness; rough, unhealthy skin
D	Salmon, sardines, fish, butter & cream products, liver oils, egg yolk, sunlight; artificial enrichment of suitable foods	Increase in utilization & retention of calcium & phosphorus, which ensures conditions favorable to normal mineralization of growing bone	400 IU	Inadequate intestinal absorption of calcium & phosphorus, demineralization of bone
E	Cereal seed oils, soybean oil, wheat germ oil, green leafy vegetables, legumes, nuts	Prevention of unwanted oxidation of polyunsaturated fatty acids & fat-soluble compounds	30 IU	Deficiencies rarely reported
K	Green leafy vegetables; most important source is intestinal bacterial flora, which provide adequate amount under normal circumstances	Synthesis of prothrombin by liver (blood-clotting mechanism)	Unknown	Deficiency rarely found

TABLE 7.4. WATER-SOLUBLE VITAMIN SOURCES, FUNCTIONS, ADULT REQUIREMENTS, AND DEFICIENCY DISORDERS

Vitamin	Sources	Functions	Adult Requirement	Deficiency Disorders
B₁ (thiamine)	Lean meats, eggs, whole-grain products, green leafy vegetables, nuts, legumes	Carbohydrate metabolism, nerve function	0.4 mg per 1000 Cal	Beriberi, neuritis
B₂ (riboflavin)	Milk, cheese, meats, eggs, green leafy vegetables, whole grains, legumes	Catalysis in cellular oxidations	0.6 mg per 1000 Cal	Fissures at angles of mouth, inflammation of tongue, visual fatigue
Niacin	Liver, meats, fish, whole grains, bread, cereals, dried peas & beans, nuts, peanut butter	Promotion of growth; important in utilization of all major nutrients	6.6 mg per 1000 Cal	Pellagra (skin disease), nervous disorders
B₆	Liver, cereals, fish, vegetables	Protein metabolism, cell function	2 mg	Nerve inflammation, skin irritations
B₁₂	Food of animal origin, fish, milk	Formation of blood; fat & sugar metabolism; promotion of growth	3 μg	Pernicious anemia, neuritis
C (ascorbic acid)	Citrus fruits and their juices, potatoes, peppers, cabbage, tomatoes, broccoli	Metablism of amino acids, healing of wounds, structural integrity of capillary walls, formation of intercellular substance of collagenous & fibrous tissue	50–100 mg	Scurvy, delayed healing of wounds, spongy gums, hemorrhages

such supplements. Claims have been made that large doses of vitamin C can prevent and cure colds; however, these findings remain controversial. Vitamin E has also been reported to prevent heart disease, reduce the serum cholesterol level, heighten sexual potency, prevent wrinkles, and perform other wonders, but research does not support these claims. Benefits of large doses of other vitamins have also been reported, but until additional research is available, avoiding large doses of any vitamins is best as some of them can seriously damage the body.

Some members of the medical profession and individuals in health-related fields recommend the daily intake of a multiple vitamin and mineral capsule.[12,38] This recommendation is based on the belief that many Americans do not eat an adequate variety of foods and that the caloric intake of some individuals may be too low to provide the necessary vitamins and minerals. Disagreeing with this position, other medical professionals believe that vitamin and mineral supplements are not necessary unless a medical doctor advises differently.[27] No danger exists in taking a multiple vitamin and mineral capsule that contains 100% of the adult requirements, but until research also resolves this disagreement, each individual must decide if such supplements are needed.

Water

One of the most important substances in the body is *water*. A variety of metabolic processes require water, and food, oxygen, and waste products enter and leave the cells with the aid of water. In addition to other functions, water serves to lubricate the joints, cushion the spinal cord and brain, and help regulate body temperature.

A person can live for some time without food but only for a few days without water. Usually the response to thirst will maintain the body's water at a safe level, but during hot weather or after vigorous exercise, adequate water replacement may not take place. Even following the practice of drinking five to eight glasses of fluids per day may not provide enough water. A good rule is to drink enough water to prevent a decrease in body weight of more than 1 or 2 lb when freely perspiring.

Diets that limit water intake should be avoided. For the purposes of weight management, however, water is Calorie-free whereas most other fluids are not.

HYPERLIPIDEMIA

Lipids (fatty materials) that are found in body tissue are also found in blood plasma. If excessive blood lipids (*cholesterol* and *triglyceride*) are present, the condition is known as **hyperlipidemia.** It usually has no outward signs and shows only in a blood test. Numerous studies have indicated that a positive relationship exists between hyperlipidemia and coronary heart disease. (See Chapter 2.)

The body needs cholesterol for several functions. A forerunner of bile salts, steroid hormones, and vitamin D, cholesterol also facilitates the absorption of fatty acids from the intestines. The body does not depend on dietary sources of cholesterol, however, because it is constantly synthesized, mainly in the liver.

As previously stated, a positive relationship exists among the quantity of dietary fat, its composition, and the serum cholesterol level. Table 7.5 lists the cholesterol value of certain foods. In the United States, plasma cholesterol levels vary widely, but a fasting level between 150 and 200 mg/100 ml of blood is considered healthy.

The triglyceride level can be raised by starches, sugars, saturated fats, and excessive alcohol intake, and is often high in overweight individuals. The triglyceride level should be below 150 mg/100 ml of blood. Many active people have less than 100 mg/100 ml of blood.

Why one individual may have hyperlipidemia while another may not, even though both have the same diet, is not clearly understood.

OTHER NUTRITIONAL CONCERNS

In addition to fats, carbohydrates, protein, minerals, vitamins, and water, the following are other concerns when planning an adequate diet.

Fiber

The undigestible component of wheat and of the roughage found in carrots, celery, apples, and other vegetables and fruits is *fiber*. It is not found in animal cells. Fiber is unaffected by the secretions of the small intestine and passes through it undigested, and therefore does not supply nutrition; however, it provides the bulk needed to move other foods through the digestive tract.

The average American is believed to consume 1 to 3 gm of fiber daily or approximately one third of the amount eaten prior to the mass production of processed food.[10] According to some nutritional experts, the daily fiber intake should be at least 6 to 10 gm. This recommendation is based on the following facts:

1. Passing through the intestine like a sponge, fiber absorbs water, cholesterol, bile salts, and other materials. This hastens the propulsion of fecal material out of the bowel; in binding with

TABLE 7.5. CALORIC AND CHOLESTEROL VALUES OF CERTAIN FOODS[a]

Food	Serving	Calories	Cholesterol
Vegetables			
Asparagus	10 stalks	25	N
Beans, baked	1 C	200	N
Beans, green	1 C	25	N
Beans, lima	1 C	150	N
Beets	1 C	75	N
Broccoli	1 C	45	N
Cabbage, cooked	1 C	45	N
Carrots, cooked	1 C	50	N
Celery	1 stalk	15	N
Corn	1 ear	100	N
Lettuce	1 head	50	N
Mushrooms	1 C	30	N
Peas, cooked	1 C	110	N
Potatoes, baked	1 med	125	N
Potato chips	10 med	100	N
Potatoes, French fried	6	100	M
Potatoes, sweet, baked	1 av	200	N
Spinach, boiled	1 C	100	N
Squash	1 C	35	N
Tomato	1 med	25	N
Turnips	1 C	45	N
Animal Meats			
Bacon	2 strips	75	L
Beef, ground	4 oz	410	H
Beef, pot roast	4 oz	250	H
Beef, roast	4 oz	200	H
Beef, steak	4 oz	200	H
Ham	1 sl	100	H

NOTE: The following abbreviations are used:

av = average	med = medium	sl = slice	sq = square
C = cup	oz = ounce	sm = small	T = tablespoon
lg = large	reg = regular		

The following symbols are used to represent cholesterol levels:
H = high   L = low
M = medium   N = none

[a] Dietary cholesterol is derived only from animal tissue or animal products (e.g., cheese, eggs, whole milk) or both.

TABLE 7.5./continued

Food	Serving	Calories	Cholesterol
Ham, smoked	4 oz	450	H
Liver, beef	4 oz	150	H
Liver, calf	4 oz	160	H
Sausage	1 link	75	H
Veal chop	4 oz	150	L
Veal cutlet	4 oz	125	L
Veal roast	4 oz	250	L
Veal steak	4 oz	250	L
Chicken			
Broiled	1/2 med	200	L
Fried	1/2 med	325	M
Livers	4 oz	150	H
Pot pie	4 oz	350	M
Salad	4 oz	225	L
Turkey			
Baked	4 oz	250	L
Hash	4 oz	175	L
Soups			
Bean	1 C	225	L
Beef broth	1 C	35	L
Chicken	1 C	100	L
Chili	1 C	350	M
Tomato	1 C	100	N
Vegetable	1 C	100	N
Beverages			
Beer	8 oz	175	N
Cider	8 oz	100	N
Coffee, black	8 oz	0	N
Grapefruit juice	6 oz	75	N
Ice cream soda	1 reg	350	M
Milk, chocolate	8 oz	225	H
Orange juice	6 oz	75	N
Pineapple juice	6 oz	95	N

continued

TABLE 7.5/*continued*

Food	Serving	Calories	Cholesterol
Soft drinks	10 oz	120	N
Tea, black	1 C	0	N
Tomato juice	6 oz	50	N
Dairy Products and Eggs			
American cheese	1 oz	105	H
Butter	1 T	100	H
Cheddar cheese	1 oz	105	H
Cottage cheese	½ C	105	L
Cream	1 T	50	H
Egg, boiled	1 med	70	H
Egg, fried	1 med	100	H
Egg, scrambled	1 med	135	H
Milk, dried skim	1 T	25	L
Milk, evaporated	1 C	200	H
Milk, skim	1 C	85	L
Milk, whole	1 C	170	H
Yogurt, skim	1 C	115	L
Seafood			
Clams, fried	2	200	L
Clams, steamed	12	100	L
Flounder, fried	4 oz	150	L
Flounder, raw	4 oz	78	L
Lobster	½ C	65	M
Lobster Newburg	av	350	H
Oysters, fried	6 med	240	M
Salmon, broiled	4 oz	140	L
Salmon, canned	½ C	200	L
Scallops	4 oz	90	L
Shrimp	10 med	100	M
Shrimp creole	av	175	M
Shrimp, fried	10 med	315	H
Tuna, canned in oil	3 oz	170	M
Breads and Cereals			
Biscuits, baking powder	1 lg	103	L
Biscuits, buttermilk	1 lg	90	L

TABLE 7.5./*continued*

Food	Serving	Calories	Cholesterol
Bread, cinnamon	1 sl	200	L
Bread, French	1 sl	50	L
Bread, protein	1 sl	40	L
Bread, raisin	1 sl	75	N
Bread, white	1 sl	65	N
Bread, whole wheat	1 sl	65	N
English muffin	1 av	150	L
Muffin	1 sm	125	M
Pancake	1 sm	100	M
Rice, brown	1 C	130	N
Rice, converted	1 C	130	N
Rice, white	1 C	200	N
Rolls, cinnamon	1 av	100	M
Rolls, hot dog	1	125	N
Rolls, plain	1	100	N
Waffle	1	225	M
Fresh Fruits[b]			
Apple	1 sm	75	N
Banana	1 med	100	N
Blueberries	1 C	80	N
Cantaloupe	½ med	40	N
Cherries, unpitted	1 C	95	N
Grapefruit	½ sm	50	N
Grapes	1 C	90	N
Orange	1 med	75	N
Peach	1 av	45	N
Pear	1 av	95	N
Pineapple	1 C	75	N
Strawberries	1 C	55	N
Watermelon	1 med sl	100	N
Candies and Nuts			
Almonds	12	100	N
Caramel	1 med	75	M
Chocolate bar	1 sm	300	H
Fudge	1 sq	110	L

[b] Frozen fruits have additional Calories.

continued

TABLE 7.5/*continued*

Food	Serving	Calories	Cholesterol
Peanuts	10	100	N
Peanut butter	1 T	100	N
Pecans	8	50	N
Popcorn, buttered	1 C	150	M
Walnuts	4	100	N
Desserts			
Cake, angel food	av	100	N
Cake, cheese	1 sm sl	350	H
Cake, chocolate	av	250	H
Cake, pound	av	200	H
Cookies, brownies	1 sq	50	H
Cookies, butter	6 sm	100	H
Cookies, chocolate chip	3 sm	65	M
Cookies, oatmeal	2 sm	50	M
Cookies, vanilla wafers	3 sm	50	L
Danish pastry	av	200	H
Doughnut	av	150	H
Eclair	av	275	H
Fruitcake	1 sm	250	L
Gelatin, sweet	av	100	N
Ice cream	1 scoop	150	M
Ice milk	1 scoop	100	L
Pie, 1 crust	av	250	M
Pie, 2 crusts	av	350	M
Sherbet	1 scoop	100	L
Sundae, fancy	av	400	H
Potpourri			
Catsup	1 T	25	N
Cranberry sauce	3 T	100	N
Honey	1 T	65	N
Jam or jelly	1 T	50	N
Maple syrup	1 T	60	N
Mayonnaise	1 T	100	M
Molasses	1 T	50	N
Mustard	1 T	10	N
Pickles, dill	av	15	N
Salad dressing, French	1 T	100	L

cholesterol and bile salts, the fiber possibly helps to reduce the levels of fats in the blood.[10]

2. When fiber levels are too low, too much water is absorbed from the large intestine, causing constipation. Outpouches called diverticula may also develop in the large intestine. These outpouches are the result of the increased pressure the colon must exert to propel the slow-moving waste matter forward. When partly digested food becomes trapped in these pouches, infection may result. This inflammatory condition, called diverticulitis, requires surgery for about one-half million Americans each year.[10]

3. A high-fiber diet requires more time and energy to chew. Because content is bulkier, the point of satisfaction is reached sooner, decreasing the caloric intake.

4. Low-fiber carbohydrates are more readily converted to glucose than high-fiber carbohydrates. The glucose enters the circulatory system quickly and increases the demand of the pancreas to produce insulin. For individuals with a genetic predisposition to diabetes, this process could be dangerous.

5. The evidence is not conclusive as to why, but in societies where food is less refined and more fiber is consumed, cancer of the colon is rare. The populations of South Africa, Japan, and Finland consume much more fiber than the typical American population, and they have a significantly lower incidence of colon and rectum cancer. Mormons living in Utah also eat a high-fiber diet and experience an extremely low incidence of colon and rectum cancer.[36] The Mormons include seasonal fresh fruits, vegetables, home preserved foods, and an ample intake of grain products in their diet.

Salt

Sodium is essential for cellular function; however, only a small amount is needed by the body. Primitive herbivorous people probably consumed no more than 0.6 gm/day, because plants contain very little sodium. Sodium chloride *(salt)* provides more than enough sodium intake for most Americans. The amount of salt that the average American consumes daily is difficult to measure exactly, but most estimates place it somewhere between 6 and 24 gm/day. Ten to 15 grams is average.[20] This is equivalent to about 4 to 6 gm of sodium. Much of the salt is consumed in processed food. In addition, more salt is added to the food when cooked or prepared.

A worldwide positive correlation exists between the quantity of salt ingested and the prevalence of hypertension in various populations. Northern Japanese eat about 2½ times as much salt as Americans, and the occurrence of hypertension is two to four times greater than in the USA.[20] Populations that consume a low amount of salt have a relatively low incidence of hypertension. Obese people who adopt special low-salt diets reduce their blood pressure before they reduce their body weight. Apparently, salt causes the body to retain fluid, producing an increase in the volume of blood. The increased amount of blood elevates the pressure within the blood vessels.

Salt intake can be decreased through removal of the salt shaker from the eating site, preparation of foods with other seasonings and spices, and limited intake of foods with a high salt content (e.g., canned foods, condiments, cured meats, and salted snacks).

Sugar

Average American intake of *sugar* is about 125 lb/person each year. Three fourths of this amount is invisible, being found in foods and beverages prepared outside the home.[24] The body needs the sugar that is obtained from the carbohydrates found in vegetables, fruits, and bread. Refined sugar does provide energy (Calories); however, it provides no protein, fat, vitamins, or fiber.

Significant problems are associated with a high sugar intake. Dental decay and excess weight are two major problems. In addition, if a large portion of an individual's caloric intake consists of sugar, too few Calories are being provided by foods from the Basic Four. Even though most people need not eliminate all sugar intake, the amount of sugar ingested should probably be limited.

Alcohol

Taken in moderation, *alcohol* does little harm. Excess consumption, however, can be detrimental to health. In addition to the well-known serious health problems (e.g., liver and kidney impairment), less-known problems are associated with alcohol abuse.

The Calories contained in alcohol supply no vitamins and minerals. If nutritious foods are not eaten because of excessive alcohol consumption, the individual will suffer a vitamin and mineral deficiency. In addition, the Calories of alcohol are used for energy before food Calories. Food Calories that are not used for energy are then stored as fat, resulting in overweight. Excessive alcohol also increases the serum triglyceride level. (See pp. 19–20 for additional information.)

Fast Foods

According to a Gallup poll, 33% of this nation's adults eat out every day, and 28% of those adults eat at fast-food establishments.[16]

Between 1970 and 1980, fast-food sales increased by more than 300%, from $6.5 billion to $23 billion annually. In 1981 there were more than 140,000 fast-food outlets nationwide, compared with 30,000 in 1971, and more than 300 regional and national restaurant chains.[1]

Fast foods really do not differ significantly from the food eaten in the average American home. That is to say, we are making the same mistake with these foods that we are making in the home. They contain too many Calories, too much fat and sugar, and too little fiber and vitamins. Most fast foods are high in protein, but few Americans are deficient in protein.

To include fast foods in the diet daily would be a mistake, but if eaten infrequently and as part of an adequate diet, they do not have to be avoided entirely. When fast foods must be eaten, avoiding fried potatoes, milk shakes, sauces, and salad dressings will decrease the fat, sugar, and salt intake. Table 7.6 lists the caloric and nutritional value of many popular fast foods.

Recommendations of Senate Select Committee

In 1977, after studying the health problems of America, the Senate Select Committee on Nutrition and Human Needs put forth the following dietary goals and recommendations.[15]

Goals

1. Reduce overall fat consumption to 30% of caloric intake.

2. Reduce saturated fat consumption to account for about 10% of caloric intake; balance that with polyunsaturated and monounsaturated fats, which should each account for about 10% of caloric intake.

3. Reduce cholesterol consumption to about 300 mg/day.

4. Increase carbohydrate consumption to account for 55 to 60% of caloric intake.

Recommendations

1. Decrease consumption of red meat and increase consumption of poultry and fish. Substitute nonfat milk for whole milk.

2. Decrease consumption of foods high in fat, and partially substitute polyunsaturated fat for saturated fat.

3. Decrease consumption of butterfat, eggs, and other high cholesterol sources.

4. Increase consumption of fruits, vegetables, and whole grains.

TABLE 7.6. CALORIC AND NUTRITIONAL VALUE OF FAST FOODS

	Calories	Fat Calories and Percentage of Total Calories[a]	Carbohydrate Calories and Percentage of Total Calories	Protein Calories and Percentage of Total Calories	Cholesterol (mg)	Sodium (mg)
Hamburgers and Hot Dogs						
Burger Chef						
Big Shef	542	316 (58%)	144 (26%)	94 (17%)	74	622
Cheeseburger	305	158 (52%)	98 (32%)	57 (19%)	44	595
Hamburger	258	118 (46%)	96 (37%)	44 (17%)	32	393
Burger King						
Cheeseburger	305	121 (40%)	116 (38%)	68 (22%)	—[b]	730
Hamburger	252	81 (32%)	115 (47%)	56 (22%)	—	525
Whopper	660	381 (58%)	201 (30%)	78 (12%)	—	1083
Whopper w/cheese	740	405 (55%)	210 (28%)	125 (17%)	—	1435
Whopper Jr	370	187 (51%)	123 (33%)	60 (16%)	—	560
Whopper Jr w/cheese	420	222 (53%)	127 (30%)	71 (17%)	—	785
Hot Dog	291	154 (53%)	93 (32%)	44 (15%)	—	—
Dairy Queen						
Big Brazier Delux	470	216 (46%)	143 (30%)	111 (24%)	—	—
Big Brazier Regular	457	205 (45%)	146 (32%)	106 (23%)	—	—
Big Brazier w/cheese	553	271 (49%)	153 (28%)	129 (23%)	—	—
Brazier Dog	273	136 (50%)	93 (34%)	44 (16%)	—	—

Jack-In-The-Box					
Cheeseburger	310	134 (43%)	112 (38%)	64 (21%)	32	875
Hamburger	263	95 (36%)	116 (44%)	52 (20%)	26	565
Jumbo Jack	538	260 (48%)	180 (33%)	98 (18%)	80	1007
McDonald's					
Big Mac	541	280 (52%)	156 (29%)	105 (19%)	86	963
Cheeseburger	306	118 (39%)	123 (40%)	65 (21%)	37	767
Hamburger	257	83 (32%)	121 (47%)	53 (21%)	24	520
Quarter Pounder	418	188 (45%)	129 (31%)	101 (24%)	67	735
Quarter Pounder w/cheese	524	276 (53%)	128 (24%)	120 (23%)	96	1236
Wendy's					
Single	470	230 (49%)	136 (29%)	104 (22%)	70	774
Double	670	358 (53%)	136 (20%)	176 (26%)	125	980
Triple	850	458 (54%)	132 (15%)	260 (31%)	205	1217

Adapted from Fast-Food Chains, *Consumer Report* 44:509-512, 1979; H. B. Falls, A. M. Baylor, and R. K. Dishman, *Essentials of fitness*, Philadelphia: Saunders College, 1980, pp. 297-300; and *Fast food and the American diet*, a report by the American Council on Science and Health, 1983.

[a] Percentage will not always total 100 owing to rounding off procedure.
[b] Dashes indicate information not available.

continued

TABLE 7.6./continued

	Calories	Fat Calories and Percentage of Total Calories	Carbohydrate Calories and Percentage of Total Calories	Protein Calories and Percentage of Total Calories	Cholesterol (mg)	Sodium (mg)
Sandwiches						
Arby's Roast Beef	370	140 (38%)	148 (40%)	82 (22%)	—	869
Burger King Chopped Beef Steak	445	121 (27%)	205 (46%)	119 (27%)	—	966
Hardee's Roast Beef	351	158 (45%)	131 (37%)	62 (18%)	—	765
Roy Rogers Roast Beef	356	112 (31%)	139 (39%)	105 (29%)	—	610
Fish						
Arthur Treacher's Original	439	251 (57%)	111 (25%)	77 (18%)	—	421
Burger King's Whaler	584	316 (54%)	205 (35%)	63 (11%)	—	968
Long John Silver's	483	251 (52%)	111 (23%)	121 (25%)	—	1333
McDonald's Filet-O-Fish	383	167 (44%)	156 (41%)	60 (16%)	47	781
Chicken						
Arthur Treacher's Original	409	214 (52%)	103 (25%)	92 (22%)	—	580
Kentucky Fried Chicken[c]						
Original Recipe (2 pieces)	393	237 (60%)	44 (11%)	112 (29%)	164	868
Original Recipe Dinner	661	337 (51%)	192 (29%)	132 (20%)	172	1536
Extra Crispy (2 pieces)	544	332 (61%)	84 (15%)	128 (24%)	168	861
Extra Crispy Dinner	808	432 (54%)	232 (29%)	144 (18%)	176	1529

Pizza[d]

Pizza Hut					
Thin'N Crisp/Cheese	450	136 (30%)	216 (48%)	100 (22%)	1386
Thick'N Chewy/Cheese	560	130 (23%)	285 (51%)	145 (26%)	—
Thin'N Crisp Supreme	506	114 (23%)	262 (52%)	130 (26%)	1848

Mexican-Style Food

Jack-In-The-Box					
Regular Taco	215	121 (56%)	70 (32%)	24 (12%)	20
Super Taco	280	152 (54%)	80 (29%)	48 (17%)	35
Taco Bell					
Bean Burrito	343	107 (31%)	192 (56%)	44 (13%)	—
Beef Burrito	466	192 (41%)	151 (32%)	123 (26%)	—
Burrito Supreme	457	199 (44%)	173 (38%)	85 (19%)	—
Wendy's					
Chili	230	72 (31%)	83 (36%)	75 (33%)	25

c Dinners include 2 pieces chicken, mashed potatoes, gravy, coleslaw and roll; figures are based on a typical combination of 1 wing and 1 thigh.
d Based on serving size of half of a 10-in. pizza.

continued

TABLE 7.6./continued

	Calories	Fat Calories and Percentage of Total Calories	Carbohydrate Calories and Percentage of Total Calories	Protein Calories and Percentage of Total Calories	Cholesterol (mg)	Sodium (mg)
French Fries						
Arby's	351	—	—	—	—	213
Arthur Treacher's	269	—	—	—	—	31
Burger Chef	275	115 (42%)	143 (52%)	17 (6%)	—	230
Burger King	314	132 (42%)	163 (52%)	19 (6%)	—	306
Hardee's	287	—	—	—	—	207
Jack-In-The-Box	349	—	—	—	—	128
Long John Silver's	320	157 (49%)	150 (47%)	13 (4%)	—	88
McDonald's	304	140 (46%)	146 (48%)	18 (6%)	9	
Roy Rogers	320	—	—	—	—	141
Wendy's	270	—	—	—	—	105

Shakes

Burger Chef Vanilla	380	88 (23%)	240 (63%)	52 (14%)	34	—
Burger King Chocolate	340	90 (27%)	218 (64%)	32 (9%)	—	280
Jack-In-The-Box Strawberry	380	88 (23%)	250 (66%)	42 (11%)	33	268
McDonald's Chocolate	383	81 (21%)	262 (68%)	40 (10%)	30	300
Wendy's Frosty	390	142 (36%)	214 (55%)	34 (9%)	45	247

Breakfast Items

McDonald's						
Egg McMuffin	327	133 (41%)	123 (37%)	71 (22%)	229	885
Scrambled Egg Breakfast[f]	697	295 (57%)	188 (27%)	112 (16%)	412	1463
Hotcakes and Sausage (w/butter and syrup)	706	262 (37%)	376 (53%)	68 (10%)	90	1685
English Muffin (w/butter)	186	46 (25%)	120 (65%)	20 (11%)	13	318
Hash Brown Potatoes	125	63 (50%)	54 (43%)	8 (6%)	7	325
Orange Juice (6 oz)	80	0 (0%)	76 (95%)	4 (5%)	0	0

e Based on 3.5-oz servings. According to *Consumer Report*, the high fat content of French fries may be due to frying the potatoes in fat or oil that is not hot enough.
f Includes scrambled eggs, sausage, English muffin with butter, and hash brown potatoes.

5. Reduce sugar consumption to about 15% of caloric intake.
6. Reduce salt consumption to approximately 3 gm/day.

5. Decrease consumption of sugar and foods high in sugar content.
6. Decrease consumption of salt and foods high in salt content.

With six of the ten leading causes of death linked to our diet, it would seem wise to follow these recommendations.

DESIRABLE BODY WEIGHT

No simple, objective, and truly accurate method can be used for determining whether one is marginally overweight or obese. Body type, total weight, and percentage of body fat are three criteria used to estimate abnormal body weight.

Body Type and Total Weight

The morphological classification of body types includes the ectomorph, the mesomorph, and the endomorph.[32] An *ectomorph* is a slender person with a light frame—the arms and legs are slender and long, the neck appears long, and muscle tissue has little definition. A *mesomorph* is an athletic-looking individual—the shoulders are broad, the hips are narrow, and muscle tissue is predominant. An *endomorph* is a thick individual—the arms and legs are short compared with the torso, the chest and waist are about the same size, and the neck is thick.

Three numbers are used to designate the components of each of the three types, with 7 as the highest and 1 as the lowest rating for each. The first number refers to endomorphic, the second to mesomorphic, and the third to ectomorphic characteristics. The rating 7-1-1 designates a pure endomorph, a 1-7-1 a pure mesomorph, and 1-1-7 a pure ectomorph. Such extreme ratings are rare, however; usually at least two components of each type are present in an individual. A 2-5-4 designation indicates less than average endomorphic, more than average mesomorphic, and an average number of ectomorphic characteristics.

Body typing can be used to determine ranges of desirable body weight. A 5 ft 11 in. endomorph, for example, should not be expected to weigh the same as a 5 ft 11 in. ectomorph.

Height-Weight Tables

Since 1959, the Metropolitan Life Insurance Company height-weight tables traditionally have been used in guiding individuals toward desirable weights. In 1983, the company released revised tables that were said to represent the weights associated with the lowest death rates among approximately 4,200,000 people observed for 22 years[25] (Table 7.7).

When the new tables were released, the American Heart Association (AHA) urged Americans to continue to use the 1959 recommendations (Table 7.8). The AHA took this position because the new tables list average weight range increases of 13 lb for short men and 10 lb for short women, with lesser increases for medium-height men and women and insignificant increases for tall men and women.[28] The AHA noted that merely looking at death rates obscured health risks associated with the increased weights. The AHA also stated that few health problems are improved by gaining weight, pointing out that the incidence of heart disease, high blood pressure, and diabetes increases in relation to weight gained. In addition, the new acceptable weights are most likely skewed upward by the fact that cigarette smokers, who tend to be thinner than nonsmokers and who die at significantly younger ages, were not taken into account in calculating the new tables.[7]

A drawback to both the old and new tables is that some individuals do not correctly determine their frame size when selecting an appropriate weight range. Many individuals with weight problems often consider themselves large-framed and do not realistically examine their problem.

The technique of body typing is best performed by a qualified individual, but there are practical methods for determining one's body frame. Two such methods are described in Laboratory 10.

Percentage of Body Fat

The best method to estimate one's desirable weight is to determine the percentage of body fat. A range of 13 to 17% body fat for men and 18 to 22% for women is generally acceptable. Individuals with numerous mesomorphic characteristics are sometimes incorrectly considered overweight even though there is a low fat percentage due to the large amount of lean tissue.

Body-fat percentage can be estimated by a procedure involving underwater weighing or by measuring subcutaneous body fat with skinfold calipers. For many years, underwater weighing has been accepted as the standard by which other methods are compared, but it requires the use of expensive laboratory equipment. Measurement with a skinfold caliper involves pinching a fold away from the underlying muscle, and applying the caliper to the fold. The thickness of the fold reflects the percentage of body fat, and therefore muscle tissue should not be included. All measurements should be taken from the right side

TABLE 7.7. 1983 METROPOLITAN HEIGHT AND WEIGHT TABLES FOR MEN AND WOMEN OF AGES 25–59

Height (with shoes on; 1-in. heels)	Small Frame (lb)	Medium Frame (lb)	Large Frame (lb)
Men (indoor clothing weighing 5 lb)			
5 ft 2 in.	128–134	131–141	138–150
5 ft 3 in.	130–136	133–143	140–153
5 ft 4 in.	132–138	135–145	142–156
5 ft 5 in.	134–140	137–148	144–160
5 ft 6 in.	136–142	139–151	146–164
5 ft 7 in.	138–145	142–154	149–168
5 ft 8 in.	140–148	145–157	152–172
5 ft 9 in.	142–151	148–160	155–176
5 ft 10 in.	144–154	151–163	158–180
5 ft 11 in.	146–157	154–166	161–184
6 ft 0 in.	149–160	157–170	164–188
6 ft 1 in.	152–164	160–174	168–192
6 ft 2 in.	155–168	164–178	172–197
6 ft 3 in.	158–172	167–182	176–202
6 ft 4 in.	162–176	171–187	181–207
Women (indoor clothing weighing 3 lb)			
4 ft 10 in.	102–111	109–121	118–131
4 ft 11 in.	103–113	111–123	120–134
5 ft 0 in.	104–115	113–126	122–137
5 ft 1 in.	106–118	115–129	125–140
5 ft 2 in.	108–121	118–132	128–143
5 ft 3 in.	111–124	121–135	131–147
5 ft 4 in.	114–127	124–138	134–151
5 ft 5 in.	117–130	127–141	137–155
5 ft 6 in.	120–133	130–144	140–159
5 ft 7 in.	123–136	133–147	143–163
5 ft 8 in.	126–139	136–150	146–167
5 ft 9 in.	129–142	139–153	149–170
5 ft 10 in.	132–145	142–156	152–173
5 ft 11 in.	135–148	145–159	155–176
6 ft 0 in.	138–151	148–162	158–179

Source of basic data: 1979 Build Study, Society of Actuaries and Association of Life Insurance Medical Directors of America, 1980. Courtesy of Metropolitan Life Insurance Company.

TABLE 7.8. 1959 METROPOLITAN LIFE INSURANCE COMPANY TABLE
OF DESIRABLE WEIGHTS (IN POUNDS) FOR MEN AND WOMEN OF AGES
25 AND OVER (INDOOR CLOTHING)

Height (with shoes on; 1-in. heels)	Small Frame (lb)	Medium Frame (lb)	Large Frame (lb)
Men			
5 ft 2 in.	112–120	118–129	126–141
5 ft 3 in.	115–123	121–133	129–144
5 ft 4 in.	118–126	124–136	132–148
5 ft 5 in.	121–129	127–139	135–152
5 ft 6 in.	124–133	130–143	138–156
5 ft 7 in.	128–137	134–147	142–161
5 ft 8 in.	132–141	138–152	147–166
5 ft 9 in.	136–145	142–156	151–170
5 ft 10 in.	140–150	146–160	155–174
5 ft 11 in.	144–154	150–165	159–179
6 ft 0 in.	148–158	154–170	164–184
6 ft 1 in.	152–162	158–175	168–189
6 ft 2 in.	156–167	162–180	173–194
6 ft 3 in.	160–171	167–185	178–199
6 ft 4 in.	164–175	172–190	182–204
Women			
4 ft 10 in.	92–98	96–107	104–119
4 ft 11 in.	94–101	98–110	106–122
5 ft 0 in.	96–104	101–113	109–125
5 ft 1 in.	99–107	104–116	112–128
5 ft 2 in.	102–110	107–119	115–131
5 ft 3 in.	105–113	110–122	118–134
5 ft 4 in.	108–116	113–126	121–138
5 ft 5 in.	111–119	116–130	125–142
5 ft 6 in.	114–123	120–135	129–146
5 ft 7 in.	118–127	124–139	133–150
5 ft 8 in.	122–131	128–143	137–154
5 ft 9 in.	126–135	132–147	141–158
5 ft 10 in.	130–140	136–151	145–163
5 ft 11 in.	134–144	140–155	149–168
6 ft 0 in.	138–148	144–159	153–173

Courtesy of the Metropolitan Life Insurance Company.
NOTE: For those between 18 and 25, subtract 1 lb for each year under 25.

of the body soon after awakening. Skinfold measurements are usually taken in several of the following areas: over the triceps and biceps muscles, below the shoulder blade, above the crest of the hip, in the chest and abdominal areas, and on the anterior thigh. (Figures 7.1 and 7.2 show sites for the measurement of skinfolds in females; Figures 7.3 and 7.4 in males.) The percentage of body fat can then be estimated through the use of the appropriate formula.[8, 33, 34] (See Laboratory 11.)

CALORIE NEEDS

The energy value of food is expressed as **Calories** (kilocalories); a Calorie is defined as the amount of heat energy required to raise the temperature of 1 kg (2.2 lb) of water 1 °C. As food is broken down, energy is made available to maintain vital functions such as brain activity, respiration, heart action, glandular secretion, and resynthesis of worn-out tissue. Collectively these functions, which result from biochemical activity in cells, are referred to as **metabolism.** If a measure of these functions is made when one has just awakened and is fasting (12 hr), reclining, and relaxing, the minimum energy required (Calories) to exist can be determined. This measure is called **basal metabolic rate (BMR).** The number of Calories required for basal metabolism varies with the age, body size, lean body mass, hormone production, and sex of the individual, with females needing fewer than males.

Normal basal metabolism requires about 1 Cal/hr for each kilogram of body weight. The number of Calories that a man requires per day can be estimated by multiplying his weight in pounds by 11; for women, whose BMR is about 10% lower than men's, multiply by 10.[13] The average adult male needs approximately 1400 to 1800 Cal/day for his basal metabolism, whereas the average adult female needs approximately 1200 to 1400. Table 7.9 presents the suggested BMRs for adults.

In proportion to body weight, BMR is highest during childhood and gradually diminishes throughout life. The decline begins during late adolescence, and its slope becomes evident at about age 25 in men and at about age 22 in women. With increasing age, muscle cells atrophy and body-fat percentage increases. The rate of decline in BMR is usually between 2 and 7% for each decade of life.[13,15]

The amount of energy needed to perform functions other than basal metabolism varies in relation to daily activities. An extremely inactive individual may need only a few hundred additional Calories, whereas a large, active man may need an extra 2000 or more. Table 7.10 shows the number of Calories needed in addition to BMR.

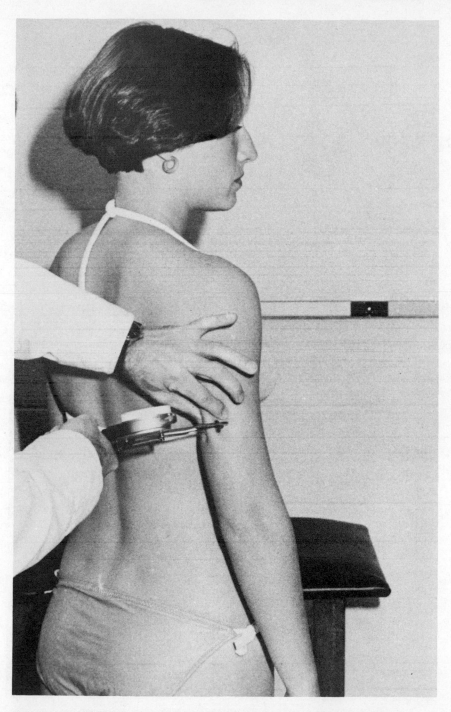

Figure 7.1. Skinfold measurement—posterior surface of arm, midtriceps

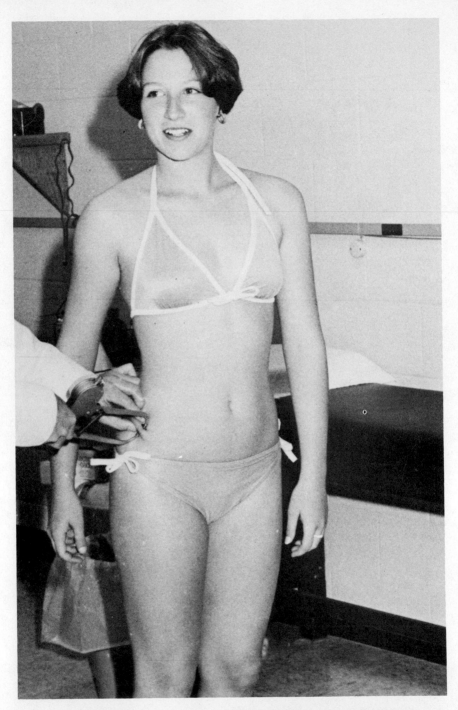

Figure 7.2. Skinfold measurement—oblique fold just above iliac crest

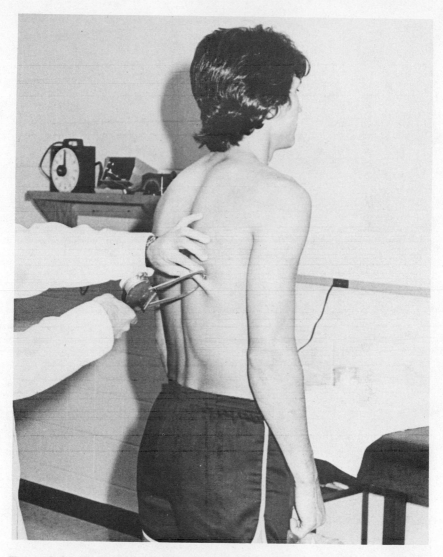

Figure 7.3. Skinfold measurement—inferior angle of scapula

Individuals generally become less active during the aging process. This reduction of activity together with the decline in BMR indicates that eating habits should be adjusted as one grows older to prevent gains in weight or increases in body-fat percentage. Consider Mr. Jones, whose case is based on experimental fact.[13]

When he leaves college, at age 22, he weighs 160 lb. He is not a letterwinning athlete but is physically active. About 12% of his weight,

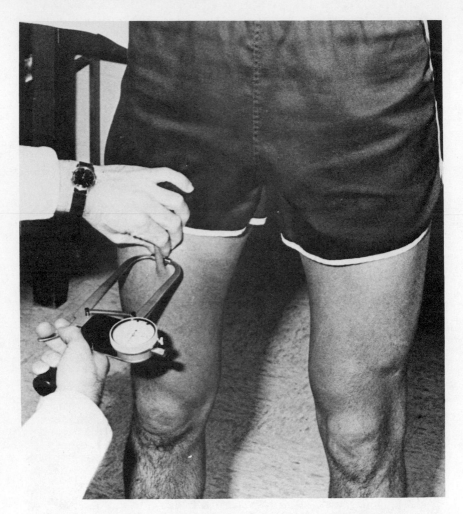

Figure 7.4. Skinfold measurement—anterior surface of midthigh

just under 20 lb, is fat. Look at Jones 35 years later, at age 57. He is proud that he weighs no more than he did when he graduated. He rarely exercises, however, and has failed to maintain a regular exercise program since graduation. His body composition is radically different—he has less muscle mass and more fat in his fat cells. Instead of 12% fat, he now has 24%, or some 40 lb.

And what if Jones had followed a more characteristic pattern? Suppose he had gained 20 lb in those 35 years, a rate of only about 9 oz per year. Those 20 lb would be fat, so that Jones would now have about 60 lb of fat out of a total weight of 180 lb—he would be one-third fat. A

TABLE 7.9. SUGGESTED BASAL METABOLIC RATES FOR ADULTS

Height		Weight		BMR
(in.)	(cm)	(lb)	(kg)	(Cal/day)
Men				
64	163	133±11	60±5	1630
66	168	142±12	64±5	1690
68	173	151±14	69±6	1775
70	178	159±14	72±6	1815
72	183	167±15	76±7	1870
74	188	175±15	80±7	1933
76	193	182±16	83±7	1983
Women				
60	152	109±9	50±4	1399
62	158	115±9	52±4	1429
64	163	122±10	56±5	1487
66	168	129±10	59±5	1530
68	173	136±10	62±5	1572
70	178	144±11	66±5	1626
72	183	152±12	69±5	1666

Reproduced from "Recommended Dietary Allowances," 9th revised edition, 1980, with permission from the National Academy Press, Washington, D.C.

very slight modification in eating habits or a regular exercise program would have prevented this accumulation.

The number of Calories required to maintain a constant weight is difficult to determine. Perhaps the best method is to keep a record of what is eaten for a week during which no weight gain or loss occurs; then calculate the number of Calories (Table 7.5) and divide by 7 to determine the average daily caloric intake. (See Laboratory 12.) Compare the result with the following estimate: moderately active adults of constant weight consume the number of Calories approximately equal to 15 times their weight in pounds.

Setpoint Theory

Many investigators now believe that there is a **setpoint** for body fat or a level of fatness that the body strives to maintain. The theory is that without external influences, the body seeks to maintain a certain amount of fat. Some individuals have a high setting (larger capacity for

TABLE 7.10. ENERGY NEED IN ADDITION TO BASAL METABOLIC RATES

| Activity | Energy Need (in Cal/kg of body weight) | |
	Men	Women
Very light	1.5	1.3
Light	2.9	2.6
Moderate	4.3	4.1
Heavy	8.4	8.0

Reproduced from "Recommended Dietary Allowances," 9th revised edition, 1980, with permission from the National Academy Press, Washington, D.C.

fat storage), some have a low setting (smaller capacity for fat storage), and a few unfortunate individuals have no setting at all.[3]

No one knows exactly what mechanism regulates fatness, but a control system that involves the fat cells and the brain seems to be in charge. Since genes influence the system, a high setpoint can be hereditary. The cells that store fat apparently release chemical signals telling the hypothalamus (small region at base of brain) how much fat they contain. The hypothalamus integrates the cells' signals with other inputs to determine what the setpoint will be.[3]

The setpoints of animals and humans are believed to change in response to two external variables: the quality or nature of available food supply and the individual's level of physical activity. For example, although rats usually eat just enough to maintain a constant weight, if they come in contact with sweet or fatty foods, their setpoint rises temporarily, enabling them to consume more food than they usually would. If the rats found their way into a bakery, they would overeat and become obese.[35]

Some evidence shows that the human setpoint rises in response to sweet foods. When provided with foods high in sugar content, many individuals eat more than they normally would. Since highly sweetened foods tend to raise the setpoint, they should be avoided.[35]

Dieting does not decrease the setpoint; exercise does. Bennett and Gurin, authors of The Dieter's Dilemma,[3] speculate that exercise lowers the setpoint by acting on the hypothalamus by means of an as yet unknown mechanism. In addition, this decrease occurs most dramatically in fat people, providing a strong argument for the importance of physical activity for preventing and treating obesity.[19] If the setpoint theory is correct, exercise appears to be the best, if not the only, method for managing a high setpoint.

Diet and Weight Reduction

Forty to fifty million Americans are estimated to be on weight-loss diets.[31] As a nation we annually spend billions of dollars attempting to lose weight. New diets continually promise startling results in an incredibly short time. Every new diet offers a new and extraordinary technique—a pill to break eating habits, a chemical reaction, a fat-burning trick, or quick weight loss through elimination of groups of foods or inclusion of only a few foods. Some of these diets are unworkable, others are dangerous to health, and almost all will be replaced by other diets.

Dr. Paul LaChance, professor of nutrition and food science at Rutgers University, and registered dietitian Michele C. Fisher, also of Rutgers, analyzed 10 of the nation's most popular diets for total Calories; selected vitamins and minerals; protein, carbohydrate, and fat (saturated and polyunsaturated); percent of total Calories from protein, fat, carbohydrate, and sugars; fiber; sodium and potassium; and cholesterol.[31] They found the following alarming facts:

1. Not one of the 10 diets met the U.S. Recommended Daily Allowance (U.S. RDA) for all 13 vitamins and minerals studied.
2. Nearly all called for more protein than is necessary.
3. Several exceeded recommended levels for cholesterol and sodium and were too low in fiber.
4. Diets that limited the intake of Calories to less than 1200/day did not provide the necessary nutrients.

Additional reasons for avoiding most diets are provided in Table 7.11.

Another problem associated with weight reduction through diet alone is that after losing the desired amount of weight, most individuals regain the weight. One study found that 90% of the people on diets regained their weight within a year, and 99% regained it within 5 years.[26]

Several reasons have been offered as to why dieting may be counterproductive. First, about 90% of all Calories burned in the body are consumed by muscle tissue. Dieting tends to reduce muscle mass, lowering the rate at which the body consumes Calories.[35]

Second, the body will attempt to protect itself against the ravages of starvation. The body has a built-in energy-conservation mechanism; when caloric intake drops significantly below the level needed to maintain weight, the metabolic rate drops also. In other words, the body begins to use less Calories to run itself. Very low-Calorie crash diets have been estimated to slow body metabolism by as much as 45%. In addition, repeated dieting trains the body to increase its ability to reduce metabolic needs, so that losing weight by cutting Calories becomes harder and harder.[21]

TABLE 7.11. TYPES OF DIETS AND REASONS FOR AVOIDING

Diet	Reasons for Avoiding
Low carbohydrate	Unbalanced; causes ketosis and other undesirable side effects; weight loss primarily due to water loss
Fruit for several days	Unbalanced; based on myths; serious side effects including diarrhea, nutrient deficiency
Very low-calorie liquid diet formula	Dangerously low in calories; serious side effects can damage health
Low carbohydrate, high protein	Unbalanced; high in fat or cholesterol; causes ketosis and other serious side effects; weight loss primarily due to water loss
Juices or teas or both or water only	Dangerous; unbalanced; effective only temporarily
Low-calorie, high-fiber diet	May be deficient in calcium and undesirably high in fiber
Low-carbohydrate diet, with relatively large intake of fructose	Fructose does not provide weight loss benefits claimed
Very low-calorie liquid protein diet	Protein of poor quality; side effects include nutrient deficiencies, abnormal heartbeat, death
Formula with low-calorie intake plan	Protein may be poor quality; unbalanced; temporary at best; nutrient deficiencies can develop
Grapefruit eaten before meals to "burn" fat	Ineffective; based on myth; successful only if calories are reduced
High-protein diet	Unbalanced; potential for developing ketosis and nutrient deficiencies
Low-calorie diet with "mood foods"	Promises unrealistic results; promotes nutrition nonsense
Liquid protein diet	Unbalanced; temporary at best; nutrient deficiencies can develop

Third, dieters tend to lose protein and regain fat, resulting in a shift of lean to fat tissue over time. When combined with a reduced metabolic rate, this tendency leads to the yo-yo syndrome, in which rapid weight loss on a crash diet is followed by equally rapid weight gain. The net result is an even higher level of fat than before the diet began.[35] After the weight is regained, the dieter may weigh no more than prior to the diet, but a larger portion of that weight will be fat.

Exercise and Weight Reduction

The need for exercise in any weight-reduction program is becoming increasingly apparent. Two fallacies concerning exercise and weight reduction often mislead the public, however. One is that exercise always increases the appetite and therefore results in no weight loss. The fact is that overweight individuals who begin an exercise program usually decrease their food intake and use stored fat for energy. If the exercise program is strenuous enough to cause an increase in food intake, the intake still does not keep up with caloric needs and weight is lost.

A second fallacy is that exercise expends so few Calories that they cannot possibly make a difference in weight. Moderate exercise programs do require limited Calories, but there are caloric benefits other than those during the exercise session. Exercise modifies the metabolic rate and the body's setpoint. For several hours after exercise, the body uses Calories at a higher rate than it would without exercise. In other words, exercise increases the body metabolism after exercise, and weight loss continues to take place.[26]

According to Dr. Peter Wood of Stanford University Medical School, very active people, such as those who jog 6 or more mi/day, eat about 600 more Calories daily than inactive people but weigh about 20% less.[39] Active individuals obviously are using Calories at a greater rate than inactive individuals.

As previously stated, Bennett and Gurin believe that exercise lowers the body's setpoint. A reduction in food intake will not lower the setpoint, and without a change in the setpoint, efforts to lose weight are continuous and usually futile.

Diet and Exercise

The best approach to weight reduction is through a program that involves exercise and a small reduction in caloric intake. With a small reduction in caloric intake, a permanent change in eating behavior is more easily made. In addition, regardless of what changes take place in the metabolism and setpoint, the expenditure of Calories through exercise is cumulative. If 250 Cal were used each day for exercise, 1750 would be used per week. Because a deficit of approximately 3500 Cal is required to lose 1 lb of body fat, this would result in the loss of 0.5 lb of body fat per week, if everything else remains equal, or 26 lb/year. The following example is for a 145-lb woman who wishes to lose 20 lb:

Caloric deficit required = 70,000 Cal
(20 lb fat × 3500 Cal/lb fat = 70,000 Cal)

Calories deducted from diet	300
Calories used in exercise	200
Daily caloric deficit	500

70,000 Cal ÷ 500 deficit Cal/day = 140 days = 20 weeks

This program takes 20 weeks to produce a loss of 20 lb. It may actually require more days, owing to the decreasing difference between total caloric demand and intake as weight is lost.

This rate of loss may appear slow to some individuals, but is sensible. Starvation or extremely hard exercise is not required. A person abstaining from one 10-oz soft drink and one average slice of pound cake can avoid the intake of 310 Cal (Table 7.5). Many desserts amount to more than 200 Cal. If this woman were to ride a bicycle for 60 min at 5 mph, she would expend 217 Cal (Table 7.12.) Furthermore, this bicycle riding would not have to be done in 60 consecutive min for this expenditure to take place; it could be done several times throughout the day if the total time amounted to 60 min. Walking for 45 min is another light exercise that would expend more than 200 Cal for this woman. It can be realized from this illustration and through the use of Tables 7.5 and 7.6 that a daily caloric deficit of 500 Cal is not an unrealistic goal.

Weight-Reduction Guidelines

The following guidelines should help the individual in a weight-reduction plan.

1. The body needs all types of nutrients, and the diet should consist of a balanced variety of sources. One of the dangers of Calorie counting for weight reduction is that it can lead to an inadequate intake of certain nutrients. Unless one is advised differently by a physician, the diet should consist of 55 to 60% carbohydrates, 10 to 15% protein, and 25 to 30% fat. At least one half to two thirds of the total fat should be unsaturated.
2. Avoid the temptation to use unsound gimmicks or diets. A reducing program should include a decrease in caloric intake and

TABLE 7.12. ENERGY EXPENDITURE FOR VARIOUS PHYSICAL ACTIVITIES

Activity	Cal/lb			METs[a]
	1 Min	15 Min	30 Min	
Archery	0.0342	0.513	1.026	4.38
Basketball	0.0530	0.795	1.590	6.80
Bicycling (level road)				
5 mph	0.0250	0.375	0.750	3.21
10 mph	0.0500	0.750	1.500	6.41
13 mph	0.0720	1.080	2.160	9.23
Bowling	0.0214	0.0321	0.0640	2.75
Calisthenics	0.0333	0.795	1.590	4.27
Golf (walking)	0.0360	0.540	1.080	4.62
Handball	0.0630	0.945	1.890	8.08
Hiking	0.0420	0.630	1.260	5.38
Jogging (level track)				
4.5 mph (13:30 min/mi)	0.0630	0.945	1.890	8.08
5.0 mph (12:00 min/mi)	0.0667	0.999	1.999	8.55
5.5 mph (11:00 min/mi)	0.0711	1.067	2.133	9.12
6.0 mph (10:00 min/mi)	0.0790	1.185	2.370	10.13
7.0 mph (8:30 min/mi)	0.0933	1.399	2.799	11.96
Paddleball	0.0690	1.035	2.070	8.85
Ping-pong	0.0304	0.456	0.912	3.90
Rope skipping (80 turns/min)	0.0752	1.1280	2.2560	9.65
Running (cross country)	0.0740	1.110	2.220	9.49
Running (level track)				
8.7 mph (6.54 min/mi)	0.1031	1.547	3.094	13.22
10.0 mph (6:00 min/mi)	0.1066	1.599	3.198	13.67
12.0 mph (5:00 min/mi)	0.1311	1.967	3.933	16.81
Running (sprints)	0.1552	2.328	4.656	19.90
Squash	0.0691	1.037	2.074	8.86
Stationary running				
50–80 counts/min	0.0780	1.170	2.340	10.00
140 counts/min	0.1622	2.433	4.866	20.79
Swimming (pleasure)	0.0724	1.086	2.172	9.28
Breast stroke (20 yd/min)	0.0319	0.479	0.958	4.09
Breast stroke (40 yd/min)	0.0639	0.959	1.918	8.19
Back stroke (25 yd/min)	0.0252	0.378	0.756	3.23
Back stroke (35 yd/min)	0.0454	0.681	1.362	5.82
Side stroke (40 yd/min)	0.0554	0.831	1.662	7.10

[a] Based on an average caloric consumption of 1.2 Cal/min for a 154-lb man sitting at rest.

continued

TABLE 7.12./*continued*

Activity	Cal/lb			METs[a]
	1 Min	15 Min	30 Min	
Crawl (45 yd/min)	0.0580	0.870	1.740	7.44
Crawl (55 yd/min)	0.0706	1.059	2.118	9.05
Tennis	0.0460	0.690	1.380	5.90
Volleyball	0.0233	0.350	0.699	2.99
Walking (level ground)				
2.27 mph (26:26 min/mi)	0.0233	0.350	0.700	2.99
3.20 mph (18:45 min/mi)	0.0313	0.470	0.940	4.01
3.50 mph (17:09 min/mi)	0.0332	0.498	0.996	4.26
4.47 mph (13:25 min/mi)	0.0524	0.786	1.572	6.72
4.60 mph (13:03 min/mi)	0.0551	0.827	1.654	7.06
5.18 mph (11:35 min/mi)	0.0627	0.941	1.882	8.04
5.80 mph (10:21 min/mi)	0.0756	1.134	2.268	9.69

Adapted from C. F. Consolazio, R. E. Johnson, and L. J. Pecora, *Physiological measurements of metabolic functions in man,* New York: McGraw-Hill, 1963, pp. 331–332.
NOTE: The number of Calories expended in any activity can be obtained by mutliplying the number of Calories per minute per pound by your weight and by the number of minutes the activity is performed.

an exercise program. By combining these, the individual does not have to cut down the caloric intake as much, the loss of fat is greater, and the percentage of lean tissue increases. If the loss of weight is accomplished strictly by means of dieting, a loss of lean tissue as well as fat results.[40]

3. Weight will be lost only if there is a **negative caloric balance** (use exceeds intake). If intake exceeds use (positive caloric balance), a weight gain results. The body stores excess Calories, whatever the source, in the form of fat.

4. Weight reduction should be gradual, with a loss of no more than 1 or 2 lb/week.

5. Base the amount of weight reduction on the percentage of excess body fat. This percentage may have to be estimated as determination of body fat without professional help is difficult.

6. Avoid heavy meals. Determine the total number of Calories per day the diet will permit and divide by the number of meals. If a between-meal snack is desired, subtract the Calories it provides

from the total number before dividing. For example, suppose that an individual who is on a diet of 2000 Cal/day eats a daily 200-Cal snack. This leaves 1800 Cal for three meals, or 600 Cal each; the individual might divide it into portions of 500, 800, and 500 Cal without a heavy meal.

7. Attempt to spread the caloric intake over several meals. Studies indicate that weight reduction is more effective when the same number of Calories is consumed in three or more meals rather than one or two meals.[17]

8. Avoid dehydration or extreme water loss. A rapid weight reduction due to water loss may take place at the beginning of an exercise program, but the body will correct this water imbalance within a few days. If thirsty, increase water intake.

9. Attempts at spot reducing are not very effective. Exercising any group of muscles leads to a mobilization of fatty acids from fat deposits throughout the body. The public has spent much money on devices designed for such programs when general exercise programs would have been better.

10. If the reduced caloric intake is constant, the rate of weight loss will decrease as time increases owing to a smaller difference between total caloric demand of the body and intake.

11. If two people are on the same caloric diet, the person with the greater lean mass will lose weight faster owing to a higher BMR.

12. If a male and a female of the same age and weight are on the same caloric diet, the male will lose weight faster than the female owing to the male's higher BMR.

Lifetime Commitment to Weight Management

Most individuals can manage their weight by eating and exercising sensibly; however, a lifetime commitment is necessary to do so. A loss of weight and a reduction in the percentage of body fat do not cure individuals of being overweight. If they revert to their old eating habits and fail to maintain a regular physical exercise program, the weight will be regained. To keep the weight down, a permanent life-style change in eating and activity habits must occur.

REFERENCES

1. American Council on Science and Health. 1983. *Fast food and the American diet.* 2d ed. Summit, N.J.: American Council on Science and Council on Science and Health.
2. American Heart Association. 1972. *The way to a man's heart.* New York: American Heart Association.

3. Bennett, W., and Gurin, J. 1982. *The dieter's dilemma.* New York: Basic Books.
4. Berg, F. M. 1983. *How to be slimmer, trimmer and happier.* Hettinger, N.D.: Flying Diamond Books.
5. Blackburn, G. L., and Pavlou, K. 1983. Fad reducing diets: Separating fads from facts. *Contemporary Nutrition* 8(7). (General Mills.)
6. Bray, G. 1979. The nutritional message must be spread. *Journal of the American Medical Association* 241:1320–1321.
7. Brody, J. April 10, 1983. Health updates say thinner is better despite charts. *N.Y. Times Service* in *Wilmington Morning Star,* Wilmington, N.C.
8. Brozek, J. et al. 1963. Densitometric analysis of body composition: Revision of some quantitative assumptions. *Annals of the New York Academy of Science* 110:113–140.
9. Bucher, C. A., Olsen, E. A., and Willgoose, C. E. 1967. *The foundations of health.* New York: Appleton-Century-Crofts.
10. Burkitt, D. P. 1980. The link between low-fiber diets and diseases. In *Readings in health 80/81.* Guilford, Conn.: Dushkin Publishing Group.
11. Burton, B. T. 1965. *The Heinz handbook of nutrition.* New York: McGraw-Hill.
12. Cooper, K. H. 1983. *The aerobics program for total well-being.* New York: Bantam Books.
13. Deutsch, R. M. 1971. *The family guide to better food and better health.* Des Moines: Meredith Corporation.
14. Eckholm, E., and Record, F. 1980. The affluent diet—a worldwide health hazard. In *Readings in health 80/81.* Guilford, Conn.: Dushkin Publishing Group.
15. Falls, H. B., Baylor, A. M., and Dishman, R. K. 1980. *Essentials of fitness.* Philadelphia: Saunders College.
16. Fast-food chains. 1979. *Consumer Report* 44:508–513.
17. Guggenheim, F. G. 1977. Basic consideration in the treatment of obesity. *Medical Clinics of North America* 61:781–796.
18. Hockey, R. V. 1973. *Physical fitness.* 2d ed. St. Louis: C. V. Mosby.
19. Hoerr, S. L. 1984. Exercise: An alternative to fad diets for adolescent girls. *The Physician and Sportsmedicine* 12(2):76–83.
20. Jacobson, M. 1980. The deadly white powder. In *Readings in health 80/81.* Guilford, Conn.: Dushkin Publishing Group.
21. Katahn, M. 1982. *The 200 Calorie solution.* New York: W. W. Norton and Company.
22. Kimber, D. C. et al. 1966. *Anatomy and physiology.* New York: Macmillan.

23. Mayer, J. 1968. *Overweight: Causes, cost and control.* Englewood Cliffs, N.J.: Prentice-Hall.
24. ———. 1980. The bitter truth about sugar. In *Readings in health 80/81.* Guilford, Conn.: Dushkin Publishing Group.
25. Metropolitan Life Insurance Company. 1983. *1983 height and weight tables announced.* New York: Metropolitan Life Insurance Company.
26. Mirkin, G. 1981. Losing weight for good. *The Runner* 3(12):16.
27. ———. 1983. *Getting thin.* Boston: Little, Brown and Company.
28. Moore, M. 1983. New height-weight tables gain pounds, lose status. *The Physician and Sportsmedicine* 11(5):25.
29. Neal, K. G. 1975. *Knowledge of health series.* Long Beach, Calif.: ELOT Publishing.
30. Ostwald, R., and Gebre-Medhin, M. 1978. Westernization of diet and serum lipids in Ethiopians. *American Journal of Clinical Nutrition* 31:1028–1040.
31. Sagon, C. February 22, 1984. Many popular diets lack nutrition needs. *Dallas Times Herald* in *The Greenville News,* Greenville, N.C.
32. Sheldon, W., Stevens, S. S., and Tucker, W. B. 1970. *The varieties of human physique.* Darien, Conn.: Hafner.
33. Sloan, A. W. 1967. Estimation of body fat in young men. *Journal of Applied Physiology* 23:311–315.
34. Sloan, W. A., Burt, J. J., and Blyth, C. S. 1962. Estimation of body fat in young women. *Journal of Applied Physiology* 17:967–970.
35. Tucker, J. B. 1982. A delicate balance. *The Runner* 4(12):84–90.
36. Upton, A. C. October 2, 1979. Status of the diet, nutrition and cancer program. Statement before the Subcommittee on Nutrition, Senate Committee on Agriculture, Nutrition and Forestry.
37. White, P. L., and Selvy, N. 1974. *Let's talk about food.* Acton, Mass.: Publishing Sciences Group.
38. Williams, R. J. 1980. Nutritional individuality. In *Readings in health 80/81.* Guilford, Conn.: Dushkin Publishing Group.
39. Wood, P. 1983. *California diet and exercise program.* Mountain View, Calif.: Anderson World Books.
40. Zuti, W. B., and Golding, L. A. 1973. Comparing diet and exercise as weight reduction tools. *The Physician and Sportsmedicine* 4(1):49–53.

Chapter Eight
STRESS AND DEPRESSION

STUDENT OBJECTIVES

On completion of this chapter, the student should be able to:

1. Define the key terms listed above
2. Describe six body changes promoted by the sympathetic nervous system and the adrenal glands in response to a stressor
3. Define epinephrine and norepinephrine, and describe the effects of these substances
4. Describe the tense individual
5. List eight stress-related diseases and disorders
6. Describe the role of exercise in the prevention of stress-related diseases
7. Determine whether he or she is a tense individual
8. Release tension through a relaxation technique
9. Describe the depressed individual
10. Describe the role of exercise in the treatment of depression

If the **homeostatic balance** (physiological equilibrium) of the body is disturbed, the individual experiences **stress.** Psychological as well as physiological conditions can promote stress, but, whatever the cause, the body does not differentiate among the **stressors.** The reaction to emotional stress appears to be physiologically identical to the reaction induced by physical stress, and continues to exist in the body until homeostatic balance is restored.

Not everyone reacts the same to stress. Some individuals thrive on stress and actually rise to the occasion to function better mentally and physically; many top executives of major businesses fall in this category. In addition, certain individuals do not react emotionally to experiences that can be considered stressful. Their personalities appear to remain calm. Others react strongly, however, and become emotionally and physically disturbed. These people often have physical problems or disorders. The difference in the reactions of people to an emotional crisis is frequently due to the various ways in which they perceive stress. Some magnify the significance of an experience, whereas others are able to perceive that the experience may not be important.

Dr. Hans Selye, a Canadian physician and endocrinologist, describes the three stages the body goes through during stress as the General Adaptation Syndrome.[19] Initially, during the alarm reaction stage, the body reacts to stress. Changes in body chemistry take place to prepare the body for the stressful experience. This stage is followed by the resistance state, in which the body attempts to adapt to the stress. If no adaptation takes place, the exhaustive stage follows, in which physical disorders, or possibly even death, are experienced.

BODY CHANGES

Sudden emotions of fear, anger, or excitement stimulate the **sympathetic nervous system** and the *adrenal glands* to instant action. The sympathetic nervous system produces the following changes in the body:[1]

1. The heart rate and stroke volume are increased, which results in increased cardiac output.
2. Blood vessels in the skin, kidneys, and most internal organs become constricted, which decreases the blood flow to these areas. Blood vessels in the skeletal muscles become dilated, which increases the flow to them.
3. Systolic blood pressure and the volume of blood circulating per minute are increased.
4. Secretions of the digestive glands and contractions of the small intestine are decreased, thus decreasing digestion.
5. Liver glycogenolysis (breakdown of glycogen to glucose) is increased, resulting in more blood glucose.
6. Breakdown of adipose-tissue triglyceride is increased.
7. The rate of ventilation is increased.
8. Muscle **tension** is increased.

The amount of epinephrine (adrenaline) and norepinephrine secreted by the adrenal medulla also rapidly and markedly rises. These two important secretions, known as **catecholamines,** help to increase and prolong the responses of the sympathetic nervous system. Epinephrine accelerates the rate and increases the strength of heart contraction, dilates coronary arteries and skeletal muscle blood vessels, and constricts vessels in many other body organs, thus raising blood pressure and redirecting blood flow to areas with increased metabolic needs. Norepinephrine is almost exclusively a vasoconstrictor for the small blood vessels of muscle tissue *(peripheral circulation)* and plays a minor role in the increase in cardiac pumping.

Stress also initiates a series of reactions that stimulate the adrenal cortex to release the hormone cortisol. Functions of cortisol are as follows:[23]

1. Stimulation of protein catabolism
2. Stimulation of the liver to convert amino acids to glucose
3. Inhibition of the oxidation of glucose by many body cells but not by the brain

These body changes promoted by the sympathetic nervous system and the adrenal glands are ideally suited to cope with stressful experiences. When primitive humans were faced with emotionally exciting and physically demanding situations, they usually had to be prepared to fight for their lives or to run to save themselves. Either choice required action and placed demands on the body. The sympathetic nervous system helped the cardiovascular and respiratory systems to supply oxygen and nutrients to the body cells and to remove waste products. The effects of cortisol enabled people to forego eating for a lengthy period, which they often had to do on occasions of danger. In addition, the amino acids liberated by the catabolism of body protein provided energy and assisted in tissue repair if injury occurred. Today, these body changes continue to take place when people are confronted with stress. Evidence suggests that the secretion of almost every known hormone can be influenced by stress.[23]

Emotional conflicts brought on by the many turmoils of our present society stimulate a person's glands, which prepare the body for a stressful experience. Urban civilization, however, makes relief of tensions within the body virtually impossible, because people are not provided with the motivation and opportunity for, or the social approval of, the vigorous activities needed to neutralize hormone secretions. Modern society has made the fight-or-flight concept obsolete, but has not changed the autonomic nervous system's response to stress. Failure to understand this response possibly may contribute to the development of stress-induced diseases.

THE TENSE INDIVIDUAL

The muscles are arranged in pairs around each joint. As one member of the pair contracts, the other should relax. If the opposing muscle is under tension, it does not relax but resists movement, which results in wasted energy, further fatigue, and increased tension. The tense individual, expending vast amounts of energy without producing results other than fatigue, is therefore not a physically efficient person and is often tired.[14]

The habitually tense individual seeks to release tension in physical actions that are unrelated to the problem created by the tension—drumming the fingers on the table aimlessly or forcibly to express irritation; continually moving in the chair to find a comfortable position; twisting a lock of hair, scratching the scalp, or pulling at an ear; gripping a pencil until the fingers become numb; twisting a handkerchief or clasping the hands in a deathlike grip; twitching the face or assuming expressions of intense concentration, grinding the teeth, and shrugging the shoulders. Sitting motionless, the tense individual twists a ring about the finger, crosses and uncrosses the legs, and wraps the feet around each other. Movement and posture appear stiff. Such a person complains of being tired, worries, and easily becomes angry or frustrated if faced with a problem for which no immediate solution is apparent.[13] (See Laboratory 13.)

STRESS-RELATED DISEASES AND DISORDERS

Emotional stress without meaningful physical movement has detrimental effects on the body. By increasing the levels of fatty acids in the bloodstream, it promotes atherosclerotic problems.[10] Prolonged tension, if frequently repeated, can lead to insomnia, colitis, and hypertension. Digestion is inhibited and acid enters the stomach, which leads to ulcers. Constipation, high serum cholesterol, and shortened time of blood coagulation are also consequences of emotional stress without physical movement. The muscle tightness that usually accompanies unpleasant emotions can create back, neck, chest, and stomach pains. Other symptoms of stress include headache, blurred vision, loss of appetite, and depression. Indeed, Selye's theory of stress postulates that almost any disease can be caused by emotional tension.

TECHNIQUES FOR RELAXATION

Relaxation is a conscious release of muscular tension. A skill that is based on an awareness of the presence of tension, relaxation is not easily performed by many persons. These individuals must learn to relax in much the same way that they would learn any other motor skill.[19]

Various relaxation techniques have been reported to be successful in the release of tension. Benson[4] proposed the following technique:

1. Sit quiety in a comfortable position and close the eyes.
2. Beginning at the feet and progressing to the head, relax all the muscles.
3. Breathe through the nose. Each time you breathe out, silently say the word *one*. Breathe easily and naturally.
4. Continue for 10 to 20 min. You may occasionally check the time but do not use an alarm. When finished, sit quietly for several minutes.
5. Maintain a positive attitude and permit relaxation to occur at its own pace. When distracting thoughts occur, try to ignore them by not dwelling on them, and continue to repeat the word *one*.

Arnheim, Auxter, and Crowe[2] reported a more involved relaxation technique.

1. Assume a supine position on a firm mat with each body curve (i.e., the neck, elbows, lower back, and knees) comfortably supported by a pillow or a towel. Spread the arms so that they do not contact the clothing or the body. Take five deep breaths; inhale and exhale slowly.
2. Curl the toes and point the feet downward. Do not bite down hard with the teeth or hold the breath. Relax. Try to relax all other parts as you tense one area of the body.
3. Curl the toes and the feet back toward the head. Breathe easily and relax.
4. Press down against the floor with the heels and attempt to curl the legs backward. Relax.
5. Straighten the legs to full extension. Let go and breathe easily.
6. Draw the thighs up to a bent position and raise the heels about 3 in. off the floor. Tension should be felt in the bend of the hip. Return slowly to the starting position and relax.
7. Forcibly rotate the thighs outward. Feel the tension in the outer hip region. Relax.
8. Rotate the thighs inward. Feel the tension deep in the inner thighs. Relax slowly and let the thighs again rotate outward.
9. Squeeze the buttocks together tightly and tilt the hips backward. Tension should be felt in the buttocks and also in the lower back. Relax.
10. Tighten the abdominal muscles and flatten the lower back. Tension should be felt in both areas. Relax.

11. Inhale and exhale slowly and deeply three times. Return to normal quiet breathing.
12. Press the head back and lift the upper back off the floor. Tension should be felt in the back of the neck and upper back. Relax.
13. Squeeze the shoulder blades together. Tension should be felt in the back of the shoulders. Relax.
14. Leaving the arms in resting position, lift and roll the shoulders inward so that tension is felt in the front of the chest. Relax.
15. Spread and clinch the fingers of both hands three times. Relax.
16. Make tight fists with both hands and slowly curl the wrists back, forward, and to both sides. Allow the fingers and thumbs to open gradually and relax.
17. Make tight fists with both hands and slowly flex the forearm against the upper arm. At the same time, lift the arm at the shoulder. Slowly uncurl the arms and return them to their original resting position. Relax.
18. Make tight fists with both hands, stiffen the arms, and press hard against the floor. Hold the pressure for 30 sec. Slowly relax.
19. Shrug the right shoulder. Bend the head sideward and touch the ear to the elevated shoulder. Slowly relax.
20. Repeat step 19 with the left shoulder.
21. Bend the head forward and touch the chin to the chest. Slowly relax.
22. Lift the eyebrows upward and wrinkle the forehead. Let the face go blank.
23. Close the eyelids tightly and wrinkle the nose. Relax the face slowly.
24. Open the mouth widely as if to yawn. Slowly relax.
25. Bite down hard and then show the teeth in a forced smile. Slowly relax.
26. Pucker the lips in a whistle position. Slowly relax.
27. Push the tongue hard against the roof of the mouth. Relax. Perform this three times.
28. Move slowly and take any position desired. Relax and rest.

With practice, either of the above techniques can successfully promote relaxation. Individuals who have difficulty in attaining a relaxed state should use a technique that is successful for them. (See Laboratory 14.)

In a study of 75 adult men, Bahrke and Morgan[3] compared the reduction of tension through exercise, quiet rest, and performance of Benson's relaxation technique. All three treatments were performed for 20 min and were equally effective in reducing tension. Possibly, for the treatment of stress, just getting away from it all may be just as important as any physiological changes that may take place through exercise.

STRESS AND PHYSICAL EXERCISE

People are designed to be physically active, and many experts believe that movement can help prevent stress-related diseases and problems. Some studies indicate that fat is cleared more rapidly from the blood after exercise, and that a physical training program increases this effect, thus preventing atherosclerosis.[24]

Michael[15] found that moderate exercise actually provides a mild type of stress for the adrenal glands, which helps to condition and fortify them so that they can manage severe stresses more effectively. The increased adrenal activity that results from repeated exercise seems to cause the formation of greater reserves of steroids, which are suitable for counteracting stress.

Other studies have indicated that repeated physical exercise decreases catecholamine uptake by the trained heart.[18] The heart responds to catecholamines with an increased pulse rate and an augmented coronary blood flow. The trained heart is more efficient in this response and more sensitive to the increased oxygen need, thus wasting less myocardial oxygen.

Studies involving mentally ill patients have verified that sports and moderate physical activity have value in the release of tension. DeVries[9] concluded that rhythmic exercise, such as walking, jogging, bicycling, and bench-stepping, with durations of 5 to 30 min and intensities of 30 to 60% of maximum heart rate, promoted significant relaxation for the tense individual. Also, through concentration on the game and on the opponent, tennis players, handball players, and participants in similar activities find a mental diversion that provides their worried minds with a new set of problems to solve; solutions to these problems, however, can be found in a short time. Habitual worry or anxiety is temporarily forgotten, and physical tensions arising from these concerns are released.[7] As previously reported, Bahrke and Morgan[3] found exercise, quiet rest, and Benson's relaxation technique equally effective in reducing tension; however, according to the researchers, tension reduction following exercise can be sustained for a longer period than that of the other two treatments.

Selye[20] classifies exercise as a potent stressor. In the first stage, the body responds to the demands of exercise. Through training and progressive amounts of reasonable exercise, an efficient response results, and the exhaustion phase of stress is deterred. Selye suggests that an individual who exercises regularly should be better prepared to resist other stressors, and that stressful situations are not as dangerous to a physically conditioned individual as to a sedentary individual.

Socially acceptable outlets for natural aggressive drives provide important physical and emotional benefits. Anger, hate, and frustration, often excluded by society from open expression, can be transformed into running, swimming, tennis, golf, or many other forms of physical activity, thus resulting in a healthier and happier life.

DEPRESSION

Depression is a common disorder. Up to 35 million Americans annually experience the symptoms of depression. Once thought of as a disease of the older population, major depression may begin in the teens and may even occur in small children.[22] Sometimes called the common cold of mental illness, depression underlies many of the physical complaints physicians are asked to treat, hospitalizing hundreds of thousands of people each year. It is also responsible for the high suicide rate among teenagers.

Depression usually relates to a loss, a disappointment, or the failure to manage stress. When depressed, the individual becomes a captive of bad moods and is unable to remain in a good or pleasant mood.

Such factors as one's job, homemaking responsibilities, financial obligations, parental responsibilities, the stress of marriage or being single, unhealthy life-styles, decline in moral values, not knowing what is expected for adequate performance of a role or task, and the failure to fulfill personal expectations contribute to depression. The traits most often exhibited by depressed individuals are poor appetite, a lonely feeling, tendency to withdraw, little interest in other people or things, trouble falling asleep or staying asleep, little energy, preoccupation with unhappiness, and thoughts about suicide.

DEPRESSION AND PHYSICAL EXERCISE

In addition to a number of effective drugs, about 250 different types of psychological treatments are available in the United States for major cases of depression.[22] With increasing frequency, however, medical authorities are prescribing physical exercise programs as therapy for mild to moderate depression.[6,10,11,16] They are impressed by the benefits that many depressed individuals obtain from extended, systematic periods of regular physical activity such as walking, jogging, swimming, bicycling, tennis, and racquetball. Males and females, young and old, have experienced a significant reduction in depression through regular exercise. Robert Brown, University of Virginia,[11] and Thaddeus Kostrubala, author of *The Joy of Running*,[12] are psychiatrists who prescribe exercise as treatment for depression. Because exercise is such effective therapy, they do not prescribe antidepressant drugs as freely as they once did.

Research has failed to show how exercise relieves depression. Some medical authorities believe that biochemical changes in the brain and other nerve tissues may help move a depressed individual toward a more functional state, but other, simpler explanations have also been proposed. Following are some examples:

1. The body and mind do not operate on different levels, independent of each other. If the body breaks down, the mind suffers; if the body is strengthened, so is the mind.[13]
2. Exercise may be antagonistic to depression. Because our mental attitude can make us feel bad physically, it can also work the other way.[13]
3. Physical activity provides depressed individuals the satisfaction of mastering what they believe to be difficult. Through exercise they can meet and accomplish a goal. Fulfilling a goal can help individuals to like themselves better.
4. Walking, running, bicycling, or other similar activities may serve to stimulate daydreaming and unconscious mind release. The mind is allowed to spin and relax, causing blue moods to leave. The exercise environment may be an important part of the healing process. The smell, touch, and feel of the outdoors provide distractions that prevent the depressed individual from concentrating on any problems.

How Much Exercise?

The antidepressant effect of exercise may depend on the type, intensity, duration, and frequency of the exercise. Brown, Ramirez, and Taub[6] demonstrated that walking 3 mi within 45 min several times a week relieved depression. In comparing the influence of tennis and jogging on depression, they found both to provide effective relief. Moreover, jogging 5 days/week for 10 weeks caused a greater reduction in depression than playing tennis or jogging for 3 days. These authors concluded that vigorous physical activities have more therapeutic value. Patients of Kostrubala also experienced better antidepressant effects with running programs of at least moderate intensity, duration, and frequency.[12]

Antidepressant benefits of exercise probably best occur when the exercise involves rhythmic movement of large muscles and is performed three to five times a week at moderate intensity. Whether performed alone or with someone is an individual decision.

EXERCISE AND MOOD CHANGES

In recent years much attention has been focused on the feelings of well-being, or state of euphoria ("runner's high"), that some individuals experience during or immediately after running and other aerobic exercises. These mood changes associated with exercise have been suggested to be due to morphine-like substances called **endorphins.**

The body contains various forms of endorphins and related compounds. Some are in the pituitary gland, some in the adrenal gland, and some in the brain substance itself. The form of endorphin found in the blood is probably derived from the pituitary gland.[5] Endorphin levels have been linked to such varied functions as pain relief, appetite control, reproduction (fertility and impotence), and heat regulation. Researchers have noted that acupuncture appears to stimulate production of endorphins, and biologists also suspect that endorphins play a part in rendering women less sensitive to pain during childbirth.[21]

In addition, researchers have measured increases in blood endorphin levels several times higher after exercise than those measured at rest. Since endorphins are potential pain-killers, it has been speculated that their presence in the blood may explain why individuals are able to continue running or exercising even after an injury occurs. Because endorphin levels are abnormally low in some cases of depression, it also has been speculated that they may have a direct relationship to the relief of depression.[8]

Medical opinion is divided on the issue of whether endorphins account for "runner's high" because at least two questions remain unanswered.[5]

1. Pain relief and other related phenomena reside primarily in the brain. The ability of endorphins to penetrate the barriers separating the brain from the blood and reach the vital sensing centers is uncertain, however.
2. Plasma endorphin levels rise soon after initiation of exercise, but the euphoric effect seems to take longer. Furthermore, the euphoria is inconsistent—some feel it, others do not.

Because of these uncertainties, no one should undertake an exercise program just for the purpose of inducing an emotional high or mystical experience. Those who have this purpose in mind may be disappointed.

Negative Addiction

Morgan[17] proposed that a person can become negatively addicted to exercise. Negative addiction is present if two basic requirements are met. First, the individual believes that he cannot live without daily exercise, and second, if deprived of exercise, the individual experiences withdrawal symptoms (e.g., depression, anxiety, and irritability). Hardcore exercise addicts exercise despite injury and give their daily exercise higher priority than job, family, or friends.

Regular exercise can no doubt provide many benefits, but an exercise program must be kept in perspective from a vocational, social, physiological, and psychological standpoint. Joggers, swimmers, bicyclists, and other exercise enthusiasts should control the exercise experience rather than let the program control them. Exercise is a means to an end—the achievement of physical and mental health.

REFERENCES

1. Anthony, C. P., and Kolthoff, N. J. 1975. *Anatomy and physiology.* 9th ed. St Louis: C. V. Mosby.
2. Arnheim, D. D., Auxter, D., and Crowe, W. C. 1969. *Principles and methods of adapted physical education.* St. Louis: C. V. Mosby.
3. Bahrke, M. S., and Morgan, W. P. 1978. Anxiety reduction following exercise and meditation. *Cognitive Therapy and Research* 2:323–333.
4. Benson, H. 1975. *The relaxation response.* New York: William Morrow and Company.
5. Bortz, W. III. 1982. The runner's high. *Runner's World* 17(4):58–59, 80.
6. Brown, R. S., Ramirez, D. E., and Taub, J. M. 1978. The prescription of exercise for depression. *The Physician and Sportsmedicine* 6(12):34–45.
7. Byrd, O. 1967. Studies on the psychological values of lifetime sports. *Journal of Health, Physical Education, Recreation* 38:35–36.
8. Cooper, K. H. 1982. *The aerobics program for total well-being.* New York: Bantam Books.
9. deVries, H. A. 1975. Physical education, adult fitness programs: Does physical activity promote relaxation? *Journal of Physical Education and Recreation* 46(7):53–54.
10. Folkins, C. H., Lynch, S., and Gardner, M. M. 1972. Psychological fitness as a function of physical fitness. *Archives of Physical Medicine and Rehabilitation* 53:503–508.

11. Higdon, H. 1978. Can running put mental patients on their feet? *Runner's World* 13(1):36–43.
12. Kostrubala, T. 1977. *The joy of running.* New York: Pocket Books.
13. Martin, J. 1977. In activity therapy, patients literally move toward mental health. *The Physician and Sportsmedicine* 5(7):84–89.
14. Methany, E. 1952. *Body dynamics.* New York: McGraw-Hill.
15. Michael, E. D. 1957. Stress adaptation through exercise. *Research Quarterly* 28:50–54.
16. Morgan, W. P. 1969. A pilot investigation of physical working capacity in depressed and nondepressed psychiatric males. *Research Quarterly* 40:859–860.
17. ———. 1979. Negative addiction in runners. *The Physician and Sportsmedicine* 7(2):56–70.
18. President's Council on Physical Fitness and Sports. 1972. Effects of chronic exercise on cardio-vascular function. *Physical Fitness Research Digest,* edited by H. H. Clark, series 2, no. 3.
19. Scott, M. A. 1963. *Analysis of human motion.* 2d ed. New York: Appleton-Century-Crofts.
20. Selye, H. 1956. *The stress of life.* New York: McGraw-Hill.
21. Strahinich, J. 1982. The endorphin puzzle. *The Runner* 4(10):48–50.
22. Trafford, A. 1983. New hope for the depressed. *U.S. News and World Report* 94(3):39–42.
23. Vander, A. J., Sherman, J. H., and Luciano, D. S. 1975. *Human physiology—the mechanism of body function.* 2d ed. New York: McGraw-Hill.
24. Watt, J. 1960. Exercise and heart disease—related fields of research. In *Exercise and Fitness,* edited by S. C. Staley et al. Chicago: Athletic Institute.

Chapter Nine
CIRCULATION

KEY TERMS

Accelerator nerve (p. 163)
Aorta (p. 163)
Atria (p. 163)
Atrioventricular (AV) node (p. 164)
Atrioventricular (AV) valve (p. 163)
Bundle of His (p. 165)
Chordae tendineae (p. 163)
Diastasis (p. 166)
Diastole (p. 166)
Interventricular septum (p. 164)

Murmurs (p. 167)
Myocardium (p. 163)
Pulmonary artery (p. 163)
Pulmonary veins (p. 163)
Purkinje fibers (p. 165)
Semilunar valves (p. 163)
Sinoatrial (SA) node (p. 164)
Systole (p. 166)
Vagus nerve (p. 164)
Venae cavae (p. 163)
Ventricles (p. 163)

STUDENT OBJECTIVES

On completion of this chapter, the student should be able to:

1. Define the key terms listed above
2. Make a schematic diagram of the heart and label the following structures
   a. Right and left atria
   b. Right and left ventricles
   c. Interventricular septum
   d. Myocardium
   e. Pulmonary artery, pulmonary veins
   f. Aorta
   g. Superior and inferior venae cavae
   h. Mitral and tricuspid valves
   i. Pulmonary and aortic valves
3. Trace blood flow from right atrium to aorta and list in order the structures passed
4. Identify basic events of the cardiac cycle and causes of the first and second heart sounds
5. List normal values for resting heart rate, systolic blood pressure, diastolic blood pressure, stroke volume, and cardiac output
6. List maximum normal values for heart rate and systolic blood pressure

The inability of one's circulatory system to deliver adequate blood with its oxygen to active muscle tissue may be the most important limitation of exercise. Although a high rate of energy turnover occurs during cardiac work, the mechanical efficiency of the heart per beat is low. Nevertheless, the amount of work accomplished by this small organ, without cessation or breakdown, is astonishing. The work performed by a normal heart during one's lifetime has been calculated to be equivalent to lifting a 30-ton weight to a height of 30,000 ft.[2]

BASIC STRUCTURE

As can be seen in Figure 9.1, the heart is a hollow organ composed of four chambers. The upper chambers are the left and right **atria,** and the lower chambers are the **ventricles. Atrioventricular (AV) valves** (mitral and tricuspid) connect the atria with the ventricles. Attached to the cusps of these valves are tendinous cords (**chordae tendineae**), which are in turn attached to small muscles located on the inner walls of the ventricles. These structures prevent inversion of the AV valves under the high pressures created by the pumping action of the heart. The **semilunar valves** (aortic and pulmonary) are located at the roots of the **aorta** and the **pulmonary artery,** respectively. These valves prevent a backflow of blood during the relaxation phase of the cardiac cycle.

Cardiac Vessels

The superior and inferior **venae cavae** return blood from the upper and lower extremities, respectively, to the right atrium. The pulmonary artery delivers blood from the right ventricle to the lungs, and **pulmonary veins** complete the circuit between the lungs and the left atrium. From the left ventricle, the aorta, the largest artery in the body, transports the blood through its branches to all parts of the body.

The blood within the chambers of the heart is for pumping purposes only. Because the **myocardium** is not capable of extracting oxygen from blood within its chambers, oxygen and other nutrients necessary for myocardial function must come by way of the coronary arteries and their branches, which encircle and perfuse the myocardium (Figure 9.2).

Cardiac Innervation

The heart is capable of contraction independent of any extrinsic nerve supply. However, two external cardiac nerves are important. The **accelerator nerve,** which belongs to the sympathetic division of the

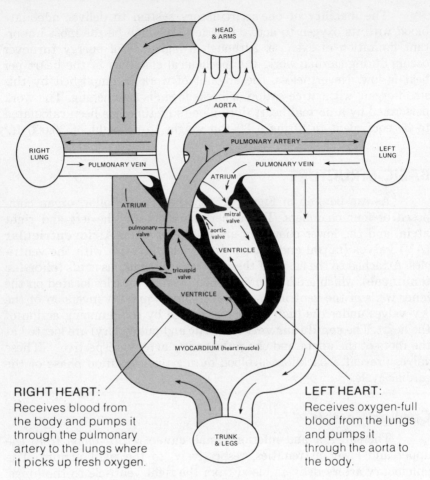

Your Heart and How it Works

Figure 9.1. Your heart and how it works (© Reproduced with permission. American Heart Association)

autonomic nervous system, provides stimuli that increase heart rate. The **vagus nerve** presents stimuli from the parasympathetic division of the autonomic nervous system and serves to reduce heart rate.

Pacing (rhythm) of the heart is normally determined by the activity of the **sinoatrial node** (also called the *SA node, sinus node,* or *pacemaker*) located in the right atrium near the superior vena cava. This mass of tissue sends out an electrical stimulus, which is conducted by the muscle cells of the atria, and which results in atrial contraction. As the conduction wave reaches the **atrioventricular (AV) node** in the base of the right atrium near the **interventricular septum,** it is

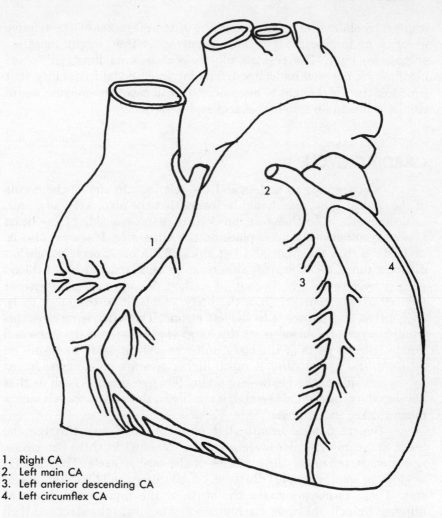

1. Right CA
2. Left main CA
3. Left anterior descending CA
4. Left circumflex CA

Figure 9.2. Coronary arteries (CA)

transmitted through the ventricular myocardium over a well-defined transmission network composed of the **Bundle of His** and the **Purkinje fibers.** Besides these major rhythm-regulating nodes, other nodes, located throughout the myocardium, can produce contraction in the event of a failure of the SA or AV nodes. Occasionally, one or more of these nodes becomes irritable and fires at random; this produces extra contractions, which are sometimes felt as extra beats or skipped beats. These are usually harmless but can be disturbing to the owner. In such cases, a physician should be consulted for accurate diagnosis. Equally important in such cases is the early establishment of an electrocardiographic baseline, which can be helpful in the diagnosis of the relative severity or innocence of similar occurrences that might manifest themselves later. The reasons for these occasional innocent "short circuits" are not well understood. The increased nodal irritability that produces them is thought to be associated with cigarette smoking, use of drinks that contain caffeine, lack of rest, or stress.

CARDIAC CYCLE

In attempting to understand the relationship among the events of the cardiac cycle, one should be aware that the atria work as a unit, as do the ventricles; therefore, an occurrence on one side of the heart almost simultaneously takes place on the other side. It should also be understood that the right and left sides of the heart serve somewhat different functions. The right side receives deoxygenated blood (blood with a relatively high content of carbon dioxide and a somewhat reduced oxygen content) from the body, pumps it to the lungs to be oxygenated, and returns it to the left atrium. The left side receives this freshly oxygenated blood from the lungs via the pulmonary veins and pumps it to all parts of the body under enough pressure to ensure its return to the right atrium. A much higher pressure must be generated by the left side of the heart—approximately five times as high as that developed by the right side—and, accordingly, the wall of the left side is much thicker and stronger.

The mechanical events that promote blood flow through the heart and cardiovascular system can be classified in three categories, which characterize the three phases of the cardiac cycle. They are (1) **systole,** or contraction, (2) **diastole,** or relaxation, and (3) **diastasis,** or rest. These terms designate the state of the myocardial fibers at different times in the cycle. Each phase first occurs in the atria and then spreads to the ventricles. Although ventricular systole follows atrial systole very closely, the two do not occur simultaneously. The contracting, relaxing, and resting of the heart muscle, together with effective action of the valves, create pressure differentials between the chambers, which facilitate blood flow in the proper direction.

In describing the events of the cardiac cycle, one might begin at any point so long as the proper sequence is followed (e.g., diastole, diastasis, systole). Increases in heart rate decrease the amount of time allowed for a particular phase and can even eliminate diastasis completely; however, the normal sequence of events is unaffected.

Beginning with atrial diastasis, a simplified account of the most important events of the cardiac cycle follows. During atrial diastasis, the fibers encircling the atria are at rest, the AV valves are open, and blood flows freely from the atria to the ventricles. At the onset of atrial systole, the stimulus from the pacemaker initiates contraction of the atrial fibers (atrial systole), which forces any blood that has collected in the atria into the ventricles. This ejection phase is followed by atrial diastole, at which time the atria are refilled. Even while the atria are contracting, the signal of the pacemaker is picked up by the AV node and is distributed to the ventricular myocardium, which initiates ventricular systole. At the onset of this phase, the AV valves, which were floated nearly closed during late diastole, are forcefully closed. The sound thus produced is fairly low pitched and is caused, in part, by vibrations set up in the walls of the heart and the blood vessels by closure of the valves. This is known as the *first heart sound.* Because the semilunar valves are also closed, ventricular blood is trapped. Pressure in the ventricles continues to build under increasing myocardial tension until it is greater than the pressure in the pulmonary artery and the aorta. At this time, the semilunar valves are forced open and the ventricles eject their blood. Immediately after ventricular systole, the fibers begin to relax, marking the beginning of ventricular diastole. Pressure in the ventricle falls below that in the aorta and pulmonary artery, and the semilunar valves forcefully close. The sound thus created is the *second heart sound;* it is higher pitched and more crisp than the first. If a valve is structurally or functionally abnormal, additional sounds (**murmurs**) usually accompany the normal heart sounds.[4,5,6] (See Chapter 2.)

VASCULAR SYSTEM

To assist the heart in delivery of blood throughout the body, three types of vessels are employed—arteries, veins, and capillaries. Functionally, the arteries carry blood away from the heart, the veins return the blood to the heart, and the capillaries are the connecting links between the arterial and venous trees, which allow respiratory gases and nutrients to be exchanged freely between the cells and the circulating blood. The duties of these vessels dictate that they be structurally different. Some of these differences are shown in Table 9.1.

CARDIOVASCULAR RESPONSES TO EXERCISE

Any discussion of cardiovascular responses to exercise must be qualified in terms of acute effects or long-term effects, because these types of responses are quite different. Furthermore, the kind of exercise employed is an important consideration. In this chapter, any reference

TABLE 9.1. CHARACTERISTICS OF ARTERIES, VEINS, AND CAPILLARIES

Vessel	Diameter[a]	Characteristics
Arteries	30 μ–2.5 cm	Walls thicker than those of corresponding veins
		Muscle tissue thicker than that in corresponding veins
		No apparent diffusion through walls
Veins	20 μ–3.0 cm	Walls thinner than those of corresponding arteries
		Muscle tissue thinner than that in corresponding arteries
		Valves present in larger veins
		No apparent diffusion through walls
Capillaries	1 μ–8 μ	Walls one cell thick, freely permit diffusion

[a] Diameters include arterioles and venules.
μ = micron (0.001 mm or 1/25,000 in.)

to exercise or training should be taken to mean dynamic exercise (e.g., running or swimming), strenuous enough to elevate the heart rate to a sustained 140 to 150 beats per minute (bpm) for more than 5 min.

To study circulatory responses to exercise, heart rate, blood pressure, stroke volume, and cardiac output are measured when the subject is at rest and again during submaximum and maximum exercise; comparisons are then made. The resting, untrained heart averages 70 to 80 bpm, but these values may range from 50 to 90 bpm and still not indicate a pathologic condition. The typical heart rate of females is between 5 and 8 bpm higher than that for males. This may be because in females the heart is somewhat smaller in relation to body size as is the stroke output per beat. If the average volume of blood ejected per stroke (70 to 80 ml) is multiplied by the average heart rate (70 to 80 bpm), the resulting output of the heart per minute (cardiac output) is approximately 4 to 6 liters of blood. The pressure generated by this outflow of blood against the artery walls is known as arterial blood pressure. Arterial pressure is pulsatile as is demonstrated by its elevation when the heart contracts and its fall when the heart relaxes. The peak resting pressure measured during contraction (systolic pressure) averages about 120 $\pm$ 20 mm Hg. The pressure measured during relaxation of the ventricle (diastolic pressure) is lower, averaging about 80 $\pm$ 10 mm Hg.

Acute Effects of Exercise

As an individual begins to exercise, the heart rate increases linearly in proportion to the severity of the work (Figure 9.3). If the

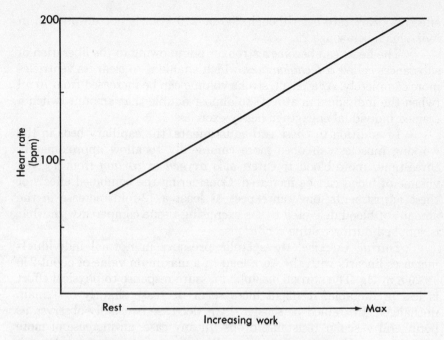

Figure 9.3. Heart rate response to increasing work loads

work is not maximal, the heart rate reaches a plateau after about 3 to 5 min and continues at that level for several minutes, again in proportion to the work load. This elevated heart rate is the result of an increased oxygen demand at the cellular level by the exercising muscles. The ultimate goal of the cardiovascular system is to increase cardiac output, thereby increasing the delivery of blood to the areas that need it so that a balance between oxygen demanded and oxygen supplied can be achieved. This is accomplished by one or all of the following compensatory adjustments:

1. Increased heart rate
2. Increased stroke volume
3. Increased perfusion of the exercising tissue by means of blood flow through previously unopened capillaries
4. Increased amount of oxygen extracted from the blood by the working cells

Most people can elevate the effective heart rate to between two and three times the resting rate. In a majority of cases, the effective heart rate range (maximum rate minus resting rate) amounts to about 100 bpm, since 170 or 180 bpm is thought by many to be the highest effective heart rate even though 200 or 210 bpm is not uncommon in individuals below age 20.[1]

The heart can become a stronger pump owing to the liberation of substances called *catecholamines,* which enable it to clear its ventricles more completely. As a result, stroke volume can be increased from 70 ml (when the individual is at rest) to almost double that amount (when a trained individual engages in heavy exercise).

In addition to these two adjustments, the capillary beds in the working muscles can open more completely to allow approximately three times more blood to enter; also *oxygen extraction* from a given volume of blood can be increased. Considering the combined effects of these adjustments, one can expect at least a 12-fold increase in the amount of blood delivered to the exercising tissue compared with what is supplied during resting conditions.

During exercise, the systolic pressure in normal individuals increases linearly with the work load to a maximum value of about 240 ± 20 mm Hg. The normal diastolic-pressure response to physical effort is less predictable; it might increase or decrease slightly or remain unchanged. In trained persons, a slight decrease is usually observed as peripheral vascular resistance drops. In any case, an increase of more than 15 mm Hg over the resting diastolic pressure is considered a hypertensive response.

Arm work elicits higher blood pressures, ventilatory volumes, and heart rates than does work by the legs for an equivalent work load.[3] The significance of this finding applied to everyday life is that, because cardiovascular stress is greater during arm work, middle-aged, untrained individuals should be extremely cautious about sporadic heavy work with the arms (e.g., shoveling snow or soil, loading heavy items, or rowing). Furthermore, isometric work (straining against heavy resistance) should be discouraged, particularly in older people, because of the extremely high blood pressures and decreased venous return this type of activity produces. Circulatory responses to endurance training are provided in Tables 4.1 and 4.2.

REFERENCES

1. Astrand, P. O., and Rodahl, K. 1977. *Textbook of work physiology.* 2d ed. New York: McGraw-Hill.
2. Burton, A. C. 1965. *Physiology and biophysics of the circulation.* Chicago: Year Book Medical Publishers.
3. Clausen, J. P., Trap-Jensen, J., and Lassen, N. A. 1970. The effects of training on the heart rate during arm and leg exercise. *Scandinavian Journal of Clinical and Laboratory Investigation* 26:295–301.

4. Franklin, M. et al. 1976. *The heart doctors' heart book.* New York: Bantam Books.
5. Guyton, A. C. 1977. *Textbook of medical physiology.* 5th ed. Philadelphia: W. B. Saunders.
6. Rushmer, R. F. 1970. *Cardiovascular dynamics.* Philadelphia: W. B. Saunders.

Chapter Ten
RESPIRATION

KEY TERMS

Aerobic capacity (p. 175)
Aerobic metabolism (p. 176)
Anaerobic metabolism (p. 176)
Maximum oxygen uptake
(p. 175)

Pulmonary ventilation (p. 174)
Steady state (p. 176)

STUDENT OBJECTIVES

On completion of this chapter, the student should be able to:

1. Define the key terms listed above
2. Describe the mechanism of oxygen delivery to the cells
3. List ranges for oxygen uptake in:
   a. Untrained young males and females
   b. Well-conditioned young males and females
   c. World class athletes

4. Explain the occurrence of a "second wind" in some people
5. Provide four factors that contribute to the runner's side stitch
6. Demonstrate the role of dead space air in reducing alveolar ventilation

---

It is unrealistic to discuss the role of the circulatory system in exercise and training without a treatment of the contributions of the respiratory system as well. In fact, increasing one's ability to deliver blood to working tissue is quite futile without a concomitant improvement in the respiratory system. Fortunately, the two systems are related so that activities that develop one also stimulate improvement in the other. Therefore, many writers combine the systems and speak of
172 the *circulorespiratory (CR) system.*

BASIC COMPONENTS OF THE RESPIRATORY SYSTEM

The basic components of the respiratory system are as follows:

1. Entryways (mouth and nose)
2. Trachea (windpipe)
3. Primary bronchi
4. Lungs (composed of many branches of *bronchioles* that through about 23 sets of subdivisions finally terminate in a *respiratory bronchiole* with its alveolar sacs)

Figure 10.1 shows these structures along with several important surrounding structures that enclose the lung in the thoracic cavity and that assist breathing. The exchange of oxygen and carbon dioxide in the lung takes place in the alveoli only. The air between the entryways and the alveoli is not involved in any exchange.

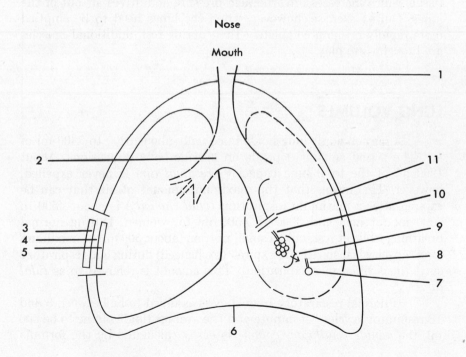

1. Trachea
2. Bronchus
3. Parietal pleura
4. Pleural cavity
5. Visceral pleura
6. Diaphragm
7. Alveolus
8. Respiratory bronchiole
9. Alveolar sacs
10. Terminal bronchiole
11. Approximately 23 generations of branching omitted

Figure 10.1. The lung

MECHANICS OF BREATHING

Breathing, also called **pulmonary ventilation,** consists of inhaling and exhaling air. At rest, inspiration is actively assisted by muscular contraction, whereas expiration is passive. The mechanics of the system require that inspiration occur when the *intercostal muscles* and the *diaphragm* contract. This causes the size of the thoracic cavity to increase, and therefore the lungs also expand because they are attached to the wall of the thoracic cavity by means of the pleura. The increase in volume results in a decrease in intrathoracic pressure, and, if the passages to the lungs are unobstructed, air flows in to equalize the pressure.

The lungs are elastic and are stretched by contraction of the inspiratory muscles. Consequently, relaxation of the muscles of inspiration results in diminished thoracic size and elastic recoil of the lung tissue, which increases intrathoracic pressure and drives air out of the lungs. During exercise, however, when the lungs need to be emptied more rapidly or more completely than during rest, additional muscles are brought into play.[1,4]

LUNG VOLUMES

A normal adult lung holds maximally about 6200 to 7400 ml of air. The actual amount depends on specific body dimensions. About 1200 ml of the total lung capacity (*residual air*) is never expelled, however. This means that the maximum amount of air that can be expired after a maximum inspiration (*vital capacity*) is about 4500 to 6000 ml for men and 3000 to 4500 ml for women. During normal breathing while at rest, only a small portion (about 500 ml) of maximum lung capacity is inspired and expired (exchanged) during one respiratory cycle (inspiration plus expiration). This amount is referred to as *tidal air.*

If normal respiratory frequency is assumed to be between 8 and 18 respiratory cycles per minute and the average tidal volume to be 500 ml, the *minute ventilatory volume* is easily calculated by the formula

$$\dot{V}_E = V_T \times f$$

where $\dot{V}_E$ is pulmonary ventilation, V_T is tidal volume (depth of breathing), and f is respiratory frequency (breaths per minute).[5]

OXYGEN AND CARBON DIOXIDE TRANSPORT

The primary function of the CR system is delivery of oxygen to cells in the quantity demanded by metabolic activity at a particular site. Equally important is the removal of carbon dioxide and other by-products of metabolism. The hemoglobin in circulating blood plays the major role in this oxygen-carbon dioxide transport function. As a result of differences in pressure of oxygen and carbon dioxide in the lungs and pulmonary capillaries and at the cellular level, diffusion gradients are established. These gradients, whose effects are enhanced by the affinity of hemoglobin for the two gases, facilitate its loading with oxygen and unloading of carbon dioxide in the capillaries of the lung and its unloading of oxygen and loading with carbon dioxide at the cellular level.

Under normal conditions of health and at normal atmospheric pressure, blood is about 98% saturated with oxygen when it leaves the lung. In a resting person, about 30% of this oxygen is removed at the cellular level, but during heavy exercise, this amount can be increased almost three times. The amount of oxygen extracted from circulating blood in 1 min is termed *oxygen uptake*. If measured during maximum exercise, this quantity is **maximum oxygen uptake,** which is believed by exercise physiologists to be the best single indicator of physical fitness because it represents the ability of the body to mobilize all its systems during physical stress.

OXYGEN REQUIREMENT

Oxygen consumption ($\dot{V}O_2$) in a 70-kg individual at rest is about 0.25 liters/min, or about 3.5 ml/kg of body weight per minute. During heavy exercise, this value can be increased 12 to 16 times depending on the relative state of CR fitness. The maximum $\dot{V}O_2$ that one can attain (**aerobic capacity**) measures the effectiveness of the heart, lungs, and vascular system in the delivery of oxygen during heavy work and the ability of the working cells to extract it. The higher the $\dot{V}O_2$ max attained, the more effective is the CR system.

Values for $\dot{V}O_2$ are usually reported in liters per minute. When comparisons between individuals are made or when classification into a fitness category is desired, however, adjustments must be made for body size. This is achieved by dividing the $\dot{V}O_2$ in milliliters per minute by the body weight in kilograms (ml/kg/min). The resulting value is expressed in milliliters of oxygen consumed per kilogram of body weight per minute of work.

Oxygen uptake in untrained young males generally ranges from 42 to 45 ml/kg/min of work. Values for females are 3 to 4 ml lower at the same level of fitness. With proper training, this value may be elevated to range from 50 to 55 ml/kg/min, which is considered to indicate excellent CR fitness. Many endurance athletes have been able to achieve oxygen uptakes as high as 65 to 70 ml/kg/min. A few biologically gifted individuals have been able to combine their hereditary traits with very hard training to develop capacities for processing more than 70 ml/kg/min. This last group describes the elite few who become world class champions in endurance events. Frank Shorter, an Olympic marathon gold medalist, and Bill Rodgers, three-time winner of the Boston Marathon, with 71 and 78 ml/kg/min, respectively, are examples of athletes in this category.

ENERGY PATHWAYS AND RECOVERY

During continuous exercise that requires less than 50% of one's aerobic capacity, the body's oxygen transport system is usually able to supply enough oxygen for muscle cells to produce energy by a process called **aerobic metabolism.** If one works below this intensity, heart rate, $\dot{V}_E$, $\dot{V}O_2$, and blood pressure are maintained at relatively constant levels for an indefinite period of time. The term **steady state** is used to describe this state of dynamic balance.

Supply and demand cannot remain balanced under all exercise conditions. Two examples are (1) at the beginning of exercise when cellular oxygen demand is greater than the *response* capability of the transport system, and (2) during high intensity work (greater than approximately 50% of aerobic capacity) when the cellular oxygen demand exceeds the *transport* capacity of the system. In these cases, some of the energy for muscle activity must be supplied from the incomplete breakdown of glucose because only limited oxygen is available (**anaerobic metabolism**). This process is inefficient, results in lactic acid formation, and accelerates fatigue, however.

For many years, it has been thought that anaerobic metabolism creates an oxygen debt, and that the debt is repaid during recovery. This concept has been supported, in part, by the observation that postexercise $\dot{V}O_2$ remains elevated for some time after an exercise bout ends. Some of the recovery $\dot{V}O_2$ has been purported to be used to oxidize the lactic acid formed during the transition from rest to work when anaerobic metabolism is the primary energy pathway. Some investigators have challenged the validity of the oxygen debt concept, however, and have offered strong evidence to the contrary.[2] Accordingly, oxygen debt appears to be a dying term and an inaccurate explanation for the elevated postexercise $\dot{V}O_2$.

In view of the preceding discussion, one is fully recovered after exercise only when blood pressure, heart rate, ventilation, $\dot{V}O_2$, and blood lactate have returned to preexercise levels. The amount of time required for recovery is a function of the intensity and duration of the exercise and the relative state of training of the individual. One recovers faster if the aerobic pathway is the primary energy source during the exercise, because less lactic acid is produced.

RESPIRATORY PHENOMENA

Several interesting respiratory phenomena have been reported by some individuals and deserve mention.

Second Wind

During the early minutes of vigorous work, uncomfortably difficult breathing (dyspnea) may occur. In some individuals, accompanying characteristics such as dizziness, heavy legs, chest discomfort, and general physical distress are also experienced. After a few minutes of continuous work at the same intensity, however, these symptoms seem to disappear, the distress subsides, and one experiences a "second wind." This phenomenon occurs more commonly in untrained persons than in well-trained athletes, or in those who have not warmed up properly. This is probably because the CR system does not become fully effective until after 3 to 5 min of work at moderate intensity. During this time lag, lactic acid accumulates. When full effectiveness is achieved, the distress subsides somewhat as a result of improved oxygen delivery to working muscles.

Side Stitch

A side stitch sometimes occurs in untrained persons during running activities. This is evident as a sharp pain in the area of the lower rib cage and is usually confined to the right side of the body. Several explanations have been offered, none of which is completely satisfactory. Any or all of the following factors may contribute to the discomfort:

1. Accumulation of lactic acid in the diaphragm
2. Severe shaking of the abdominal contents, which causes pain in the supporting structures
3. Formation of gas in the ascending colon
4. Reduced blood flow to the affected area due to the rerouting of blood to other areas

As with second wind, side stitch occasionally occurs in trained individuals. Relief may be hastened by application of pressure on the affected side while the exercise is continued. If the pain becomes too severe, the only alternative is to terminate the work.

VENTILATION DURING RUNNING

Runners are often concerned about the efficiency of their methods of ventilating the lungs during exercise. They wonder whether they should breathe faster as the demands of exercise increase or whether they should breathe deeper. While the answer is not clear for all levels of exercise, some insight into the problem might be gained from the following example.

Assume that a runner at rest is breathing at a rate (f) of 10 times/minute and at a depth (V_T) of 0.5 liter/breath. From the ventilation equation found on page 174, it can be seen that the pulmonary ventilation ($\dot{V}_E$) is 5.0 liters/min.

$$\dot{V}_E = V_T \times f$$
$$= 0.5 \text{ liter/breath} \times 10 \text{ breaths/min}$$
$$= 5.0 \text{ liters/min}$$

Suppose that, during exercise, the runner's ventilatory demand increases to 20 liters/min. The question is whether the demand should be satisfied by an increase in tidal volume or in rate or both. At this low level, the answer clearly favors an increase in the depth if the runner wishes to remain efficient. The reason concerns repeated involvement of dead space air (DSA) and can be explained as follows.

Although pulmonary ventilation describes the air flow to and from the lungs, alveolar ventilation ($\dot{V}_A$) represents the portion of pulmonary ventilation that actually reaches the alveolar level to participate in the oxygen-carbon dioxide exchange with pulmonary capillary blood. DSA is the volume of air that is contained in the respiratory passageways. Because it amounts roughly to 1 ml/lb of body weight, this volume is estimated to be 150 ml for the so-called reference man. DSA might be considered stagnant because it never reaches the alveoli nor is it completely flushed out during expiration. Consequently, DSA does not contribute to effective ventilation of the alveoli. Its volume must be deducted from the tidal volume per breath to arrive at a value for alveolar ventilation.[3] In terms of the preceding example, the runner's ventilatory requirement of 20 liters/min could be satisfied, on the one hand, by an increase in rate alone as follows:

$$\dot{V}_E = V_T \times f$$
$$= 0.500 \text{ liters/breath} \times 40 \text{ breaths/min}$$
$$= 20 \text{ liters/min}$$

$$\dot{V}_A = (V_T - DSA) \times f$$
$$= (0.500 - 0.150) \times 40$$
$$= 0.350 \times 40$$
$$= 14 \text{ liters/min}$$

On the other hand, the requirement could be met by an increase in tidal volume alone:

$$\dot{V}_E = V_T \times f$$
$$= 2.000 \text{ liters/breath} \times 10 \text{ breaths/min}$$
$$= 20 \text{ liters/min}$$

$$\dot{V}_A = (V_T - DSA) \times f$$
$$= (2.000 - 0.150) \times 10$$
$$= 1.850 \times 10$$
$$= 18.5 \text{ liters/min}$$

From this example, alveolar ventilation is clearly enhanced more by an increase in tidal volume than by an increase in frequency. While this holds true for most submaximum levels of work, there is a point at which the metabolic cost of deep breathing outweighs its advantage. At any rate, it appears helpful to consciously attempt to increase tidal volume to satisfy greater ventilatory demands during submaximum work. Many distance runners advocate that this increase in tidal volume be accomplished by belly breathing, which they claim is more efficient than intercostal (chest) breathing.

REFERENCES

1. Astrand, P. O., and Rodahl, K. 1977. *Textbook of work physiology.* 2d ed. New York: McGraw-Hill.
2. Brooks, G. A., and Fahey, T. D. 1984. *Exercise physiology: Human bioenergetics and its applications.* New York: John Wiley and Sons.
3. Comroe, J. H. 1965. *Physiology of respiration.* Chicago: Yearbook Medical Publishers.
4. Guyton, A. C. 1977. *Textbook of medical physiology.* 5th ed. Philadelphia: W. B. Saunders.
5. Slonim, N. B., and Hamilton, L. H. 1971. *Respiratory physiology.* 2nd ed. St. Louis: C. V. Mosby.

Chapter Eleven
THE MUSCULAR SYSTEM

STUDENT OBJECTIVES

On completion of this chapter, the student should be able to:

1. Define the key terms listed above
2. Describe the characteristics of skeletal, smooth, and cardiac muscle tissue
3. Identify and describe the components of the gross structure of skeletal muscle
4. Diagram a skeletal muscle fiber, and label and define the sarcomere, actin, and myosin filaments, Z-line, H-zone, A-band, and I-band
5. Describe the sliding-filament theory and the role of adenosine triphosphate
6. Identify the factors responsible for gradation of muscular contraction
7. List and define the types of muscular contraction

People cannot do anything without using some muscle, or muscles, as all movement and body functions depend on the contraction of muscle tissue. The human body has three types of muscle tissue—skeletal, smooth, and cardiac.

Skeletal, striated muscle performs the functions of moving and stabilizing the skeletal system. It is innervated by the voluntary (somatic) nervous system and consists of long, cylindrical **muscle fibers.** Each fiber, or cell, has several hundred nuclei and is structurally independent of other fibers. Skeletal muscle is called *striated* because of its parallel layers of alternating light and dark bands.

Smooth, nonstriated muscle is found in the walls of the hollow **180** organs and blood vessels. It is innervated by the involuntary (autonomic) nervous system and ordinarily is not under voluntary control. Smooth muscle consists of long, spindle-shaped cells, and each cell usually has only one nucleus.

Cardiac muscle, the heart muscle, is a network of striated fibers. The arrangement of the fibers enables the cardiac muscle to contract as a unit, obeying the **all-or-none law.** Cardiac muscle also contracts rhythmically and automatically because the impulse for contraction originates within the heart itself.

GROSS STRUCTURE OF SKELETAL MUSCLE

Skeletal muscle has an outside covering of connective tissue called the *epimysium,* which merges with a tendon at the ends of the muscle. The tendon connects the muscle to a bone.

Within a muscle, the fibers are grouped into bundles, referred to as *fasciculi,* which are covered by a connective tissue called the *perimysium.* The fasciculi vary in length and ordinarily do not run the full length of a large muscle. A fasciculus may have only a few muscle fibers or as many as 150 or more (Figure 11.1).

MICROSCOPIC STRUCTURE OF SKELETAL MUSCLE

Each fiber is surrounded by connective tissue, the *endomysium.* One fiber rarely runs the entire length of a muscle or even of a fasciculus. Hence, the connective tissue of a muscle is necessary for the

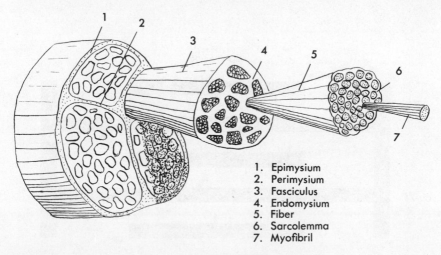

1. Epimysium
2. Perimysium
3. Fasciculus
4. Endomysium
5. Fiber
6. Sarcolemma
7. Myofibril

Figure 11.1. Construction of a skeletal muscle

transmission of the force of contraction from one fiber to another, from the fibers to a fasciculus, from one fasciculus to another, and from the fasciculi to the tendon or tendons connected to the bone.

The smallest fibers cannot be seen with the naked eye, and the largest are as thick as a human hair. They range in length from 1 to 50 mm, which in some cases is the entire length of the muscle.

Beneath the endomysium, the muscle cell is covered by a tough, exceedingly thin, elastic sheath, the **sarcolemma,** and beneath it are

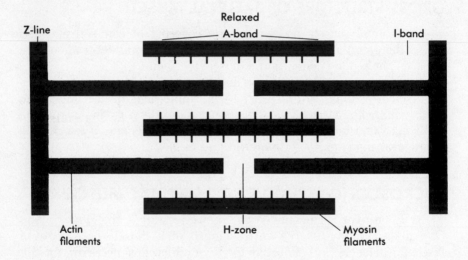

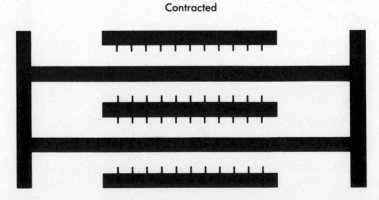

Figure 11.2. Structure of a sarcomere

located the numerous nuclei. Embedded in the muscle-fiber protoplasm (**sarcoplasm**) are columnlike structures called **myofibrils.** (It is the myofibrils, with alternating segments of light and dark, that provide the striated appearance of skeletal muscle.) Each myofibril is subdivided into *sarcomeres.* These are the functional units of the myofibrils and are composed of two types of parallel, proteinaceous filaments—thick filaments containing *myosin* and thin ones containing *actin.*

As shown in Figure 11.2, the thin filaments of actin form a light zone, called the *I-band,* and the thick myosin filaments form the denser, darker *A-band.* The actin filaments arise from a membrane called the *Z-line,* which forms the boundary between the sarcomeres. The spaces between pairs of actin filaments form a lighter band within the A-band, called the *H-zone.*

THE CONTRACTILE PROCESS

The most widely accepted explanation of muscle contraction is the *sliding-filament theory.* It contends that the actin filaments slide between the myosin filaments, which pulls the Z-lines of the sarcomere toward the A-band and shortens the I-band. The length of the A-band is not changed; that is, the myosin filaments remain constant in length. The H-zone disappears in the sliding process, however. (See Figure 11.2.) The exact manner in which this process occurs is not completely understood, but cross-bridges from the myosin filaments are believed to form a chemical bond with selected sites on the actin filaments.

Energy for muscle contraction is derived from the breakdown of *adenosine triphosphate (ATP).* Nerve impulses sent to the muscle cell stimulate this breakdown, and the energy yielded is used when the actin filaments slide between the myosin filaments. The liberation of energy occurs in the following reaction: ATP → *adenosine diphosphate* (ADP) + phosphate + energy. ATP for further contraction is synthesized from nutrient substances and creatine phosphate. The latter, found only in muscle tissue, is broken down by enzymes during exercise. Its by-products combine with ADP to form ATP:

$$\text{creatine phosphate} \overset{\text{enzyme}}{\rightleftharpoons} \text{creatine} + \text{phosphates} + \text{energy}$$
$$\text{phosphates} + \text{energy} + \text{ADP} \rightleftharpoons \text{ATP}$$

THE MOTOR UNIT

The basic unit of muscular contraction is the **motor unit,** which consists of a group of muscle cells innervated by the fiber of a single nerve cell. On entering the muscle through the epimysium, the nerve fiber branches and distributes itself among the muscle cells. The need for this arrangement can be seen in the huge difference that exists between the number of *motor nerves* entering a muscle and the number of muscle fibers (cells) within the muscle. (About 250,000,000 separate muscle fibers make up the human skeletal muscles, but there are only approximately 420,000 motor nerves.[1]) As every muscle fiber must be innervated, nerve fibers must branch repeatedly.

The number of muscle fibers in a motor unit varies from muscle to muscle in relation to the function of the muscle. Muscles performing fine and delicate work, such as those of the eye, may have ratios of one nerve fiber to five or fewer muscle fibers, whereas muscles used for heavy work may have 150 or more muscle fibers per motor unit.

THE ALL-OR-NONE LAW

A muscle rarely contracts to its maximum as an entire unit, but a single fiber can only contract maximally. On receiving a nerve impulse that is strong enough to cause contraction, an individual muscle fiber responds to its fullest extent. A muscle fiber has no partial contractions. Because a single nerve cell supplies all the muscle fibers of a motor unit, the motor unit also follows the all-or-none law.

The contraction force of the entire muscle varies in relation to a given set of conditions at the time of contraction. If appropriate nutrients are available and the muscle is warm and not fatigued, the contraction can be strong. A weak contraction results if the muscle is cold and fatigued and the needed nutrients are not present.

MUSCLE FATIGUE

Fatigue occurs when the contractile and metabolic processes of muscle fibers are no longer able to maintain an established work rate. Exercise physiologists do not agree on the site of muscular fatigue. Its causes may include changes in the chemical properties of the muscle fibers, breakdown of the ATP/ADP system, depletion of the glycogen stores, and inability to remove excess lactic acid produced during anaerobic work.

GRADATION OF MUSCULAR CONTRACTION

The strength, or gradation, of contraction is determined not by the individual motor unit but by two other factors. One is the number of motor units stimulated. A muscle might contain hundreds of motor units and, although all the fibers of a single motor unit must contract together, the many motor units of one muscle do not have to contract at the same time. The size of the work load is evaluated by the brain, which stimulates an appropriate number of motor units. Sometimes an incorrect judgment is made, and more motor units are stimulated than are needed, as happens when one lifts an empty box that was believed to contain a heavy load. Conversely too few motor units are stimulated when one first lifts a heavy box that was believed to be light.

The second factor in the gradation of muscular response is the frequency of stimulation, or the number of times per second that each motor unit is stimulated. If the muscle fibers are stimulated a second time before they relax from the first contraction, a second contraction will be added to the first. The total response to the two stimuli, which are close together, is larger than the response to a single stimulus.

TYPES OF CONTRACTION

Muscular contraction occurs when the muscle shortens, maintains a static position, or lengthens under certain conditions. Examples of these types of contraction follow.

During *isotonic,* or *dynamic, contraction,* the muscle changes in length while a constant tension is applied to it. Two types of isotonic contraction, concentric and eccentric, result. *Concentric contraction* takes place when the muscle shortens. Push-ups (extension phase), work with weights, and sit-ups require this type of contraction. The gradual lengthening of a muscle against resistance from a shortened position is *eccentric contraction.* The triceps undergo eccentric contraction as one returns to the down position during push-ups, as do the biceps brachii when the body is slowly lowered during chin-ups.

If a muscle remains a constant length during contraction, *isometric,* or *static, contraction* takes place. Pushing and pulling against an immovable object produce isometric contraction.

All three types of contraction have been used to increase strength; however, each has recognized advantages and disadvantages. Training regimens employing these types of contraction are discussed in greater detail in Chapter 4.

REFERENCE

1. Mathews, D. K., and Fox, E. L. 1976. *The physiological basis of physical education and athletics.* 2d ed. Philadelphia: W. B. Saunders.

Chapter Twelve
SUMMARY

In this book, we have attempted to provide the reader with information about human response to a regular exercise program (training), the benefits as well as the risks associated with engagement in such a program, and some of the biological and psychological consequences of failure to remain physically active throughout life. Exposure to this information should convince the reader to make a commitment to a lifetime exercise program.

This program should be based on sound scientific principles and should be developed to meet the needs of each individual. A summary of these principles and the procedures for development of an exercise program are provided below.

For persons under age 35 with no previous history of cardiovascular disease and without any of the coronary heart disease primary risk factors, no medical clearance is required before participation in a physical exercise program. All persons over age 35 are advised to receive medical clearance before they begin training.

Once the individual has determined that no contraindications to an exercise program exist, a personal fitness goal should be established and either a graded exercise test or a self-evaluation technique for circulorespiratory endurance should be administered. A physical exercise program can then be planned with consideration given to (1) the type of exercise to be conducted, (2) the frequency of training, (3) the intensity, and (4) the duration of each work period.

The type of exercise program is dictated by the particular components of physical fitness that the person wishes to develop or maintain—circulorespiratory endurance, muscular endurance and strength, flexibility, and weight management. Ideally, a regular exercise program would emphasize all these components. If one cannot devote enough time and effort to pursue an all-encompassing program, however, the components of circulorespiratory endurance, flexibility, and weight management should take precedence.

Circulorespiratory endurance is developed through aerobic activities, such as running, walking, swimming, or bicycling for a relatively long distance, or jumping rope for an extended period at an appropriate intensity. Individuals should select an aerobic activity or activities that they enjoy and to which they can make a commitment to continue. Running is perhaps the most convenient aerobic activity for development and maintenance of circulorespiratory endurance although some people find it boring. In addition, individuals with joint problems (in the back, knees, and ankles) and foot disorders are unable to run for an extended period. Although some sports activities and forms of training require intense effort for short periods of time, they are inappropriate for development of circulorespiratory endurance because they are not aerobic. These activities can, however, provide other exercise benefits and are highly recommended for these benefits.

An exercise program designed to develop circulorespiratory endurance should be performed a minimum of 3 (nonconsecutive) days/week, although a daily program is preferable. Many individuals exercise 5 to 7 days/week but prefer to modify the intensity or the duration or both on alternate days—they exercise with greater intensity or for a longer period every other day, or 3 or 4 days/week.

Determining the intensity at which one should exercise is critical; however, if training effects are to occur, the principle of overload must be observed. Sedentary persons who initiate an exercise program should begin at a relatively low intensity and gradually increase the level of exertion. With great expectations of physical development, many persons undertake a program but they mistakenly begin their activity at an intensity that is too high for them. Their efforts result in soreness and discomfort, which hinder continuation of the program, and, upon recovery from the soreness, these persons have no desire to resume.

Monitoring the heart rate is the easiest method of determining the intensity at which one is working. Unless advised differently by a qualified physician, one should exercise at a minimum of 60% of one's maximum heart rate range. As the level of circulorespiratory endurance increases, this percentage can be increased. The heart rate can be used to indicate the intensity of all aerobic activities.

The duration of each exercise period is determined by the objectives of the program. The individual should devote 5 to 10 min to flexibility exercises and a minimum of 20 min to aerobic activity. As the level of circulorespiratory endurance improves, the duration of the exercise period can and perhaps should be increased.

Flexibility is known to be specific to particular joints and to particular sports, and it decreases during the aging process; therefore, the individual should maintain a flexibility program for the entire body, with special emphasis on neck and shoulder flexibility, back extension, hip flexion, and posterior leg extension. Participants in a regular exercise program should be aware that many aerobic activities do not contribute to flexibility and, in fact, can actually decrease it; for example, jogging decreases flexibility of the posterior upper and lower leg muscles. For these reasons, static stretching for each specific flexibility should be performed several times throughout the day rather than all at once.

Weight management involves a combination of diet and exercise because caloric intake must be balanced by caloric expenditure (energy needs). A combination of moderately decreased caloric intake and moderately increased physical activity is the most effective procedure for weight loss. The distance one walks, runs, bicycles, or swims, rather than the intensity of performance, is important for weight loss. Approximately the same number of Calories is used whether one walks or runs for a specified distance. For effective development of circulorespiratory endurance and weight management, one should consider both the intensity and the duration of the exercise program.

Participation in a regular exercise program must be based on a personal decision. Excuses that are often given for not doing so—lack of time, of facilities, of motivation—should be reexamined in relation to the benefits of such a program. To enhance the quality of life, everyone should make regular, vigorous exercise a lifetime commitment.

Appendix A
12-MINUTE WALK-RUN TEST

The 12-min walk-run is a test of circulorespiratory function. It should be performed only after the safety precautions (contraindications to exercise) described in Chapter 3 have been considered. It is important to reemphasize that all-out effort on the 12-min walk-run test should not be attempted until moderate aerobic exercises have been employed for a few weeks.

The object of the test is to cover the greatest possible distance, measured in miles, during a 12-min period. The test may be administered in any area in which the distance can be measured.

TABLE A.1. COOPER'S FITNESS CATEGORIES FOR 12-MIN WALK-RUN TEST (MILES COVERED)

Fitness Category	Age (years)					
	13-19	20-29	30-39	40-49	50-59	60+
Men						
Very poor	<1.30ª	<1.22	<1.18	<1.14	<1.03	<.87
Poor	1.30-1.37	1.22-1.31	1.18-1.30	1.14-1.24	1.03-1.16	.87-1.02
Fair	1.38-1.56	1.32-1.49	1.31-1.45	1.25-1.39	1.17-1.30	1.03-1.20
Good	1.57-1.72	1.50-1.64	1.46-1.56	1.40-1.53	1.31-1.44	1.21-1.32
Excellent	1.73-1.86	1.65-1.76	1.57-1.69	1.54-1.65	1.45-1.58	1.33-1.55
Superior	>1.87	>1.77	>1.70	>1.66	>1.59	>1.56
Women						
Very poor	<1.0	<.96	<.94	<.88	<.84	<.78
Poor	1.00-1.18	.96-1.11	.94-1.05	.88-.98	.84-.93	.78-.86
Fair	1.19-1.29	1.12-1.22	1.06-1.18	.99-1.11	.94-1.05	.87-.98
Good	1.30-1.43	1.23-1.34	1.19-1.29	1.12-1.24	1.06-1.18	.99-1.09
Excellent	1.44-1.51	1.35-1.45	1.30-1.39	1.25-1.34	1.19-1.30	1.10-1.18
Superior	>1.52	>1.46	>1.40	>1.35	>1.31	>1.19

From THE AEROBICS PROGRAM FOR TOTAL WELL-BEING by Dr. Kenneth H. Cooper. Copyright © 1982 by Kenneth H. Cooper. Reprinted by permission of the publisher, M. Evans and Company, Inc., New York, NY 10017.

ª < = less than, > = more than.

Appendix B
1.5-MILE RUN

The 1.5-mi run is a test of circulorespiratory function. It should be performed only after the safety precautions (contraindications to exercise) described in Chapter 3 have been identified. It is important to reemphasize that all-out effort on the 1.5-mi run test should not be attempted until moderate aerobic exercises have been employed for a few weeks.

The object of the test is to cover 1.5 mi in as little time as possible. The test may be administered in any area in which 1.5 mi can be measured.

TABLE B.1. COOPER'S FITNESS CATEGORIES FOR 1.5-MI RUN TEST (MIN AND SEC)

Fitness Category	Age (years)					
	13–19	20–29	30–39	40–49	50–59	60+
Men						
Very poor	>15:31ª	>16:01	>16:31	>17:31	>19:01	>20:01
Poor	12:11–15:30	14:01–16:00	14:46–16:30	15:36–17:30	17:01–19:00	19:01–20:00
Fair	10:49–12:10	12:01–14:00	12:31–14:45	13:01–15:35	14:31–17:00	16:16–19:00
Good	9:41–10:48	10:46–12:00	11:01–12:30	11:31–13:00	12:31–14:30	14:00–16:15
Excellent	8:37–9:40	9:45–10:45	10:00–11:00	10:30–11:30	11:00–12:30	11:15–13:59
Superior	<8:37	<9:45	<10:00	<10:30	<11:00	<11:15
Women						
Very poor	>18:31	>19:01	>19:31	>20:01	>20:31	>21:01
Poor	16:55–18:30	18:31–19:00	19:01–19:30	19:31–20:00	20:01–20:30	20:31–21:31
Fair	14:31–16:54	15:55–18:30	16:31–19:00	17:31–19:30	19:01–20:00	19:31–20:30
Good	12:30–14:30	13:31–15:54	14:31–16:30	15:56–17:30	16:31–19:00	17:31–19:30
Excellent	11:50–12:29	12:30–13:30	13:00–14:30	13:45–15:55	14:30–16:30	16:30–17:30
Superior	<11:50	<12:30	<13:00	<13:45	<14:30	<16:30

From THE AEROBICS PROGRAM FOR TOTAL WELL-BEING by Dr. Kenneth H. Cooper. Copyright © 1982 by Kenneth H. Cooper. Reprinted by permission of the publisher, M. Evans and Company, Inc., New York, NY 10017.

ª < = less than, > = more than.

Appendix C
SAMPLE EXERCISE PRESCRIPTION

Name: _Scott Burgess_   Age: _19_   Exercise preference: _Jogging_

Resting HR: _75_   Max HR: _195_   Training HR: 60% _147_ ;
70% _159_ ; 80% _171_

CR evaluation by _12–min run_   Results: _Fair (1.3 mi)_

Comments: _Negligible regular physical activity during previous 3 years._

Fitness goal: _Run 3 mi continuously at 8.5 min/mi pace without undue stress._

Exercise Recommendations

General: _Precede all exercise sessions with warm-up of light calisthenics and flexibility exercises. End all workouts with 10 to 15 min of cool-down activities before entering a warmer environment. Use caution when exercising in adverse environmental conditions (e.g., high heat and humidity)._

Specific:

Exercise style and type: _Continuous activity—walk/jog—eventually full jog at 8.5 min/mi pace._

Frequency: _Initially triweekly, symmetrically spaced. After 3 to 5 weeks, increase to 4 to 5 workouts/week if desired._

Intensity: _60 to 75% of max HR range._

Duration: *20 min/workout initially (excluding warm-up and cooldown). After 8 to 10 weeks increase to 30 to 40 min if desired.*

GLOSSARY

Adenosine diphosphate. A compound [ester] composed of one molecule each of adenine and D-ribose and two molecules of phosphoric acid. It is formed as a result of the breakdown of adenosine triphosphate and is used in the resynthesis of adenosine triphosphate.

Adenosine triphosphate. A compound [ester] composed of one molecule each of adenine and D-ribose and three molecules of phosphoric acid. Its breakdown by hydrolysis is accompanied by the release of energy for muscular and other types of cellular activity.

Adrenal glands. Endocrine glands, one located immediately above each kidney. They produce epinephrine and norepinephrine and many steroidal hormones involved in electrolyte and fluid balance.

Aerobic power (aerobic capacity). The capacity of one's heart, lungs, and vascular system to deliver oxygen to working muscles.

Anabolic androgenic steroids. Synthetically produced drugs that are associated with tissue building. They have masculinizing properties, decrease normal testosterone production, increase fluid retention, cause personality changes, and may increase the incidence of kidney and liver tumors.

Asymptomatic. Presenting none of the symptoms usually connected with the identification of particular diseases.

Baroreceptors. Nerve endings in various arteries that respond to pressure (e.g., blood pressure, stretching, touching).

Beriberi. A disease caused by deficiency of thiamine (vitamin B_1). It is characterized by cardiovascular abnormalities, edema, and cerebral manifestations and other nerve damage.

Body image. The feelings and attitudes an individual has toward own body.

Catecholamines. One of a group of similar compounds that mimic responses to activity of the sympathetic nervous system. Examples are epinephrine and norepinephrine.

Distributed practice. A system of practice schedules separated by either rest or some activity that is different from the one being practiced.

Dynamic contraction. Isotonic contraction—a type of muscle contraction in which the muscle fibers shorten. Movement is involved.

Eccentric contraction. A type of muscle contraction in which the muscle fibers gradually lengthen from a shortened position against resistance.

Endothelial injury-platelet aggregation hypothesis. Damage to inner blood vessel walls (endothelium) from a variety of sources causes platelet aggregation, vessel wall changes, and eventual atherosclerosis.

Extracellular fluid. Fluid found outside the body cells.

Fibrinolysis. The activity of the fibrinolysin system, which removes small clots from tiny vessels throughout the body.

Glucose. A simple sugar belonging to the monosaccharide group, which is oxidized in the body to liberate heat and energy.

Glycogen. Animal starch, which is stored in the animal body for future conversion into sugar (glucose) and for subsequent use as a source of energy.

Hemodynamic. Related to circulation or to the cardiovascular system.

Histological. Pertaining to microscopic structure.

Homeostatic balance. The presence of physiological equilibrium in which body functions and conditions are within an acceptable and safe range.

Hyperextension. Extreme extension or overextension of a joint of the body.

Hypokinetic disease. Malady due to lack of movement.

Interventricular septum. Tissue separating the left side of the heart from the right side.

Intracellular fluid. Fluid found within the cell wall.

Isokinetic contraction. A type of muscle contraction in which the speed of the contraction and the resistance encountered are unchanged during the entire range of motion.

Isometric contraction. Static contraction—a type of muscle contraction in which no shortening of the muscle fibers occurs, thus producing no movement.

Isotonic contraction. See **Dynamic contraction.**

IU. International unit, a quantity of a substance (e.g., a vitamin) that produces a particular biological effect agreed on as an international standard.

Lactic acid. A by-product of anaerobic metabolism resulting from incomplete oxidation of glucose during muscular work. It is capable of terminating muscular contraction if its concentration is high enough.

Lesion. Any pathological or traumatic discontinuity of tissue or loss of function of a part.

Lipid. Any one of a group of organic substances that are insoluble in water but soluble in alcohol, ether, chloroform, and other fat solvents. It has a greasy feel.

Lipid infiltration hypothesis. Elevated serum lipids lead to deposition of lipid material in artery walls and eventual atherosclerosis.

Massed practice. A system of practice schedules that have little or no rest or alternate activity between the beginning and the end of the activity being practiced.

MET. The metabolic equivalent of resting oxygen uptake expressed in terms of milliliters per kilogram of body weight per minute.

Metabolism. The sum of all physical and chemical processes by which living organized substance is produced and maintained; also, the transformation by which energy is made available for the uses of an organism.

Monoclonal cell proliferation theory. Proliferating cells of an atherosclerotic plaque stem from one mutated cell.

Motor nerves. Fibers of tissue that conduct impulses from the brain to the muscle tissue. The impulse must be transmitted if movement is to take place.

Murmur (heart). One of various sounds produced by the heart during specific events of the cardiac cycle, usually the result of a leaky or narrowed valve. It may or may not be pathologic.

Neuritis. Inflammation of a nerve or nerves, which is marked by pain, sensory disturbances, and impaired reflexes.

Neuromuscular efficiency. Control of the muscles by the motor-nerve stimuli in the least wasteful manner.

Oxygen consumption. The amount of oxygen processed by the body. Usually expressed in liters per minute but sometimes in milliliters per kilogram of body weight per minute to allow interpersonal comparisons to be made. Also called **oxygen intake** and **oxygen uptake.**

Oxygen extraction. The amount of oxygen extracted from 100 ml of blood.

Palpation. The act of feeling with the hand by light finger pressure.

Peripheral circulation. Blood flow through small vessels surrounded by muscles.

Pernicious anemia. A progressive decrease in the number and increase in the size of red blood cells resulting in weakness and gastrointestinal and nervous disturbances.

Relaxation. The relief or reduction of tension in the body. It reduces muscle tonus.

Repetition max (RM). The maximum number of times that an exercise can be repeated with a specified amount of weight.

Self-concept. An individual's perception of the kind of person he or she is.

Self-esteem. An individual's success or failure as defined by himself or herself.

Self-image. An individual's view of himself or herself at a particular time and place.

Static contraction. See **Isometric contraction.**

Stress. Any situation in which the body's homeostatic balance is disturbed.

Stressor. Any psychological or physical condition that disturbs the homeostatic balance of the body; anything that causes stress.

Stretch reflex. The reflex contraction of a muscle in response to being suddenly stretched beyond its normal length. This reflex action serves to prevent injury owing to overstretching.

Sympathetic nervous system. A division of the autonomic, or involuntary, nervous system, which is responsible for promoting the body's reactions to a stressor.

Symptomatic. Presenting symptoms of a known condition, usually pathologic.

Tension. Increased muscle tonus, in which the muscles are contracted more than is necessary to maintain posture.

Viscera. Internal organs.

Work/relief ratio. The proportion between time spent working and time spent recovering. A work/relief ratio of 1:2 means that the recovery period is twice as long as the work period.

Laboratory 1

KNOWLEDGE AND ATTITUDE ABOUT THE PURPOSE AND VALUE OF PHYSICAL ACTIVITY

Name _____   Instructor _____

Class and section _____   Date _____

Purpose

The purpose of this laboratory session is to evaluate your knowledge and attitude about the purpose and value of physical activity.

Equipment Needed

None

Procedure

Read each of the questions listed below and check yes or no the answer that best indicates your knowledge or attitude.

Yes   No

_____ _____   1. Do you avoid the use of labor-saving devices whenever possible (e.g., riding lawn mowers and riding golf carts)?

_____ _____   2. Do you regularly perform work that requires vigorous physical exertion?

_____ _____   3. Do you regularly (at least three times per week) participate in physically active lifetime sports (e.g., tennis, racquetball, handball, or badminton)?

_____ _____   4. Do you regularly (at least three times per week) participate in aerobic activities that involve a minimum of 20 min of continuous movement (e.g., jogging, jumping rope, bicycling, or swimming)? **199**

Yes	No	
___	___	5. Do you believe that you can jog 2 miles and continue your daily activities without experiencing fatigue in the evening?
___	___	6. Do you know the guidelines and precautions that should be followed when you first begin an exercise program?
___	___	7. Can you plan a scientifically sound exercise program for a 40–year-old sedentary individual?
___	___	8. Are you able to describe the benefits of a regular exercise program?
___	___	9. Are you able to estimate the energy expenditure of various physical activities?
___	___	10. Do you know the differences among circuit, interval, and aerobic training?
___	___	11. Are you able to develop an individualized training program for strength improvement?
___	___	12. Are you able to identify the primary and secondary risk factors associated with the development of coronary heart disease?
___	___	13. Are you able to identify safe ranges for blood pressure, serum cholesterol, and serum triglycerides?
___	___	14. Are you able to describe the role of exercise in the prevention of, and the rehabilitation after, coronary heart disease?
___	___	15. Are you able to select and self-administer a suitable test for classification of the functional capacity of the circulorespiratory system?
___	___	16. Are you able to determine your target heart rate for training?

Yes   No

_____ _____ 17. Are you able to state the physiological adaptations to endurance training and to strength training?

_____ _____ 18. Are you able to develop an individualized training program for improvement of circulorespiratory endurance?

_____ _____ 19. Are you aware of the problems and disorders associated with lack of flexibility?

_____ _____ 20. Are you able to determine your flexibility in the neck, shoulder, chest, trunk, lower back, hips, and hamstring muscles?

_____ _____ 21. Are you able to design an individualized program to develop flexibility?

_____ _____ 22. Do you know the major reasons why individuals are overweight?

_____ _____ 23. Do you know the effects of being overweight?

_____ _____ 24. Do you know the difference between saturated and unsaturated fat?

_____ _____ 25. Are you able to describe an adequate diet in relation to carbohydrate, protein, and fat percentages?

_____ _____ 26. Are you able to describe a weight reduction plan in relation to caloric intake and exercise?

_____ _____ 27. Do you know the characteristics of a tense individual?

_____ _____ 28. Can you identify any stress-related diseases and disorders?

_____ _____ 29. Can you describe the role of exercise in helping to prevent stress-related disorders?

_____ _____ 30. Are you able to release tension through a relaxation technique?

_____ _____ 31. Are you able to state the maximum normal values for heart rate and systolic blood pressure?

_____ _____ 32. Are you able to describe the changes in respiratory function that result from long-term endurance training?

Yes   No

_____   _____   33. Do you avoid the use of alcohol and tranquilizers after a stressful experience or a bad day?

_____   _____   34. Do you believe you have good eating habits?

_____   _____   35. Are you able to relax immediately when you go to bed at night?

_____   _____   36. Do you enjoy social interaction through participation in sports?

_____   _____   37. Do you have a socially acceptable way of releasing aggressive drives and hostile feelings?

_____   _____   38. Is your typical day free from an unusual number of stressful experiences?

_____   _____   39. Have you avoided any weight gain during the past year?

_____   _____   40. Do you know the relationship of percentage of body fat and acceptable body weight?

_____   _____   41. Do you like yourself?

_____   _____   42. Do you enjoy mental and physical challenge?

_____   _____   43. Are you physically fit?

_____   _____   Response totals

Results

In today's society most people need to participate in a regular physical activity program; however, many fail to do so owing to their lack of knowledge about the value of physical fitness and their attitude toward physical activity.

Observe the number of questions you answered no. These answers indicate a lack of knowledge about physical activity. They may also indicate a negative attitude.

Do you believe that an increased knowledge about the value of physical fitness and participation in a regular physical activity program can improve one's attitude toward physical activity? _____

Laboratory 2
FLEXIBILITY EVALUATION

Name _____   Instructor _____

Class and section _____   Date _____

Purpose

The purpose of this laboratory session is to evaluate your flexibility in the neck, shoulders and shoulder girdle, chest muscles, trunk extension, trunk and hips, lower back and hips, and hamstring muscles.

Equipment Needed

1. Bench
2. Ruler or yardstick

Procedure

1. Take the flexibility tests described on pp. 81–84.
2. Report the first three tests (shoulder lift, trunk extension, and sit and reach) in inches. Report the remaining four tests as passed (P) or failed (F).
3. Use Table 6.1 (p. 81) to determine your flexibility classification for the first three tests.

Test	Score	Classification
Shoulder lift (Fig. 6.1, p. 81)	_____	_____
Trunk extension (Fig. 6.2, p. 82)	_____	_____
Sit and reach (Fig. 6.3, p. 82)	_____	_____
Neck flexibility (Fig. 6.4, p. 83)	_____	
Hips and lower back (Fig. 6.5, p. 83)	_____	
Hamstring muscles (Fig. 6.6, p. 84)	_____	
Chest muscles (Fig. 6.7, p. 84)	_____	

203

Results

Flexibility is not a general factor but is specific to given joints and sports or physical activities. Active individuals tend to be more flexible than inactive individuals. Do you need to develop additional flexibility? _____

Laboratory 3
FLEXIBILITY EXERCISES

Name _____   Instructor _____

Class and section _____   Date _____

Purpose

The purposes of this laboratory session are:

1. To provide the opportunity to practice the flexibility exercises described on pp. 84–102.
2. To guide you in the formation of a flexibility program that can be conducted throughout your lifetime.

Equipment Needed

Towels

Procedure

Perform each of the flexibility exercises described on pp. 89–102. Follow all the instructions concerning duration and mechanics.

Results

1. Did you experience difficulty with any of the exercises?

   _____

2. Do you believe you should perform certain flexibility exercises daily? _____

3. What do you think will happen to your flexibility as you grow older? _____

Stating how much flexibility is desirable is impossible; however, everyone should strive to prevent loss of flexibility because the lack of it can create disorders or functional problems.

Laboratory 4
ESTIMATION OF HEART ATTACK RISK

Name _____   Instructor _____

Class and section _____   Date _____

Purpose

The purpose of this laboratory session is to provide you with an estimate of your chances of suffering a premature heart attack now or in the future. You will make this estimate by rating your blood levels of "good" cholesterol (HDL) and "bad" cholesterol (LDL) and by playing the game RISKO.

Equipment Needed

1. Sphygmomanometer
2. Stethoscope

Procedure

1. Complete the cholesterol quiz. (See p. 208–210.)
2. Play RISKO as the directions indicate for your present age. (See pp. 211–213.)
3. Play RISKO a second time with data you estimate to be descriptive of your mother (for women) or your father (for men).

Results

1. What are your totals for the cholesterol quiz? _____
2. What do your cholesterol quiz totals estimate your heart disease

   risk to be? _____

3. What is your RISKO score? _____
4. What does your RISKO score estimate your heart attack risk to

   be? _____

207

5. What is your parent's RISKO score? _____
6. What does your parent's RISKO score estimate her or his heart attack risk to be? _____
7. List the risk factors that you might be able to change to decrease your chances of suffering a premature heart attack.

GOOD OR BAD CHOLESTEROL: RATE YOURSELF

This quiz will enable you to rate your blood levels of "good" cholesterol (HDL) and "bad" cholesterol (LDL). For each factor, choose the category that best fits you. Enter the first number given (positive, negative, or zero) under HDL and the second number under LDL. Then total your two scores.

Factor	Starting Score:	HDL 50	LDL 140
Sex			
• Male	−5/+10	☐	☐
• Female	+5/−10		
Family History			
• Heart disease before 55 in immediate family	−5/+10	☐	☐
• No heart disease before 55 in immediate family	0/0		
Exercise			
• Sedentary	−2/+10		
• Some regular exercise	+10/0	☐	☐
• Regular aerobic exercise	+20/−10		
Weight			
• Ideal weight* or less	0/0		
• Overweight (ideal plus 1–29 lb)	−2/+5	☐	☐
• Overweight (ideal plus 30 lb or more)	−5/+10		

* Roughly, your height in inches $\times$ 2.1 for men or 2.0 for women

	HDL	LDL
Smoking		
• 10 cigarettes per week or more $-5/+5$	☐	☐
• 9 cigarettes per week or less $0/0$		
Dietary Fat		
• Heavy fat intake $+5/+10$	☐	☐
• Light fat intake $-2/-10$		
Dietary Cholesterol		
• Heavy intake of eggs, meats, dairy products $+5/+20$	☐	☐
• Light intake of eggs, meats, dairy products $0/-10$		
Vegetarianism		
• Strict vegetarian $-5/-20$	☐	☐
• Not a strict vegetarian $0/0$		
Totals:	☐	☐

About Your Score: A: HDL—60 and above, LDL—120 and below

         B: HDL—35 to 59, LDL—121 to 199

         C: HDL—34 and below, LDL—200 and above

Low Risk	*Medium Risk*	*High Risk*
A score of two As or one A and one B predicts low risk of coronary heart disease. Your lifestyle is probably already good with respect to heart disease. Blood ceasurements of HDL and LDL are unnecessary.	A score of two Bs or one A and one C: Your risk is in the average range for LDL or HDL, but could probably be improved by life-style changes. Blood measurements of HDL and LDL are worthwhile, but not crucial.	One score in B and one from C predict increased risk of heart disease. Two scores in C suggest high risk. Lifestyle changes are indicated. Blood measurements of HDL and LDL are a good investment.

Note: This quiz applies to adults (18 or older). It provides a *guide* to your blood levels of HDL and LDL, and your corresponding risk of developing coronary heart disease. The results may not reflect your actual blood levels, since there are many unknown variables. Alcohol consumption, estrogen supplementation (in women), and use of several other medications may affect HDL or LDL levels in blood, but their significance is not yet clear. Laboratory error of HDL and LDL measurements can also be considerable.

Source: P. Wood, The cholesterol controversy is over, *Runner's World* 19(3):76–80, 1984. Courtesy of Peter Wood.

RISKO

The purpose of this game is to give you an estimate of your chances of suffering heart attack.

The game is played by marking squares which—from left to right—represent an increase in your risk factors. These are medical conditions and habits associated with an increased danger of heart attack. *Not all risk factors are measurable enough to be included in this game.*

Rules:

Study each risk factor and its row. Find the box applicable to you and circle the large number in it. For example, if you are 37, circle the number in the box labeled 31-40.

After checking out all the rows, add the circled numbers. This total—your score—is an estimate of your risk.

If you score:

6-11—Risk well below average
12-17—Risk below average
18-24—Risk generally average
25-31—Risk moderate
32-40—Risk at a dangerous level
41-62—Danger urgent. See your doctor now.

Heredity:

Count parents, grandparents, brothers, and sisters who have had heart attack and/or stroke.

Tobacco smoking:

If you inhale deeply and smoke a cigarette way down, add one to your classification. Do not subtract because you think you do not inhale or smoke only a half inch on a cigarette.

Exercise:

Lower your score one point if you exercise regularly and frequently.

Cholesterol or saturated fat intake level:

A cholesterol blood test is best. If you can't get one from your doctor, then estimate honestly the percentage of solid fats you eat. These are usually of animal origin—lard, cream, butter, and beef and lamb fat. If you eat much of this, your cholesterol level probably will be high. The U.S. average, 40%, is too high for good health.

Blood pressure:

If you have no recent reading but have passed an insurance or industrial examination, chances are you are 140 or less.

Sex:

This line takes into account the fact that men have from 6 to 10 times more heart attacks than women of childbearing age.

RISKO SCORE

Name _____ Sex _____ Date _____
Place the correct score for each factor on the appropriate line.

	Yourself	*Dad or Mom*
Age		
Heredity		
Weight		
Tobacco smoking		
Exercise		
Cholesterol or fat percentage in diet		
Blood pressure		
Sex		
Total		
Classification		

Factor						
Age	1 10 to 20	2 21 to 30	3 31 to 40	4 41 to 50	6 51 to 60	8 61 to 70 and over
Heredity	1 No known history of heart disease	2 1 relative with cardiovascular disease Over 60	3 2 relatives with cardiovascular disease Over 60	4 1 relative with cardiovascular disease Under 60	6 2 relatives with cardiovascular disease Under 60	7 3 relatives with cardiovascular disease Under 60
Weight	0 More than 5 lb below standard weight	1 −5 to +5 lb standard weight	2 6–20 lb overweight	3 21–35 lb overweight	5 36–50 lb overweight	7 51–65 lb overweight
Tobacco smoking	0 Nonuser	1 Cigar and/or pipe	2 10 cigarettes or less a day	4 20 cigarettes a day	6 30 cigarettes a day	10 40 cigarettes a day or more
Exercise	1 Intensive work & recreational exertion	2 Moderate work & recreational exertion	3 Sedentary work & intense recreational exertion	5 Sedentary work & moderate exertion	6 Sedentary work & light recreational exertion	8 Complete lack of all exercise
Cholesterol or fat % in diet	1 Cholesterol below 180 mg%. Diet contains no animal or solid fats	2 Cholesterol 181–205 mg%. Diet contains 10% animal or solid fats	3 Cholesterol 206–230 mg%. Diet contains 20% animal or solid fats	4 Cholesterol 231–255 mg%. Diet contains 30% animal or solid fats	5 Cholesterol 256–280 mg%. Diet contains 40% animal or solid fats	7 Cholesterol 281–300 mg%. Diet contains 50% animal or solid fats
Blood pressure	1 100 upper reading	2 120 upper reading	3 140 upper reading	4 160 upper reading	6 180 upper reading	8 200 or over upper reading
Sex	1 Female under 40	2 Female 40–50	3 Female over 50	4 Male	6 Stocky male	7 Bald stocky male

Laboratory 5
EVALUATION OF CIRCULORESPIRATORY FITNESS (12-MINUTE RUN)

Name _____ Instructor _____

Class and section _____ Date _____

Purpose

The purpose of this laboratory session is to evaluate your present level of circulorespiratory fitness. Research has shown that the distance one can cover in 12 min correlates highly with maximum oxygen uptake measured during treadmill exercise.

Equipment Needed

1. Timing device that will run continuously for 12 min
2. Area that can be used to measure the distance covered (Suggestion: A standard collegiate basketball playing floor is 50 × 94 ft. One lap equals 288 ft. If an additional 12 ft are allowed for rounding the corners, a distance of approximately 300 ft can be used for one lap. This offers a convenient alternative to measuring straight-line distance when a running track is not available.)

Procedure

1. Select a running area where distance covered can be easily measured.
2. Start the timer and run, jog, or walk for 12 consecutive min. (Be sure to warm-up first!)
3. Record the distance covered in miles.
4. If laps around a 50 × 94-ft basketball floor (described in step 2 above) were counted, convert laps to miles using Table L5.1. **215**

TABLE L5.1. FITNESS CATEGORIES BASED ON COOPER'S 12-MIN RUN (LAPS COVERED)[a]

Fitness Category	Age (years)					
	13–19	20–29	30–39	40–49	50–59	60+
Men						
Very poor	<22.9[b]	<21.5	<20.8	<20.1	<18.1	<15.3
Poor	22.9–24.1	21.5–23.1	20.8–22.9	20.1–21.8	18.1–20.4	15.3–18.0
Fair	24.3–27.5	23.2–26.2	23.1–25.5	22.0–24.5	20.6–22.9	18.1–21.1
Good	27.6–30.3	26.4–28.9	25.7–27.5	24.6–26.9	23.1–25.3	21.3–23.2
Excellent	30.4–32.7	29.0–31.0	27.6–29.7	27.1–29.0	25.5–27.8	23.4–27.3
Superior	>32.9	>31.2	>29.9	>29.2	>28.0	>27.5
Women						
Very poor	<17.6	<16.9	<16.5	<15.5	<14.8	<13.7
Poor	17.6–20.8	16.9–19.5	16.5–18.5	15.5–17.2	14.8–16.4	13.7–15.1
Fair	20.9–22.7	19.7–21.5	18.7–20.8	17.4–19.5	16.5–18.5	15.3–17.2
Good	22.9–25.2	21.6–23.6	20.9–22.7	19.7–21.8	18.7–20.8	17.4–19.2
Excellent	25.3–26.6	23.8–25.5	22.9–24.5	22.0–23.6	20.9–22.9	19.4–20.8
Superior	>26.8	>25.7	>24.6	>23.8	>23.1	>20.9

Source: Adapted from THE AEROBICS PROGRAM FOR TOTAL WELL-BEING by Kenneth H. Cooper, M.D., M.P.H. Copyright © 1983 by Kenneth H. Cooper. Reprinted by permission of the publisher, M. Evans & Co., Inc., New York, NY 10017.

[a] Assuming 17.6 laps/mi. Laps are rounded off to nearest tenth.

[b] < = less than, > = more than.

Results

1. Distance covered _____ laps or _____ miles
2. Fitness category _____ (From Table L5.1, p. 216 or Appendix A, p. 189.)
3. Are you pleased, satisfied, or dissatisfied with your performance?

_____

Scores for additional 12–min runs:

Date	Laps (distance)	Score
_____	_____	_____
_____	_____	_____
_____	_____	_____
_____	_____	_____
_____	_____	_____

Laboratory 6

EVALUATION OF CIRCULORESPIRATORY FITNESS (HARVARD STEP TEST)

Name _____   Instructor _____

Class and section _____   Date _____

Purpose

The purpose of this laboratory session is to evaluate your circulorespiratory fitness by means of the Harvard Step Test. This test is based on the fact that the speed at which you recover from hard exercise is a reliable indicator of your level of circulorespiratory fitness.

Equipment Needed

1. One sturdy 20-in. bench; one sturdy 18-in. bench
   (If gymnasium bleachers are used, 2-in. by 10-in. boards bolted into place on top of the seat increase the step height sufficiently to permit substitution for the 20-in. bench.
2. Metronome
3. Timer with a second hand that will run for 8.5 min consecutively

Procedure

The male subject steps up and down on the 20-in. bench 30 times/min for 5 min. The female steps up and down on the 18-in. bench 30 times/min for 4 min.

At the end of the test, the subject sits immediately. The pulse is counted and recorded during 30-sec intervals after 1, 2, and 3 min of recovery. Use the following score sheet to calculate your score for the test.

Recovery Period	Pulse Count
1 to 1.5 min	_____
2 to 2.5 min	_____
3 to 3.5 min	_____
Sum of 3 pulse counts	_____

Long Form

$$\text{Index} = \frac{(\text{duration of exercise in seconds}) \times 100}{2 \times (\text{sum of pulse counts during recovery})}$$

$$= \frac{(\qquad) \times 100}{2 \times (\qquad)}$$

$$= \underline{\qquad}$$

$$\text{Index} = \underline{\qquad}$$

Short Form

$$\text{Index} = \frac{(\text{duration of exercise in seconds}) \times 100}{5.5 \times (\text{pulse count, 1 to 1.5 min})}$$

$$= \frac{(\qquad) \times 100}{5.5 \times (\qquad)}$$

$$= \underline{\qquad}$$

$$\text{Index} = \underline{\qquad}$$

Classification

Below 55	Poor
55–64	Low average
65–79	Average
80–89	Good
90 and above	Excellent

Results

1. What is your classification? _____
2. How do the results of this test compare with your performance on the 12-min run? _____
3. Which test do you perceive to be physically more demanding?

   _____

4. Are you pleased or displeased with your score? _____

Laboratory 7

CAROTID PULSE MONITORING AND TARGET HEART RATE DURING TRAINING

Name _____   Instructor _____

Class and section _____   Date _____

Purpose

The purposes of this laboratory session are to practice palpation of the carotid pulse, to determine how high you must elevate your heart rate (HR) to achieve a training stimulus, and to get a feel for a training pace that elicits your target heart rate.

Equipment Needed

Stopwatch or wristwatch with a second hand

Procedure

1. Use the first two fingers on your preferred hand to find your carotid artery. (See Figure 3.2, p. 35.)
2. Press lightly until you can feel your carotid pulse.
3. Count your pulse for 30 sec, then multiply by 2 to get your HR for 1 min. (Note: Resting HR should be counted for at least 30 sec. Exercise HR must be counted during the first 10 sec following cessation of exercise.)
4. Try this several times during a 10–min rest period while you are either seated or reclining.
5. Assume that the lowest value obtained is your resting HR. Using that value, calculate your target HR for training by inserting the appropriate values in the spaces provided below.

		Example	Your Values
a. Maximum HR*		200	___
b. Resting HR	minus	70	− ___
c. Maximum HR range		130	___
d. Desired % maximum HR range for training	×	0.60	× 0.60
e. Answer (from step c multiplied by step d)		78	___
f. Resting HR (from step b)	plus	70	+ ___
g. Minimum training HR		148	___

h. Repeat process to get zone for long, slow distances (LSD) and interval training
(Use 60 and 75% for limits of LSD; 80 and 90% for limits of interval training.)

* Use 220 − age if maximum HR is not known.

Results

Once you develop a feel for your own pace, you should be able to maintain the desired rate comfortably for 10 to 15 min. After a few training sessions, you will need to reexamine your resting HR to see if a new target HR should be determined. In each training session, it is desirable to monitor your HR both during and immediately after the exercise to ensure that the intensity level is adequate, but not too great.

The preexercise warm-up should bring you close to the lower limit of your training zone. You should be about halfway into your training zone by the middle of the workout. Postexercise HR should not exceed the upper limit of your training zone.

Record your zone rates below.

	Lower limit	Upper limit
LSD	___	___
Interval	___	___

Laboratory 8
INTERVAL TRAINING

Name _____   Instructor _____

Class and section _____   Date _____

Purpose

The purpose of this laboratory session is to demonstrate the use of interval (intermittent) training, as might be used indoors or outdoors in a relatively small area.

Equipment Needed

1. Timing device with a second hand, such as wall clock, lab timer, stopwatch, or wristwatch
2. Marked area approximately 94 × 50 ft (the size of an official basketball court)

Procedure

Progress through an interval-style workout as outlined below. The work consists of a series of activities that are interspaced with recovery periods. The work will become progressively harder, will reach a peak, and then will taper off.

1. Begin with 3 to 5 min of stretching and flexibility exercises as described on pp. 84–102
2. Walk 2 laps around the perimeter of the basketball court (or a rectangle 94 × 50 ft) at a vigorous pace.
3. Walk 1 lap at a vigorous pace while you make swimming movements with your arms.
4. Racing-walk 0.5 lap, then walk regularly for the remainder of the lap.
5. Walk 1 lap very slowly.
6. Jog 1 lap very slowly.
7. Walk 1 lap to recover.

8. Jog 1 lap at a moderate pace (25 to 30 sec/lap).
9. Walk 1 lap to recover.
10. Jog 1 lap at a moderate pace.
11. Walk 1 lap to recover.
12. Jog 2 laps at a moderate pace. Walk 1 lap to recover.
13. Jog 3 laps. Walk 1 lap to recover.
    Note: Check heart rate (HR) during first 10 sec after jogging 3 laps and remember the value. (HR should be in 60 to 70% range.)
14. At center court, execute the following high-intensity exercises consecutively. No rest intervals. Exercises are to be executed as fast as possible!
    a. Running, in place, knees waist-high for 15 sec
    b. 10 push-ups
    c. Repeat step a
    d. Supine flutter kicking for 15 sec
    e. Repeat step a
    f. Prone flutter kicking for 15 sec
    g. Repeat step a
    h. 10 sit-ups
    i. Repeat step a
    j. 10 squat jumps
    k. Repeat step a
    l. Check HR immediately. (HR should be in 80 to 85% range.)
15. Walk 1 lap to recover.
16. Jog 3 laps at a moderate pace. Walk 1 lap to recover.
17. Jog 2 laps at a moderate pace. Walk 1 lap to recover.
18. Jog 1 lap. Walk 3 laps to recover.
19. Cool down for 5 to 10 min before showering.

Results

This program produces varying degrees of stress depending on how vigorously the steps are executed and the physical condition of the participant. If your HR was not within the 60 to 70% range at the end of step 13, you should increase the pace (e.g., to 20 sec per lap) and increase the number of consecutive laps (e.g., to 4 or 5 laps) before you proceed to the high-intensity exercises (step 14). After the high-intensity exercises are completed, your HR should be at least as high as your target HR (85%) as calculated by Karvonen's method. (See p. 36.) In the early stages of training, most people prefer to intersperse work with frequent rest periods. As your body adapts to the repeated stress over a period of days or weeks, you will need to increase the stimulus by (1) increasing the pace, (2) progressively increasing the number of consecutive laps, or (3) removing the recovery laps to make the program more continuous than intermittent.

Laboratory 9
CIRCUIT TRAINING FOR STRENGTH

Name _____   Instructor _____

Class and section _____   Date _____

Purpose

The purpose of this laboratory session is to demonstrate a modification of the circuit-training approach as applied to strength training.

Equipment Needed

A Universal Gym or some similar weight-training apparatus

Procedure

1. Determine the maximum amount of weight that can be handled through five repetitions (5 RM) of each of the following exercises:
   a. Leg curls
   b. Weighted chins
   c. Leg press
   d. Bench press
   e. Weighted sit-ups
   f. Military press
2. Begin with step 1a. Complete the 5 RM.
3. Proceed to step 1b. Repeat the 5 RM.
4. Continue the pattern until all steps (a through f) have been completed three times (three sets). Note: In the second and third sets, initially you might not be able to complete 5 RM owing to fatigue. As you increase in strength, you will find that you can do much beyond the initial 5 RM, particularly in the first set. To keep the work uniformly distributed over the three sets, you must adhere to the following regulations.
   a. Do not exceed eight repetitions in the first or second sets no matter how strong you feel.

b. If you execute eight repetitions in the first and second sets and you can exceed eight repetitions in the third set of a particular exercise, you must establish a new 5 RM for that lift. To find the new 5 RM, simply add weight until five repetitions are once again the maximum you can lift without a pause for rest.

c. Remember to stagger the lifts so that the same muscle groups are not used in successive exercises.

Results

This type of weight training is very strenuous and should be engaged in only triweekly on nonconsecutive days. As resistance increases, you may need some slight assistance to overcome the inertia of a weight at rest.

Laboratory 10
METHODS OF ESTIMATING DESIRABLE BODY WEIGHT

Name _____   Instructor _____

Class and section _____   Date _____

Purpose

The purpose of this laboratory session is to estimate your body frame size and desirable weight.

Equipment Needed

1. Measurement tape
2. Ruler
3. Scales

Procedure

1. Determine your height and weight

   Height _____ in. (without shoes)

   Weight _____ lb

2. Estimate your body frame size (small, medium, or large) with one or both of the following techniques:

   Elbow Breadth

   Extend your right arm and bend the forearm upward at a 90-degree angle. Keep the fingers straight and turn the palm away from the body. Place the thumb and index finger of the left hand on the two prominent bones on either side of the right elbow. Now measure the space between the thumb and index finger of the left hand with a ruler or tape measure. Record the measurement in the space below and compare the measurements with the standards in Table L10.1.

   Elbow breadth measurement _____ in.

   Body frame _____

TABLE L10.1. STANDARDS FOR ESTIMATING MEDIUM FRAME USING ELBOW BREADTH AND HEIGHT[a]

Men		Women	
Height (in.)	Elbow Breadth[b] (in.)	Height (in.)	Elbow Breadth[b] (in.)
61–62	$2^1/_2$–$2^7/_8$	57–58	$2^1/_4$–$2^1/_2$
63–66	$2^5/_8$–$2^7/_8$	59–62	$2^1/_4$–$2^1/_2$
67–70	$2^3/_4$–3	63–66	$2^3/_8$–$2^5/_8$
71–74	$2^3/_4$–$3^1/_8$	67–70	$2^3/_8$–$2^5/_8$
75–above	$2^7/_8$–$3^1/_4$	71–above	$2^1/_2$–$2^3/_4$

[a] Height without shoes.
[b] Measurements lower than those listed indicate a small frame and higher measurements indicate a large frame. (Adapted from the Metropolitan Life Insurance Company.)

Ankle Girth

Measure the girth of the right ankle at the smallest point just above the bony prominences, pulling the tape as snug as possible. Record the measurement in the space below and compare the results with the standards in Table L10.2.

Ankle girth measurement _____ in.

Body frame _____

3. Estimate your desirable body weight using Tables 7.7 (p. 132) and 7.8 (p. 133) and by the Cooper method described below. Because heights in Tables 7.7 and 7.8 are with 1-in. heel shoes, add 1 in. to the height that you determined previously.

Desirable body weight (Table 7.7) _____

Desirable body weight (Table 7.8) _____

TABLE L10.2. STANDARDS FOR ESTIMATING BODY FRAME SIZE FROM ANKLE GIRTH (in.)

Sex	Small	Medium	Large
Men	Less than 8	8 –9.25	More than 9.25
Women	Less than 7.5	7.5–8.75	More than 8.75

Source: P. B. Johnson, W. F. Updike, M. Shaefer, and D. C. Stolberg, *Sport, exercise and you.* New York: Holt, Rinehart and Winston, 1975.

Cooper method
Men

Multiply your height in inches (without shoes) by 4 and subtract 128.

$$\text{Height} = \underline{\hspace{4cm}} \text{ in.}$$

$$\times \underline{\hspace{3cm} 4 \hspace{1cm}}$$

$$- \underline{\hspace{2cm} 128 \hspace{1cm}}$$

Desirable body weight
for medium frame $\underline{\hspace{4cm}}$

Women

Multiply your height in inches (without shoes) by 3.5 and subtract 108.

$$\text{Height} = \underline{\hspace{4cm}} \text{ in.}$$

$$\times \underline{\hspace{3cm} 3.5 \hspace{1cm}}$$

$$- \underline{\hspace{2cm} 108 \hspace{1cm}}$$

Desirable body weight
for medium frame $\underline{\hspace{4cm}}$

These calculations will give men of medium bone structure a weight with approximately 15 to 19% body fat, and women of average build a weight with body fat in the 18 to 22% range. Large-framed individuals should add 10% to the figure they have identified as their desirable body weight, and small-framed individuals should subtract 10% from the figure. Use the body frame size that you determined through measurement of your elbow breadth or ankle girth.*

4. The Overweight Index (OW)** may be used to estimate whether you are overweight. Values of 100 or less are considered to indicate a good weight, and values greater than 110 are considered to indicate overweight.

---

*Data from K. H. Cooper, *The aerobics program for total well-being.* New York: Bantam Books, 1983.

**Index from P. B. Johnson, W. F. Updike, M. Schaefer, and D. C. Stolberg, *Sport, exercise and you.* New York: Holt, Rinehart and Winston, 1975.

$$\text{OW index} = \frac{45 \times \text{body wt (lb)}}{(2.5 \times \text{ht (in.)}) - 100}$$

$$= \frac{45 \times \rule{2cm}{0.4pt}}{(2.5 \times \rule{2cm}{0.4pt}) - 100}$$

$$= \frac{\rule{3cm}{0.4pt}}{(\rule{2cm}{0.4pt}) - 100}$$

$$= \rule{4cm}{0.4pt} \text{ (fraction)}$$

OW index = \rule{4cm}{0.4pt}

Results

Summarize all values that you determined.

Height \rule{2cm}{0.4pt} in.

Weight \rule{2cm}{0.4pt} lb

Elbow breadth measurement \rule{3cm}{0.4pt}

Body frame \rule{2cm}{0.4pt}

Ankle girth measurement \rule{3cm}{0.4pt}

Body frame \rule{2cm}{0.4pt}

Desirable body weight (Table 7.7) \rule{3cm}{0.4pt}

Desirable body weight (Table 7.8) \rule{3cm}{0.4pt}

Desirable body weight (Cooper method) \rule{3cm}{0.4pt}

OW index \rule{2cm}{0.4pt}

Note: Desirable body weight is best estimated when considered in conjunction with percentage of body fat. When methods for measurement of body fat are unavailable, the techniques described in this Laboratory can be used as alternatives. Is your weight acceptable to you compared with the standards given above? \rule{3cm}{0.4pt}

Laboratory 11
ESTIMATION OF BODY-FAT PERCENTAGE

Name _____   Instructor _____

Class and section _____   Date _____

Purpose

The purpose of this laboratory session is to estimate your percentage of body fat and to help determine a reasonable body weight based on percentage of fat.

Equipment needed

Skinfold calipers
Scales

Procedure

1. Have your skinfold thickness measured as described on pp. 131 and 134.
2. Use appropriate equations (step 1) to determine your body density.
3. Use the formula in step 2 to determine your percentage of fat.
4. Use the equations in step 3 to determine your optimal weight range.

Note: Tables L11.1 and L11.2 may be used for determining percentage of fat in place of the calculation procedure.

SAMPLE CALCULATION: PERCENTAGE OF BODY FAT

Step 1. Calculation of body density (B.D.)

FEMALE

Skinfolds: Suprailiac average = _13_ : Triceps average = _10_

B.D. = 1.0764 − (0.00081 × suprailiac) − (0.00088 × triceps)

= 1.0764 − (0.00081 × _13_) − (0.00088 × _10_

= 1.0764 − (_0.01053_) − (_0.0088_)

B.D. = _1.05707_

MALE

Skinfolds: Thigh average = _10_ : Subscapula average = _10_

B.D. = 1.1043 − (0.001327 × thigh) − (0.00131 × subscapula)

= 1.1043 − (0.001327 × _10_) − (0.00131 × _10_)

= 1.1043 − (_0.01327_) − (_0.0131_)

B.D. = _1.07793_

Step 2. Calculation of fat percentage

FEMALE

B.D. = _1.057_ (From Step 1)

$$BF \% = \left(\frac{4.570}{B.D.} - 4.142\right) \times 100$$

$$= \left(\frac{4.570}{1.057} - 4.142\right) \times 100$$

$$= (4.324 - 4.142) \times 100$$

$$= 0.182 \times 100$$

BF % = _18.2%_

MALE

B.D. = _1.078_ (From Step 1)

$$BF \% = \left(\frac{4.570}{B.D.} - 4.142\right) \times 100$$

$$= \left(\frac{4.570}{1.078} - 4.142\right) \times 100$$

$$= (4.240 - 4.142) \times 100$$

$$= 0.098 \times 100$$

BF % = _9.8%_

WORKSHEET: PERCENTAGE OF BODY FAT

Name _____

Step 1. Calculation of body density (B.D.)

FEMALE

Skinfolds: Suprailiac average = ____ : Triceps average = ____

B.D. = $1.0764 - (0.00081 \times$ suprailiac$) - (0.00088 \times$ triceps$)$

$\quad = 1.0764 - (0.00081 \times$ ____$) - (0.00088 \times$ ____$)$

$\quad = 1.0764 - ($ _____ $) - ($ _____ $)$

B.D. = _____

MALE

Skinfolds: Thigh average = ____ : Subscapula average ____

B.D. = $1.1043 - (0.001327 \times$ thigh$) - (0.00131 \times$ subscapula$)$

$\quad = 1.1043 - (0.001327 \times$ ____$) - (0.00131 \times$ ____$)$

$\quad = 1.1043 - ($ _____ $) - ($ _____ $)$

B.D. = _____

Step 2. Calculation of fat percentage

FEMALE   MALE

B.D. = _____ (From Step 1)   B.D. = _____ (From Step 1)

$BF \% = \left(\dfrac{4.570}{B.D.} - 4.142\right) \times 100$ $BF \% = \left(\dfrac{4.570}{B.D.} - 4.142\right) \times 100$

$\quad = \left(\dfrac{4.570}{\rule{1cm}{0.4pt}} - 4.142\right) \times 100$ $\quad = \left(\dfrac{4.570}{\rule{1cm}{0.4pt}} - 4.142\right) \times 100$

$\quad = ($ _____ $- 4.142) \times 100$ $\quad = ($ _____ $- 4.142) \times 100$

$\quad = ($ _____ $) \times 100$ $\quad = ($ _____ $) \times 100$

$BF \% =$ _____ % $BF \% =$ _____ %

SAMPLE CALCULATION: OPTIMAL WEIGHT RANGES

Use the formulas and the fat percentages given below to calculate your desirable weight range. Desirable fat percentages range from 13 to 17% for males and from 18 to 22% for females. In no case should body fat percentage fall below 3 and 12% for males and females, respectively.

Sample Calculation

Given: Body weight = 150 lb; % fat = 13%

Step 3. Calculation of fat weight (FW)

$$FW = \text{Body wt} \times (\% \text{ fat} \div 100)$$
$$= \underline{150} \times (\underline{13\%} \div 100)$$
$$= \underline{150} \times \underline{.13}$$
$$FW = \underline{19.5} \text{ lb}$$

Calculation of lean body weight (LBW)

$$LBW = \text{Body wt} - FW$$
$$= \underline{150} - \underline{19.5}$$
$$LBW = \underline{130.5} \text{ lb}$$

Calculation of desirable body weight (DBW)

$$DBW = \frac{LBW}{1.00 - (\text{desired} \% \text{ fat} \div 100)}$$

$$= \frac{130.5}{1.00 - \underline{17\%} \div 100)}$$

$$= \frac{130.5}{1.00 - .17}$$

$$= \frac{130.5}{.83}$$

$$DBW = \underline{157.2} \text{ lb}$$

WORKSHEET: CALCULATION OF OPTIMAL WEIGHT RANGE

Name _____; Weight = _____; % Fat = _____%

Step 3. Calculation of fat weight (FW)

$$FW = \text{Body wt} \times (\% \text{ fat} \div 100)$$
$$= \underline{\quad} \times (\underline{\quad} \div 100)$$
$$= \underline{\quad} \times \underline{\quad}$$
$$= \underline{\quad} \text{ lb}$$

Calculation of lean body weight (LBW)

$$LBW = \text{Body wt} - FW$$
$$= \underline{\quad} - \underline{\quad}$$
$$LBW = \underline{\quad} \text{ lb}$$

Calculation of desirable body weight (DBW)

Minimum DBW*   Maximum DBW**

$$DBW = \frac{LBW}{1.00 - \left(\frac{\text{desired}}{\% \text{ fat}} \div 100\right)} \qquad DBW = \frac{LBW}{1.00 - \left(\frac{\text{desired}}{\% \text{ fat}} \div 100\right)}$$

$$= \frac{}{1.00 - (\underline{\quad}\% \div 100)} \qquad = \frac{}{1.00 - (\underline{\quad}\% \div 100)}$$

$$= \frac{}{1.00 - (\underline{\quad})} \qquad = \frac{}{1.00 - (\underline{\quad})}$$

$$= \underline{\quad\quad} \qquad\qquad = \underline{\quad\quad}$$

DBW = _____ lb   DBW = _____ lb

My body weight should remain between _____ and _____ lb.

* Use 13% for men and 18% for women.
** Use 17% for men and 22% for women.

Skinfold thickness at scapula (in mm) (left margin) — **Thigh skinfold** (top margin)

	6	6.5	7	7.5	8	8.5	9	9.5	10	10.5	11	11.5	12	12.5	13	13.5	14	14.5
4	5	5	5	5	6	6	6	6	7	7	7	7	8	8	8	8	9	9
4.5	5	5	5	6	6	6	6	7	7	7	7	8	8	8	8	9	9	9
5	5	5	6	6	6	6	7	7	7	7	8	8	8	9	9	9	9	10
5.5	5	6	6	6	6	7	7	7	7	8	8	8	9	9	9	9	10	10
6	6	6	6	6	7	7	7	7	8	8	8	9	9	9	9	10	10	10
6.5	6	6	6	7	7	7	7	8	8	8	9	9	9	10	10	10	10	10
7	6	6	7	7	7	7	8	8	8	8	9	9	9	10	10	10	10	11
7.5	6	7	7	7	7	8	8	8	8	9	9	9	10	10	10	10	11	11
8	7	7	7	7	8	8	8	8	9	9	9	10	10	10	10	11	11	11
8.5	7	7	7	8	8	8	8	9	9	9	10	10	10	10	11	11	11	11
9	7	7	8	8	8	8	9	9	9	10	10	10	10	11	11	11	11	12
9.5	7	8	8	8	8	9	9	9	10	10	10	10	11	11	11	11	12	12
10	8	8	8	8	9	9	9	9	10	10	10	11	11	11	11	12	12	12
10.5	8	8	8	9	9	9	9	10	10	10	11	11	11	11	12	12	12	12
11	8	8	9	9	9	9	10	10	10	11	11	11	11	12	12	12	12	13
11.5	8	9	9	9	9	10	10	10	11	11	11	11	12	12	12	12	13	13
12	9	9	9	9	10	10	10	11	11	11	11	12	12	12	12	13	13	13
12.5	9	9	9	10	10	10	11	11	11	11	12	12	12	12	13	13	13	13
13	9	9	10	10	10	11	11	11	11	12	12	12	12	13	13	13	13	14
13.5	9	10	10	10	11	11	11	11	12	12	12	12	13	13	13	13	14	14
14	10	10	10	11	11	11	11	12	12	12	12	13	13	13	13	14	14	14
14.5	10	10	11	11	11	11	12	12	12	12	13	13	13	13	14	14	14	14
15	10	11	11	11	11	12	12	12	12	13	13	13	13	14	14	14	14	15
15.5	11	11	11	11	12	12	12	12	13	13	13	14	14	14	14	15	15	15
16	11	11	11	12	12	12	12	13	13	13	13	14	14	14	14	15	15	15
16.5	11	11	12	12	12	12	13	13	13	13	14	14	14	14	15	15	15	16
17	11	12	12	12	12	13	13	13	13	14	14	14	14	15	15	15	16	16
17.5	12	12	12	12	13	13	13	13	14	14	14	14	15	15	15	16	16	16
18	12	12	12	13	13	13	13	14	14	14	14	15	15	15	16	16	16	16
18.5	12	12	13	13	13	13	14	14	14	14	15	15	15	16	16	16	16	17
19	12	13	13	13	13	14	14	14	14	15	15	15	16	16	16	16	17	17
19.5	13	13	13	13	14	14	14	14	15	15	15	16	16	16	16	17	17	17
20	13	13	13	14	14	14	14	15	15	15	16	16	16	16	17	17	17	17
20.5	13	13	14	14	14	14	15	15	15	16	16	16	16	17	17	17	17	18
21	13	14	14	14	14	15	15	15	16	16	16	16	17	17	17	17	18	18
21.5	14	14	14	14	15	15	15	16	16	16	16	17	17	17	17	18	18	18
22	14	14	14	15	15	15	15	16	16	16	17	17	17	17	18	18	18	18
22.5	14	14	15	15	15	15	16	16	16	17	17	17	17	18	18	18	18	19
23	14	15	15	15	15	16	16	16	17	17	17	17	18	18	18	18	19	19
23.5	15	15	15	15	16	16	16	17	17	17	17	18	18	18	18	19	19	19
24	15	15	15	16	16	16	17	17	17	17	18	18	18	18	19	19	19	20

Directions for use of Table L11.1.
1. Record skinfold measures to nearest 0.5 mm
   Scapula _____ mm   Thigh _____ mm
2. Locate scapula measurement along left margin of table. Locate thigh measurement along top margin.

thickness (in mm)																		
15	15.5	16	16.5	17	17.5	18	18.5	19	19.5	20	20.5	21	21.5	22	22.5	23	23.5	24
9	10	10	10	10	11	11	11	11	12	12	12	12	13	13	13	13	14	14
10	10	10	10	11	11	11	11	12	12	12	12	13	13	13	13	14	14	14
10	10	10	11	11	11	11	12	12	12	12	13	13	13	13	14	14	14	15
10	10	11	11	11	11	12	12	12	12	13	13	13	13	14	14	14	15	15
10	11	11	11	11	12	12	12	12	13	13	13	13	14	14	14	15	15	15
11	11	11	11	12	12	12	12	13	13	13	13	14	14	14	15	15	15	15
11	11	11	12	12	12	12	13	13	13	13	14	14	14	15	15	15	15	16
11	11	12	12	12	12	13	13	13	13	14	14	14	15	15	15	15	16	16
11	12	12	12	12	13	13	13	13	14	14	14	15	15	15	15	16	16	16
12	12	12	12	13	13	13	14	14	14	15	15	15	15	16	16	16	16	16
12	12	12	13	13	13	13	14	14	14	15	15	15	15	16	16	16	16	17
12	12	13	13	13	13	14	14	14	15	15	15	15	16	16	16	16	17	17
12	13	13	13	13	14	14	14	15	15	15	15	16	16	16	16	17	17	17
13	13	13	13	14	14	14	15	15	15	15	16	16	16	16	17	17	17	17
13	13	13	14	14	14	15	15	15	15	16	16	16	16	17	17	17	17	18
13	13	14	14	14	15	15	15	15	16	16	16	16	17	17	17	17	18	18
13	14	14	14	14	15	15	15	16	16	16	16	17	17	17	17	18	18	18
14	14	14	14	15	15	15	16	16	16	16	17	17	17	17	18	18	18	19
14	14	14	15	15	15	16	16	16	16	17	17	17	17	18	18	18	19	19
14	14	15	15	15	16	16	16	16	17	17	17	17	18	18	18	19	19	19
14	15	15	15	16	16	16	16	17	17	17	17	18	18	18	19	19	19	19
15	15	15	16	16	16	16	17	17	17	17	18	18	18	19	19	19	19	20
15	15	16	16	16	16	17	17	17	17	18	18	18	19	19	19	19	20	20
15	16	16	16	16	17	17	17	17	18	18	18	19	19	19	19	20	20	20
16	16	16	16	17	17	17	17	18	18	18	19	19	19	19	20	20	20	20
16	16	16	17	17	17	17	18	18	18	19	19	19	19	20	20	20	20	21
16	16	17	17	17	17	18	18	18	19	19	19	19	20	20	20	20	21	21
16	17	17	17	17	18	18	18	18	19	19	19	20	20	20	20	21	21	21
17	17	17	17	18	18	18	18	19	19	19	20	20	20	20	21	21	21	22
17	17	17	18	18	18	18	19	19	19	20	20	20	20	21	21	21	22	22
17	17	18	18	18	18	19	19	19	20	20	20	20	21	21	21	21	22	22
17	18	18	18	18	19	19	19	20	20	20	20	21	21	21	21	22	22	22
18	18	18	18	19	19	19	20	20	20	20	21	21	21	21	22	22	22	23
18	18	18	19	19	19	20	20	20	20	21	21	21	21	22	22	22	23	23
18	18	19	19	19	20	20	20	20	21	21	21	21	22	22	22	23	23	23
18	19	19	19	20	20	20	20	21	21	21	21	22	22	22	23	23	23	23
19	19	19	20	20	20	20	21	21	21	21	22	22	22	23	23	23	23	24
19	19	20	20	20	20	21	21	21	21	22	22	22	23	23	23	23	24	24
19	20	20	20	20	21	21	21	21	22	22	22	23	23	23	23	24	24	24
20	20	20	20	21	21	21	21	22	22	22	23	23	23	23	24	24	24	25
20	20	20	21	21	21	21	22	22	22	23	23	23	23	24	24	24	25	25

3. Identify percentage fat within the matrix at the point where lines from scapula and thigh values intersect.

4. Record % fat = _____.

Skinfold thickness

	4	4.5	5	5.5	6	6.5	7	7.5	8	8.5	9	9.5	10	10.5	11	11.5	12	12.5
6	14	14	14	14	14	15	15	15	15	15	15	16	16	16	16	16	16	17
6.5	14	14	14	14	15	15	15	15	15	15	16	16	16	16	16	16	17	17
7	14	14	14	15	15	15	15	15	16	16	16	16	16	16	17	17	17	17
7.5	14	14	15	15	15	15	15	15	16	16	16	16	16	17	17	17	17	17
8	14	15	15	15	15	15	16	16	16	16	16	16	17	17	17	17	17	17
8.5	15	15	15	15	15	15	16	16	16	16	16	17	17	17	17	17	17	17
9	15	15	15	15	15	16	16	16	16	16	17	17	17	17	17	17	18	18
9.5	15	15	15	15	16	16	16	16	16	16	17	17	17	17	17	18	18	18
10	15	15	15	16	16	16	16	16	17	17	17	17	17	17	18	18	18	18
10.5	15	16	16	16	16	16	16	16	17	17	17	17	17	17	18	18	18	18
11	16	16	16	16	16	16	17	17	17	17	17	17	17	18	18	18	18	18
11.5	16	16	16	16	16	17	17	17	17	17	17	18	18	18	18	18	18	19
12	16	16	16	16	17	17	17	17	17	17	18	18	18	18	18	18	19	19
12.5	16	16	16	17	17	17	17	17	17	18	18	18	18	18	18	19	19	19
13	16	16	17	17	17	17	17	17	18	18	18	18	18	18	19	19	19	19
13.5	16	17	17	17	17	17	17	18	18	18	18	18	18	19	19	19	19	19
14	17	17	17	17	17	17	18	18	18	18	18	18	19	19	19	19	19	19
14.5	17	17	17	17	17	18	18	18	18	18	18	19	19	19	19	19	19	20
15	17	17	17	17	18	18	18	18	18	18	19	19	19	19	19	19	20	20
15.5	17	17	17	18	18	18	18	18	18	19	19	19	19	19	19	20	20	20
16	17	17	18	18	18	18	18	18	19	19	19	19	19	19	20	20	20	20
16.5	17	18	18	18	18	18	18	19	19	19	19	19	19	20	20	20	20	20
17	18	18	18	18	18	18	19	19	19	19	19	19	20	20	20	20	20	20
17.5	18	18	18	18	19	19	19	19	19	19	20	20	20	20	20	20	21	21
18	18	18	18	19	19	19	19	19	19	20	20	20	20	20	20	21	21	21
18.5	18	18	19	19	19	19	19	19	20	20	20	20	20	20	21	21	21	21
19	18	19	19	19	19	19	19	20	20	20	20	20	20	21	21	21	21	21
19.5	19	19	19	19	19	19	20	20	20	20	20	20	21	21	21	21	21	21
20	19	19	19	19	19	20	20	20	20	20	20	21	21	21	21	21	21	22
20.5	19	19	19	19	20	20	20	20	20	20	21	21	21	21	21	21	22	22
21	19	19	19	20	20	20	20	20	20	21	21	21	21	21	21	22	22	22
21.5	19	19	20	20	20	20	20	20	21	21	21	21	21	21	22	22	22	22
22	19	20	20	20	20	20	20	21	21	21	21	21	21	22	22	22	22	22
22.5	20	20	20	20	20	20	21	21	21	21	21	21	22	22	22	22	22	23
23	20	20	20	20	20	21	21	21	21	21	22	22	22	22	22	22	23	23
23.5	20	20	20	21	21	21	21	21	21	22	22	22	22	22	22	23	23	23
24	20	20	21	21	21	21	21	21	22	22	22	22	22	22	23	23	23	23
24.5	20	21	21	21	21	21	21	22	22	22	22	22	22	23	23	23	23	23
25	21	21	21	21	21	21	22	22	22	22	22	22	23	23	23	23	23	23
25.5	21	21	21	21	21	22	22	22	22	22	23	23	23	23	23	23	23	24
26	21	21	21	21	22	22	22	22	22	23	23	23	23	23	23	24	24	24
26.5	21	21	21	22	22	22	22	22	23	23	23	23	23	23	24	24	24	24
27	21	21	22	22	22	22	22	22	23	23	23	23	23	23	24	24	24	24

Skinfold thickness at triceps (in mm)

Directions for use of Table L11.2.
1. Record skinfold measures to nearest 0.5 mm
   Triceps _____ mm   Iliac _____ mm
2. Locate triceps measurement along left margin of table. Locate iliac measurement along top margin.

OF ILIAC CREST AND TRICEPS
TO PERCENTAGE OF BODY FAT

at iliac crest (in mm)																		
13	13.5	14	14.5	15	15.5	16	16.5	17	17.5	18	18.5	19	19.5	20	20.5	21	21.5	22
17	17	17	17	17	18	18	18	18	18	18	19	19	19	19	19	19	20	20
17	17	17	17	18	18	18	18	18	18	19	19	19	19	19	19	20	20	20
17	17	17	18	18	18	18	18	18	19	19	19	19	19	19	20	20	20	20
17	17	18	18	18	18	18	18	19	19	19	19	19	19	20	20	20	20	20
17	18	18	18	18	18	18	19	19	19	19	19	19	20	20	20	20	20	20
18	18	18	18	18	18	19	19	19	19	19	19	20	20	20	20	20	20	21
18	18	18	18	18	19	19	19	19	19	19	20	20	20	20	20	20	21	21
18	18	18	18	19	19	19	19	19	19	20	20	20	20	20	20	21	21	21
18	18	18	19	19	19	19	19	19	20	20	20	20	20	20	21	21	21	21
18	18	19	19	19	19	19	19	20	20	20	20	20	20	21	21	21	21	21
18	19	19	19	19	19	19	20	20	20	20	20	20	21	21	21	21	21	21
19	19	19	19	19	19	20	20	20	20	20	21	21	21	21	21	21	22	22
19	19	19	19	20	20	20	20	20	20	21	21	21	21	21	21	22	22	22
19	19	19	20	20	20	20	20	20	21	21	21	21	21	21	22	22	22	22
19	19	20	20	20	20	20	20	21	21	21	21	21	21	22	22	22	22	22
19	20	20	20	20	20	20	21	21	21	21	21	21	22	22	22	22	22	22
20	20	20	20	20	20	21	21	21	21	21	21	22	22	22	22	22	22	23
20	20	20	20	20	21	21	21	21	21	21	22	22	22	22	22	22	23	23
20	20	20	20	21	21	21	21	21	21	22	22	22	22	22	22	23	23	23
20	20	20	21	21	21	21	21	21	22	22	22	22	22	22	23	23	23	23
20	20	21	21	21	21	21	21	22	22	22	22	22	22	23	23	23	23	23
20	21	21	21	21	21	21	22	22	22	22	22	22	23	23	23	23	23	24
21	21	21	21	21	22	22	22	22	22	22	23	23	23	23	23	23	24	24
21	21	21	21	22	22	22	22	22	22	23	23	23	23	23	23	24	24	24
21	21	21	22	22	22	22	22	22	23	23	23	23	23	23	24	24	24	24
21	21	22	22	22	22	22	22	23	23	23	23	23	23	24	24	24	24	24
21	22	22	22	22	22	22	23	23	23	23	23	23	24	24	24	24	24	24
22	22	22	22	22	22	23	23	23	23	23	23	24	24	24	24	24	24	25
22	22	22	22	22	23	23	23	23	23	23	24	24	24	24	24	24	25	25
22	22	22	22	23	23	23	23	23	23	24	24	24	24	24	24	25	25	25
22	22	22	23	23	23	23	23	23	24	24	24	24	24	24	25	25	25	25
22	22	23	23	23	23	23	23	24	24	24	24	24	25	25	25	25	25	25
22	23	23	23	23	23	24	24	24	24	24	24	25	25	25	25	25	25	26
23	23	23	23	23	24	24	24	24	24	24	25	25	25	25	25	25	26	26
23	23	23	23	24	24	24	24	24	24	25	25	25	25	25	25	26	26	26
23	23	23	24	24	24	24	24	24	25	25	25	25	25	25	26	26	26	26
23	23	24	24	24	24	24	24	25	25	25	25	25	25	26	26	26	26	26
23	24	24	24	24	24	24	25	25	25	25	25	25	26	26	26	26	26	26
24	24	24	24	24	24	25	25	25	25	25	25	26	26	26	26	26	27	27
24	24	24	24	24	25	25	25	25	25	25	26	26	26	26	26	27	27	27
24	24	24	24	25	25	25	25	25	25	26	26	26	26	26	27	27	27	27
24	24	24	25	25	25	25	25	26	26	26	26	26	26	27	27	27	27	27
24	25	25	25	25	25	25	26	26	26	26	26	26	27	27	27	27	27	27

3. Identify percentage fat within the matrix at the point where lines from triceps and iliac values intersect.

4. Record % fat = _____.

Laboratory 12

SEVEN-DAY RECORD OF CALORIC CONSUMPTION AND CALORIC EXPENDITURE

Name _____   Instructor _____

Class and section _____   Date _____

Purpose

The purpose of this laboratory session is to determine your caloric consumption and caloric expenditure for a 7-day period.

Equipment Needed

None

Procedure

Maintain a record of your weight, food intake, Calories in, physical activity, and Calories out for a 7-day period on pp. 243–249. Use Tables 7.5 (p. 116) and 7.6 (p. 124) for this purpose.

Results

1. Are your caloric intake, BMR, and caloric expenditure in balance? _____
2. Did you gain weight, lose weight, or maintain the same weight during the 7 days? _____
3. Should you adjust your food intake and physical activity for good weight management? _____
4. List the more caloric-dense foods in your diet.

_____

5. List the items that you could or would do without to reduce caloric intake.

_____

6. Estimate the number of empty (no nutritional value) Calories consumed during the 7-day period and calculate daily average.

_____

SUMMARY OF TOTAL CALORIC INTAKE AND CALORIC EXPENDITURE

Name _____ Body weight _____

Instructor _____ Estimated BMR (see Table 7.9, p.139) _____

Date _____ Class and section _____

Time	Food Intake	Calories In	Physical Activity	Calories Out
	Total _____		Total _____	

Laboratory 12

Name _____   Date _____

Time	Food Intake	Calories In	Physical Activity	Calories Out
		Total _____		Total _____

Laboratory 12

Name _____ Date _____

Time	Food Intake	Calories In	Physical Activity	Calories Out
	Total		Total	

Laboratory 12

Name _____ Date _____

Time	Food Intake	Calories In	Physical Activity	Calories Out
	Total		Total	

Laboratory 12

Name _____   Date _____

Time	Food Intake	Calories In	Physical Activity	Calories Out
		Total _____		Total _____

Laboratory 12

Name _____   Date _____

Time	Food Intake	Calories In	Physical Activity	Calories Out
		Total	Total	

248

Laboratory 12

Name _____ Date _____

Time	Food Intake	Calories In	Physical Activity	Calories Out
		Total _____		Total _____

Laboratory 12

Date _____

Time	Food Intake	Calories In	Physical Activity	Calories Out
		Total _____		Total _____

Laboratory 13
THE TENSE INDIVIDUAL

Name _____   Instructor _____

Class and section _____   Date _____

Purpose

The purpose of this laboratory session is to determine if you are a tense individual.

Equipment Needed

None

Procedure

1. Read each of the questions listed below and check the answer that describes you most often.
2. Have a friend answer the questions to reflect how he or she perceives you.

Yes	No	
_____	_____	1. Do you often experience headaches or backaches?
_____	_____	2. When sitting in a chair and talking to someone, do you continually move in the chair to seek a comfortable position?
_____	_____	3. When retiring for the night, are you usually unable to fall asleep immediately?
_____	_____	4. Do you often grind your teeth when you are confronted with an unpleasant experience?

Yes   No

5. Do you easily become angry or frustrated when you are faced with a problem for which there is no immediate solution?

6. Do you often complain of being tired?

7. Does your face often hold expressions of intense concentration?

8. Do you often drum your fingers aimlessly or forcibly to express irritation?

9. Does your posture appear stiff when you sit or walk?

10. Are you unable to concentrate on one problem at a time?

11. Are you unable to relax voluntarily?

12. Do you often experience nervousness and uneasy feelings?

13. Do you become upset when your plans are interrupted or must be changed?

14. Are you highly competitive in sports, in your test grades, and in your daily responsibilities?

15. Are you time conscious?

16. Do you experience extreme dissatisfaction and anxiety when you fail to achieve success in your endeavors?

17. Are you an aggressive person?

18. Are you often too busy to allow time for physical activity?

19. Do you plan your day's activities and often budget your time?

20. Are you critical of yourself when you make a mistake?

21. Do you feel "uptight" at the end of the day?

22. Are you impatient when others are late for an appointment with you?

Yes   No

____   ____   23. Do you often set high goals or levels of achievement for yourself?

____   ____   24. Do you experience bad moods very often?

____   ____   25. Are you unyielding when others disagree with your beliefs or convictions?

Results

Tense people seek to release their tension in physical actions that are in no way related to the problem created by the tension. If you answered yes to 5 or more of the questions, you may need to reexamine your perception of the stressor, seek diversions to provide your worried mind with new problems that can be solved, participate in physical activity to provide a release for the tension, and participate in some form of relaxation technique.

Laboratory 14
RELAXATION TECHNIQUES

Name _____   Instructor _____

Class and section _____   Date _____

Purpose

The purpose of this laboratory session is to practice the conscious release of muscular tension (relaxation). It is a skill that is not easily performed by many individuals.

Equipment Needed

1. Mats
2. Pillows or towels

Procedure

1. Practice the Benson relaxation technique described on p. 154.
2. Have a partner or group leader guide you through the Arnheim relaxation technique described on pp. 154–155.

Results

1. Did either of the relaxation techniques help you release muscular tension? _____

2. Do you need to develop the skill to consciously relax? _____

Laboratory 15
PREPARING A PERSONALIZED EXERCISE PRESCRIPTION

Name _____   Instructor _____

Class and section _____   Date _____

Purpose

The purpose of this laboratory session is to provide practice in preparing a personalized exercise prescription.

Equipment Needed

None

Procedure

Using the steps provided in Chapter 3 and the sample found in Appendix B, develop your own exercise prescription.

Name: _____ Age: _____ Exercise Preference: _____

Resting HR: _____ Max HR: _____

Training HR: 60% _____; 70% _____; 80% _____

CR evaluation by _____; Results: _____

Comments:

Fitness goal:

EXERCISE LOG

Name _____   Instructor _____

Date	Exercise type	Distance	Duration	Mid-HR	Post-HR

EXERCISE LOG

Name _____ Instructor _____

Date	Exercise type	Distance	Duration	Mid-HR	Post-HR

EXERCISE LOG

Name _____   Instructor _____

Date	Exercise type	Distance	Duration	Mid-HR	Post-HR

EXERCISE LOG

Name _____ Instructor _____

Date	Exercise type	Distance	Duration	Mid-HR	Post-HR

EXERCISE LOG

Name _____ Instructor _____

Date	Exercise type	Distance	Duration	Mid-HR	Post-HR

EXERCISE LOG

Name _____ Instructor _____

Date	Exercise type	Distance	Duration	Mid-HR	Post-HR

EXERCISE LOG

Name _____   Instructor _____

Date	Exercise type	Distance	Duration	Mid-HR	Post-HR

EXERCISE LOG

Name _____   Instructor _____

Date	Exercise type	Distance	Duration	Mid-HR	Post-HR

EXERCISE LOG

Name _____   Instructor _____

Date	Exercise type	Distance	Duration	Mid-HR	Post-HR

EXERCISE LOG

Name _____   Instructor _____

Date	Exercise type	Distance	Duration	Mid-HR	Post-HR

INDEX

A-band, 183
Accelerator nerve, 163
Actin filaments, 183
Adenosine diphosphate (ADP), 183, 184
Adenosine triphosphate (ATP), 183, 184
Adipose tissue, 106
Adrenal cortex, 152
Adrenal glands, 151, 156, 159
Adrenal medulla, 151
Adrenaline, 151
Aerobic capacity, 33, 175, 176
Aerobic dance, 70, 71
    clothing, 74
    shoes, 74
Aerobic metabolism, 176
Aerobic power, 31, 33, 46, 47–48
Aerobic program, 70
Aging, activity, 40–41, 137
Alcohol, 19–20, 122
All-or-none law, 181, 184
Alveolar sacs, 173
Alveolar ventilation, 178–179
American Heart Association (AHA), 4, 5, 8, 12, 17, 131
Amino acids, 152
Anabolic androgenic steroids, 54–55
Anaerobic metabolism, 176
Angina pectoris, 9
Aorta, 163
Appetite, 143
Arteries, 167
Arteriosclerosis, 106, 156
Asymptomatic, 27–28
Atherosclerosis, 9, 10–11
Atria, 163, 166–167
Atrioventricular (AV) node, 164–166, 167

Atrioventricular (AV) valves, 163, 166–167
    mitral, 163, 164
    tricuspid, 163, 164
Autonomic nervous system, 152, 164, 180

Ballistic stretch, 79
Baroreceptors, 34
Basal metabolic rate (BMR), 134, 137, 147
Bicycling 70, 71, 186
Blood pressure, 11–12, 14, 21, 106, 131, 168
    arm work, 170
    diastolic, 168
    isometric contraction, 170
    systolic, 151, 168
Blood vessels, 106, 151, 167, 168
Body fat, 105, 107, 131, 134, 137–138, 139–140, 143, 146
Body image, 3
Body type
    ectomorph, 130
    endomorph, 130
    mesomorph, 130
Breast soreness, 62
Bronchi, 173
Bronchioles, 173
Bundle of His, 165

Caloric
    balance, 105
    expenditure, 188
    intake, 105, 123, 139, 141, 147, 188
    negative balance, 146
    positive balance, 105, 106
Calories, 36–37, 71, 73, 107, 115–119, 122, 123, 124–129, 139, 141, 143–144, 146, 188